JN092417

世代間交流の理論と実践 3

新たな社会創造に向かうソーシャルネットワークとしての世代間交流活動

The Theory and Practices of Intergenerational Learning; Series 3

Intergenerational Exchange Activities as a Social Network toward the Creation of a New Society

草野篤子・溝邊和成・内田勇人・村山陽・作田はるみ　編著

三学出版

はじめに

現在、直面しているパンデミックが警鐘となり、森林を保護する動きが、各国で出てきている。新型コロナウイルス感染症の拡大は、人口増加による農地化、産業化、住宅地の拡大などの影響によるもので、以下のようなことを考慮する必要がある。森林伐採などにより、人はコウモリをはじめとした動物と共存せざるを得ない危機的な問題を抱えてしまっている。動物から人に広がる感染症は、最近では、SARS、MERS、エボラ出血熱、そして現在の新型コロナウイルスがある。いずれの病気も、非常に感染力が強く、世界中で脅威となっている。しかし、医療技術の急速な進歩があるにもかかわらず、日本では、保健所、病院などの公衆衛生･医療行政関連施策などの縮小、半減化、非正規化などが全国的に進んでおり、現在、公的な保健衛生･医療機関拡充へと政策を転換する必要性に迫られている。

国際的な次元での世代間交流

世代間交流プログラムや実践に対する関心は、日本だけではなく、国際的な広がりを持っている。この分野では、国際的な組織としてICIP :The International Consortium for Intergenerational Programsがあり、米国のGU: Generations United、ヨーロッパのEMIL：European Map of Intergenerational Learningの存在を、忘れることはできない。また、国際的な雑誌としては、Journal of Intergenerational Relationships (Taylor &Francis)が、出版されている。

コロナ禍の下、米国の世代間交流と子ども、若者、高齢者擁護の団体、Generations Unitedの国際大会が、昨年(2021)年6月15日から17日の3日間、オンラインで開催された。初めてのオンライン開催にもかかわらず、18カ国、500人に近い参加者が熱い討論と情報を共有した。最大の難問は、世界各国・各地との時差で、例えば、日本の場合には、米国の東海岸の朝が、日本では深夜になってしまうということである。それにもかかわらず、熱心な日本世代間交流学会の会員は、発表、参加することができ、コロナ禍でも、世代間交流の実践と研究の交流が、止まることなく続けられてきている。

世代間交流に焦点を当てた国際会議は、多数開催されており、その中には、国連が主催するものも含まれている。国連は 1999 年を「国際高齢者年」と定め、多世代間関係を４つの基本コンセプトの１つとし、「すべての人のための社会を目指して」(Toward a Society for All) と表わし、この年の統合テーマとして “Ages” が選ばれた。

世代間を扱うテーマは、他の国連の会議でも中心的なテーマとなっている。「第２回高齢化に関する世界会議」(2002 年４月、マドリード)、「ユースデー」(2004 年のテーマは「世代間交流社会における若者」) などがある。前者では、国連はマドリッド国際会議の２つのレビューと評価を行った。世界会議の成果としては、「高齢化に関する国際行動計画」がある。これらの評価では、国際的な世代間交流プログラムや世代間交流の特徴として、以下の点が挙げられ、過去 10 年間の政策を、次のように統括している (Kaplan, M. & Sánchez, M. 2014)。

- 高齢者政策に割り当てられている予算が限られていることから、「各国政府は特定のグループに焦点を当てるのではなく、若い世代と高齢者世代の幸福を向上させることができる手段を検討する」(United Nation, 2007, p.7)。
- 「世代間の責任とサポートがどのように交渉されているかを理解すること。ニーズや資源と同様に、この点に関して高齢者が果たす役割がある。個人、家族、コミュニティにとって、高齢化対策は非常に重要である。世代間の次元を考慮する」(Ibid, p.9)。
- コミュニティの中で世代間の連帯を育む必要がある。とはいえ、世代間の連帯は、利他主義や善意から生じる自然なものに見えるかもしれないが、異なる世代間の絆は、意図的に作り上げられ、促進されなければならない」(Ibid, p.10)。
- 世代間対話プログラムを実施した南アフリカは、高齢者プログラムを通じて、世代間プログラムを支援する資源を利用できるようにした。各国が世代間の連帯を促進している例として、「高齢アメリカ人法」が挙げられている (United

Nations, 2011）。

人々の暮らしの中にある関係、文化の違いを超えて不変なのは、人間という生き物が社会的な動物であり、他の人間とのつながりを求める中核的なニーズを持っている。研究成果に基づいて、あらゆる世代の人々にとっていかに重要であるかを述べている。

「私たちは幼少期から他人を信頼する経験を積んでいる。私たちを育み、世話をしてくれる」（Bateson, 2010, p.8）。もちろん、何が「有意義」であるとみなされるかは、文化的・社会的文脈に影響を受けている（op. cit. Kaplan M., Sanchez M.）。

世代間交流分野への私信（メッセージカード）

スペイン、グラナダ大学教授、マリアーノ・サンチェス博士の日本世代間交流学会第12回大会（2021年10月）での発表は、世代間交流研究分野における自身がたどった軌跡を振り返るというアプローチで行われた。その表題は、「世代間交流研究の分野における私の過去、現在、未来をつなぐ12の省察」である。

この省察は、現在の世代間交流分野における研究と実践において、非常に的確な示唆を与えるものなので、ここで、マリアーノ・サンチェス博士の考えとは、必ずしも一致するものではないと思われるが、この枠組みに沿って、私なりの考えをカードにして述べさせていただきたい。カードは、「過去から学ぶ　－4つの古い信念－」「現在の見解　－4つの現在の信条－」「未来へ身を乗り出す　－4つの前進への道－」とし、それぞれ4枚ずつで構成している。

過去から学ぶ　－4つの古い信念－

カード1

世代間交流プログラムは、主に人間の高齢化と関係がある。

1960年代の米国における高齢者差別（Ageism）を起源としている。米国では、職場を離れた高齢者たちは、経済能力を失い、また、核家族を基本とする国であるので、身の回りの世話をしてくれる人もあまり周りにおらず、「臭い、汚い」という扱われ方をされる場合が多々見られたという。このような事態に直面し、ピッツバーグ大学教授のサリー・ニューマン博士を中心として、世代間交流の研究と実践が始められた。米国での最初の高齢者と子どもの世代間交流は、フロリダ大学 Yonge Laboratory School で実行に移され、1965 年には低所得で健康な大人と、特別な支援が必要な子どもの学習をサポートする祖父母里親プログラム (the Foster Grandparent Program) が、ニューヨークのスターテン島で、コミュニティー・サービス・プロジェクトとして始まった。資金は、主に米国連邦政府、地元の基金などによって運営された。

カード2

世代間交流プログラムは、主に家族の外、コミュニティの領域に属する。

米国やヨーロッパの国々では、日本のような三世代、四世代の家族が同じ屋根の下で生活を共にすることは、あまり見られなかった。特に、米国は、ヨーロッパから若い世代がフロンティア・ムーブメントによって移住して建国された国家であるし、ヨーロッパでも、特にイギリスでは、産業革命期に、夫婦共働きをするために、親世代を都市に呼び寄せて、子どもの世話をしてもらった経験があったようであるが、それは、イギリスの家族には定着しなかったという歴史がある。人は、高齢になることによって、多くの場合、労働市場において経済的価値を生み出すことはできないが、高齢者がコミュニティにおいて子どもや青年を主な対象とした世代間交流を行うことで、社会的な貢献を行うことができる。

カード3

世代間交流プログラムは、主に互恵的な交流を中心に組織されるべきである。

世代間交流は、高齢者や、子ども、若者が一方的に利益を得るものではなく、その双方が利益を得る WIN-WIN な関係であるべきである。持続的、継続的なプログラムは、一つの世代が他の世代に対して一方的に働きかけるのではなく、双方が互恵的な関係を作り上げることによって、安定的なプログラムが出来上がる。

カード４

世代間交流プログラムは、主に活動を行うことである。

世代間交流には、様々なプログラムや、まだプログラムには至っていないイニシアティブがあるが、例えば、子どもや若者が高齢者ホームを訪問するとか、高齢者が幼稚園・保育園、小・中・高等学校などを訪問するなど、世代間交流プログラムは、理論だけでなく活動を伴うことが特徴である。

現在の見解　－４つの現在の信条－

カード５

世代間交流プログラムは、主に、全体を通じて最初から最後まで、時を超えて、人間の相互依存に関係している。

人は、地域社会に生きる社会的な動物であるから、この世に生を受けた時から、死に至るまで、相互依存関係の下で暮らしており、一人では生きていけない。したがって、世代間交流プログラムは、一生を通じて、子ども、青年、中年世代、高齢者に至るまで、相互依存関係に依拠している。

カード６

世代間交流プログラムは、家族内領域と家族外領域の橋渡しになる。

世代間交流プログラムは、かつて言われていたような家族外領域に留まるものではなく、家族内領域においても、言えることである。家族外領域の世代間交流が家族内領域の世代間交流に影響を与えることもあり、また逆の場合もある。

カード７

世代間交流プログラムは、主に多様な関係性を軸に編成されるべきである。

世代間交流プログラムは、ただ単に一つの関係性に基づいたものではなく、様々な関係と絡み合って編成されることが望まれる。例えば、地域との関係、そこに住む住民、その人たちの文化、歴史、社会などと関係する場合が多い。したがって、そこでの多様な軸を理解し、それにふさわしい世代間交流プログラムを、世代間交流コーディネーターが、計画、実施していくことが、重要となってくる。

カード 8

世代間交流プログラムは、主に異なる世代の人々が出会い、交流できるようにすることである。

現代社会は、学校、職場、地域社会においても、同一の世代が生活を共にする場合が多い。この限られた人間関係では、人間発達においても、また、多世代で構成されている地域社会が上手く機能しなくなる。そのためにも、学校、職場、地域社会で世代間交流を実施することによって、多様な世代が出会い交流することによって、現場が抱えている問題を解決することができる。

未来へ身を乗り出す　－４つの前進への道－

カード 9

より直線的でない筋の通ったロジックモデル、より関係性を重視した実践

世代間交流は、相互依存の関係を構築するものであるから、元々、直線的関係ではあり得ないが、お互いがお互いを理解し、WIN-WIN な関係を重視した実践を行うことが肝要である。多世代のおかれた環境を十分に配慮し、思いやり、その関係性を重視したプログラムを作成していくことが必要である。そういった交流を実施する上では、世代間交流コーディネーターの存在が重要となる。そのためには、日本世代間交流協会 (JIUA: Japan Intergenerational Unity Association) が、ここ 10 数年実施している「世代間交流コーディネーター養成講座」のような理論と実践の両方を身につけられる講座が、多くの場所で開催されることが望まれる。

カード 10

年代を重視せず、ライフコースを重視した世代間交流プログラム

Erikson E. H.（エリクソン E.H.）は、人間の一生を８つの発達段階にわけ、その段階ごとに心理的課題と危機、課題達成により獲得する要素などを分類した。後に 91 歳までの長寿を得たこともあって、第９段階を追加し、世代間交流理論にも、大きな影響を与えてきた。日本では特に、例えば、20 代前半までには、学校教育を修了、結婚し、家族を形成するといった、年代別のライフサイクル論が、規範意識として潜在的な影響を与えていた。しかし、年功序列や終身雇用などの労働関係にも変化がみられ、女性も、高学歴を求め、結婚・出産後も、働き続けたいと希望する者が増加した。従って、今までのような、年齢によって規定していくライフサイクルに基づいた人生設計が不可能となっている。特に米国やヨーロッパ諸国では、人生の中で転職、離婚・再婚など多様なライフイベントが生じている場合がみられる。したがって、世代間交流においても、年代ではなく、ライフコースを重視したプログラムを展開する必要が出てきている。

カード 11

我々の分野における模範的な世代間交流関係　―今まで我々が説いてきたことの実践―

Mariano Sanches 博士によると、これからの世代間交流は、集団的絆、社会的絆の確立に大きな役割を果たす社会的統合、他者とのつながりの感情、社会的構成員の間に一体感を生み出すネットワークとの関連で、幸福を追求する関係を構築する実践を行うことが重要であるという。

カード 12

より質の高い、持続的な国際協力

ICIP（国際世代間交流協会）を生み出す契機となった The First International Conference on Intergenerational Programs to Promote Social Change（第１回国際的社会改革を促進する世代間交流国際会議）は、1999 年 10 月 14 日に、オランダのヴァールスで開催され ICIP が創設された。その目的は、次のようなものであった。①世代間交流プログラムの研究と実践を促し、開発していく　②世代間交流プログラムの理論と実践の体系的な開発を、コーディネートする。いくつかの問題は、国境を超えた問題であり、その普遍的な性質を認めた異なった国家間のパートナーシップを通して、問題が解決できることを確認した。ICIP は、多様な文化的パートナーシップを反映したものであり、次のように機能されていくことが必要である。

・情報交換を促す。
・優れた実践例は、他への適用を広げていく。
・社会問題に対する世代間交流を通じた解決策の重要性を深く理解することに加えて、調査を行う。
・世代間交流の発展を支える国際的ネットワークを創出する。

最後に示したカード 12 の ICIP は、世代間交流プログラムを通して、世界的な規模の社会改革を促す媒体としての役割を担うことになる (Newman S. 2002)。ICIP の世界大会は、第 1 回大会は、2002 年に英国のキール大学で、第 2 回は、2004 年カナダのヴィクトリア大学、第 3 回は、2006 年に、オーストラリアのメルボルン大学など、第 4 回大会は、2007 年にニューヨーク、第 5 回はシンガポール国立大学などで開催されている。第 6 回大会を、2020 年に日本で開催を予定し、準備委員会が結成され、準備を着々進めていたが、COVID-19 が世界的に蔓延し、やむなく中止をせざるを得なくなった。

世界は、残念ながら COVID-19 の蔓延で、世代間交流の歩みが停滞しがちであり、人と人とのネットワークを分断する逆風となっている。しかし、多くの世代間交流プログラムでは、ネットワークや交流において、今まではこれ程、利用されてこなかったオンラインなどを様々な形で利用することによって、社会参加の幅、種類、そして広がりによって、地域の概念をも変えていく可能性が出てきている。多世代の多様な価値観を持つ多くの人々との繋がりを持続的に発展させ、相互支援や協働を通して、多世代のあらゆる人々に居場所があり、出番があり、主役になれる住みやすい地域や社会を構築する努力を精力的に継続していくことが、今、私たちに与えられた使命と考える。

感謝を込めて

さて、本書には、米国 Generations United（ジェネレーションズ・ユナイテッド）代表 Donna M. Butts 氏をはじめ、シンガポール国立大学教授 Leng Leng Thang 博士、米国ペンシルヴァニア州立大学教授 Matt Kaplan 博士、スペイングラナダ大学教授 Mariano Sanchez 博士、国立台湾大学准教授 Shin Tsen Liu 博士、そして米国ノースウエスタンリザーブ大学およびトロント大学教授 Peter Whitehouse 博士からメッセージが届いている。それらのメッセージは、日本の世代間交流が世界へつながる道標となっている。心より感謝申し上げる次第である。

また、上記の世代間交流の研究・実践において世界的に著名な各氏から、各国で現在実践されている顕著なプログラムや実践例を推薦していただいた。まさに、海外で、世代間交流の研究や実践において先駆的に活躍している方々からの、先見性のある示唆に富んだ事例が盛りだくさん織り込まれている。感謝と敬意を込めて、ここに名前を記しておきたい。

Derenda Schubert 氏・Lindsay Magnuson 氏・Renee Moseley 氏（Chap.1）、Rick Lathrop 氏・David Blake Willis 氏（Chap.2）、A. Patricia Aguilera-Hermida 氏（Chap.3）、Theresa Southam 氏（Chap.4）、Grace Hampton 氏（Chap.5）、Mariano Sánchez 氏・Andrés Rodríguez 氏（Chap.6）、Ryan McKay 氏・Denise Milne 氏（Chap.7）、Sammy How 氏・Lim Wei Loong 氏（Chap.8）、Gaspar Mayor Pascual 氏（Chap.9）、Kristin Bodiford 氏・Cory Elliott 氏（Chap.10）

さらに、日本国内からも、30 名近くの方々からの貴重な報告を得ることができた。同じく感謝の意を表し、名前を記しておく。

齋藤美保子氏（第１章）、小林久人氏（第２章）、瀧口優氏（第３章）、杉啓以子氏（第４章）、飯塚あい氏（第５章）、佐々木剛氏・草野篤子氏（第６章）、廣田直子氏（第７章）、森田久美子氏・青木利江子氏・小林美奈子氏・山本晴美氏・呂暁衛氏・永嶺仁美氏・佐々木明子氏（第８章）、田渕恵氏・小西順子氏（第９

章)、草野篤子氏(第 10 章)、松本大佑氏・濱口雅行氏・濱口郁枝氏・内田勇人氏(第 11 章)、糸井和佳氏(第 12 章)、矢野真理氏･作田はるみ氏･坂本薫氏･内田勇人氏(第 13 章)、村山陽氏(第 14 章)、叶内茜氏・筧敏子氏(第 15 章)、溝邊和成氏(第 16 章)

世代をつなぎ地域を再生するために、地域や社会が抱える諸問題に取り組み、すべての世代、女性、障碍者、マイノリティーなどが抱える諸問題を、社会的ネットワーク、共生、社会的に排除するのではなく、社会的に包摂していくことによって、解決していくことが重要である。市民的参加のネットワークでは、当事者間のコミュニケーションが活発であればあるほど、信頼関係が構築される傾向が強い。市民度が高いコミュニティでは、ボランティア活動が盛んにおこなわれ、そのなかで地域、学校や保育園、子育て支援、福祉施設などにおける世代間交流が展開されている。世代間交流における人間関係は、垂直的・支配的人間関係では決してなく、水平的・互恵的な人間関係を基本としている。平和な社会を維持するためにも、将来にわたって、生涯を通じて人を支え、包摂的・持続的な社会の構築に、あらゆる世代が生涯を通じて携わり、人々を支えていける地域を切に期待する。そして本書が、少しでも役に立ってくれれば、これ以上の喜びはない。

草野篤子

Introduction

The COVID-19 pandemic that the world is currently facing has become a warning, and the movement to protect the forest has finally come out in a lot of countries. The spread of COVID-19 is due to the effects of population growth on farmland, industrialization, and the expansion of residential areas, and it is necessary to consider the following: Deforestation and other causes have led to a critical problem in which people are forced to coexist with bats and other animals. Infectious diseases that spread from animals to people are, more recently, SARS, MERS, Ebola, and the current COVID-19. These diseases are highly contagious and pose a threat around the world. In Japan there is rapid progress in medical technology, public health centers and hospital services expansion, however, we are faced with a global problem, and there is a need for global efforts and collaboration to shift policies and expand medical innovation and services worldwide.

Intergenerational exchange in an international dimension

The interest in intergenerational exchange programs and practices is not limited to Japan, but has an international scope. In this field, there are international organizations such as ICIP: The International Consortium for Intergenerational Programs, GU: Generations United in the U.S., EMIL: European Map of Intergenerational Learning, and there is an internationally published journal: The Journal of Intergenerational Relationships (Taylor &Francis).

Under the COVID 19, an international convention spearheaded by Generations United, a U.S. intergenerational relations and advocacy organization for children, youth, and the elderly, was held last June 15-17, 2021, on line. Despite being held online for the first time, close to 500 participants from 18 countries engaged in heated discussions and shared information. The biggest challenge was the time difference with other countries around the world, for example, in Japan, the morning on the U.S. East Coast time falls in the middle of the night in Japan. Nevertheless, enthusiastic members of the Japan Society for Intergenerational Studies were able to present and participate, and the exchange of practice and research on intergenerational exchange has continued unabated despite the Corona Virus disaster.

A number of international conferences focusing on intergenerational exchange have been held, including some sponsored by the United Nations. The United Nations designated 1999 as the International Year of Older Persons, with multigenerational relations as one of the four basic concepts, expressed as "Toward a Society for All," and the year's unifying theme was “solidarity and cooperation between generations.”

Themes dealing with intergenerational issues have been a central theme at other UN conferences. These include the Second World Conference on Aging (Madrid, April 2002) and Youth Day (the 2004 theme was "Youth in an Intergenerational Society"). In the former, the UN reviewed and evaluated two Madrid international conferences. The outcome of the World Conference was the International Plan of Action on Aging. These evaluations identified the following features of international intergenerational programs and intergenerational exchanges, and they oversee the policies of the past decade as follows (Kaplan, M. & Sánchez, M. 2014).

- Given limited budgets allocated to policies for older persons, ‘Governments are considering instruments that can improve the well-being of young and older generations rather than focusing on one particular group’ (United Nations, 2007, p. 7).
- Understanding how generational responsibility and support is negotiated, the role played by older persons in this regard, ‘as well as the needs and resources of individuals, families and communities, is crucial for ageing policies that take an intergenerational dimension into account’ (ibid., p. 9).
- There is a need to foster intergenerational solidarity within communities: ‘Though intergenerational solidarity may appear natural and result from altruism and good will, bonds between different generations must be created and promoted intentionally’ (ibid., p. 10).
- South Africa, through the drafting of a national policy on its living heritage and the implementation of an intergenerational dialogue program, and the USA, which made available resources to support intergenerational programs through the Older Americans Act, are cited as examples of how countries are promoting intergenerational solidarity (United Nations, 2011).

In terms of relationships in people's lives, what is constant across cultural differences is that the human creature is a social animal and there is a core need to connect with other humans. Based on the research findings, Bateson describes how important this is for people of all ages. She said, "From an early age, we have the experience of trusting others. They nurture and care for us" (Bateson, 2010, p. 8). Of course, what is considered "meaningful" is influenced by cultural and social contexts (op. cit. Kaplan M., Sanchez M.).

Personal letter (message card) to the field of Intergenerational exchange

Dr. Mariano Sanchez, Professor, University of Granada, Spain, at the 12th Annual Conference of the Japan Society for Intergenerational Studied (October 2021), reflected on his own trajectory in the field of intergenerational exchange research. The title of his paper was "Twelve reflections that link my past, present, and future in the field of intergenerational exchange research."

I would like to share some of my own messages (card style) within this framework, which may not necessarily coincide with Dr. Mariano Sánchez's ideas, as they are very pertinent to current research and practice in the broader field of intergenerational exchange.

Learning from the Past - Four Old Beliefs

card 1

Intergenerational programs have mainly to do with human aging.

It has its origins in discrimination against the elderly (Ageism) in the U.S. in the 1960s. In the U.S., elderly people who had aged out of the workforce often lost their economic capacity and were treated as "smelly and dirty" because there was no one around to take care of them since the country was based on the nuclear family. Faced with this situation, Dr. Sally Newman, professor at the University of Pittsburgh, and others began to study and practice intergenerational exchange. The first intergenerational exchange between the elderly and children in the U.S. was implemented at the Yonge Laboratory School of the University of Florida, and in 1965, the Foster Grandparent Program was established to support the learning of low-income, healthy adults and children with special needs. The program began as a community service project on Staten Island, New York. Funding came primarily from the U.S. federal government and local foundations.

card 2

Intergenerational programs belong mainly to the extrafamilial/communitarian sphere.

In the U.S. and European countries, it was not common to see three or four generations of families living together under the same roof as in Japan. This was especially the case in the U.S., a nation founded by the immigration of younger generations from Europe by the Frontier Movement, and in Europe, especially in England, where there is a history of the Industrial Revolution period in which couples had the experience of taking their parents' generation to the cities to work together and take care of their children, but this did not take root in the English family.

Although people often do not create economic value in the labor market as they age, the elderly can make a social contribution by engaging in intergenerational exchanges in their communities, primarily with children and adolescents.

card 3

Intergenerational programs are usually framed as one generation providing a service to another generation.

Intergenerational exchanges should be win-win relationships in which the elderly, children, and youth do not benefit unilaterally, but both parties benefit. Sustained and ongoing programs will not be created by one generation working unilaterally on the other, but by both creating a mutually beneficial relationship that is stable.

card 4

Intergenerational programs are mainly to do with carrying out activities.

There are various intergenerational exchange programs and initiatives that have not yet resulted in programs, but intergenerational exchange programs are characterized by the fact that they involve activities as well as theory, for example, children and youth visiting homes for the elderly, or the elderly visiting kindergartens, nursery schools, elementary, middle, and high schools, etc.

The Present Views- Four Current Beliefs

card 5

Intergenerational programs have mainly to do with human interdependence throughout (from beginning to end, across time).

Since humans are social animals living in a community, they are intertwined in interdependent ways, from birth till death. Therefore, intergenerational exchange programs rely on interdependent relationships throughout life, from children, adolescents, and middle-aged to the elderly.

card 6

Intergenerational programs can bridge familial and extrafamilial spheres.

Intergenerational exchange programs are not confined to the extrafamilial sphere, as was once said, but also within the intrafamilial sphere. Intergenerational exchange in the extrafamilial realm can influence intergenerational exchange in the intrafamilial realm. And vice versa.

card 7

Intergenerational programs should be organized mainly around a diversity of relationships.

Intergenerational exchange programs should not be organized around just one relationship but should be intertwined with a variety of relationships. For example, they may be related to how one experiences the community, other inhabitants, their culture, history, society, etc. An intergenerational exchange coordinator can play an important role in ensuring that programs are planned and evolve in ways that reflect the relationships (and issues) that are most important to participants.

card 8

Intergenerational programs are mainly to do with facilitating that people from different generations can meet and interact.

In today's society, the same generations often live together in schools, workplaces, and communities. This lack of age diversity in many of the setting where people spend much of their time limits opportunities to meet and form meaningful relationships with people of other generations.

Leaning into the Future-Four Paths Forward

card 9

Less linear, logic models, more relation-centered practices

Since intergenerational exchange builds a relationship of interdependence, it cannot be a linear relationship in nature, but it is vital that both parties understand each other and practice a win-win relationship-oriented approach. It is necessary to create programs that give full consideration to the environment of other generations, and that emphasize compassion and relationships with them.

In addition, the presence of an intergenerational exchange coordinator is indispensable in conducting exchanges. For this purpose, courses that enable participants to acquire both theoretical and practical skills, such as the "Intergenerational Exchange Coordinator Training Course" that the Japan Intergenerational Unity Association (JIUA) has been carrying out annually.

For this purpose, courses that provide both theory and practice, such as the "Intergenerational Exchange Coordinator Training Course" that the Japan Intergenerational Unity Association (JIUA) has been conducting for the past decade or so, should be held in many places. It is desirable that the organizations that run intergenerational programs will be able to provide a more effective and efficient service to its customers.

card 10

Less (chronological) age-focused and more life course -focused in intergenerational programs.

Erikson E. H. divided the human life into eight developmental stages, classifying psychological challenges, crises, and factors to be acquired through task achievement at each stage, and later added a ninth stage, partly due to his longevity up to 91 years, which has had a significant impact on intergenerational exchange theory. In Japan, in particular, the life-cycle theory of chronological stages, for example, completing schooling, getting married, and forming a family by the early 20s, influenced, if only subconsciously, the normative consciousness. However, labor relations, such as seniority-based systems and lifetime employment, have changed, and an increasing number of women are seeking higher education and wishing to continue working after marriage and childbirth. Therefore, it is no longer possible to plan one's life based on a life cycle defined by age. Especially in the U.S. and European countries, there are cases where various life events, such as job change, divorce and remarriage, occur during a person's life. Therefore, in intergenerational exchanges, it has become necessary to develop programs that emphasize the life course rather than the age.

card 11

Exemplary intergenerational relationships between generations in our field (practicing what we preach)

According to Dr. Mariano Sanchez, the intergenerational exchanges of the future will be about the practice of building relationships that pursue well-being in relation to collective ties, social integrations.

card 12

Higher quality, sustainable international cooperation

The First International Conference on Intergenerational Programs to Promote Social Change was held on October 14, 1999, in Vaals, the Netherlands, and ICIP was founded. Its objectives were to (1) To encourage and develop research and practice of intergenerational exchange programs (2) To coordinate the systematic development of theory and practice of intergenerational exchange programs. The ICIP, which reflects a diverse cultural partnership, should function to coordinate the development of a global network of intergenerational exchange programs. The following are some of the key points of emphasis project (Newman S. 2002).

- Encourage the exchange of information.
- We will expand the application of good practices to other areas.
- In addition to a deep understanding of the importance of intergenerational solutions to social problems, we will conduct research.
- Create an international network to support the development of intergenerational exchange.

ICIP (International Consortium for Intergenerational Programs) shown on the last card 12, will serve as a medium for promoting social reform on a global scale through its intergenerational exchange programs, it concludes (Newman S.2002).

Subsequently, the first ICIP World Congress was held at Keele University in the United Kingdom in 2002, the second at the University of Victoria, Canada in 2004, the third in Melbourne, Australia in 2006, and the fourth in New York City in 2007. The fifth conference was held in Singapore. The sixth conference was scheduled to be held in Japan in 2020, and a preparatory committee was formed and preparations were steadily underway, but the worldwide spread of COVID 19 forced the cancellation of the conference.

Unfortunately, the world tends to stagnate in the progress of intergenerational exchange due to the COVID-19 epidemic, a headwind that divides networks of people. However, many intergenerational exchange programs are beginning to use various forms of networking and interaction, such as online platforms, which have not been used to such an extent in the past, yet have the potential to change the concept of community through the breadth, variety, and extent of social participation. We believe that our mission now is to sustainably develop connections among many people with diverse values from multiple generations, and through mutual support and collaboration, to vigorously continue our efforts to build livable communities and societies where all people have a place, a place to come in, and plentiful opportunities to engage people across the age continuum in ways that they deem as meaningful.

With thanks,

We have received messages from the following people from overseas for this publication.
Ms. Donna M. Butts, Executive Director of Generations United, USA
Dr. Leng Leng Thang, Professor of National University of Singapore
Dr. Matt Kaplan, Professor at Pennsylvania State University, USA
Dr. Mariano Sanchez, Professor at the University of Granada, Spain
Dr. Shih Tsen Liu, Associate Professor at National Taiwan University
Dr. Peter Whitehouse, Professor at Northwestern Reserve University and University of Toronto, USA

These messages are a beacon of intergenerational exchange in Japan to the world. I would like to thank them from the bottom of my heart.

In addition, each of the world-renowned experts in intergenerational exchange researches and practices mentioned above recommended outstanding programs and practices currently being implemented in their respective countries. The book is indeed a wealth of visionary and thought-provoking papers from those who are pioneering researches and practices in intergenerational exchange overseas. With gratitude and respect, I would like to note their names here.

Chapter 1: Derenda Schubert, Lindsay Magnuson, and Renee Moseley
Chapter 2: Rick Lathrop and David Blake Willis
Chapter 3: A. Patricia Aguilera-Hermida
Chapter 4: Theresa Southam
Chapter 5: Grace Hampton
Chapter 6: Mariano Sanchez, Andres Rodriguez, and Carolina Campos

Chapter 7: Ryan McKay and Denise Milne
Chapter 8: Sammy How and Lim Wei Loong
Chapter 9: Gaspar Mayor Pascual
Chapter 10: Kristin Bodiford and Cory Elliott

Then we were able to obtain valuable reports from nearly 30 Japanese people. We likewise express our gratitude and note their names.
Chapter 1: Mihoko Saito
Chapter 2: Hisato Kobayashi
Chapter 3: Masaru Takiguchi
Chapter 4: Keiko Sugi
Chapter 5: Ai Iizuka
Chapter 6: Tsuyoshi Sasaki and Atsuko Kusano
Chapter 7: Naoko Hirota
Chapter 8: Kumiko Morita, Reiko Aoki, Minako Kobayashi, Harumi Yamamoto, Xiaowei Lyu, Hitomi Nagamine, and Akiko Sasaki
Chapter 9: Megumi Tabuchi and Junko Konishi
Chapter 10: Atsuko Kusano
Chapter 11: Daisuke Matsumoto, Masayuki Hamaguchi, Ikue Hamaguchi, and Hayato Uchida
Chapter 12: Waka Itoi
Chapter 13: Mari Yano, Kaoru Sakamoto, Harumi Sakuda, and Hayato Uchida
Chapter 14: Yoh Murayama
Chapter 15: Akane Kanouchi and Toshiko Kakehi
Chapter 16: Kazushige Mizobe

In order to connect generations and regenerate the community, it is important to address the various issues facing the community and society, and to solve the problems faced by all generations, women, the physically challenged, and minorities, with social networks, new modes of collaboration, and interventions that promote social inclusion rather than social exclusion. In a network of civic participation, the more active the communication between the parties involved, the stronger the tendency to build trust. Communities with a high level of civic participation are active in volunteer activities, and intergenerational exchanges in communities themselves, nursery schools, childcare support, and welfare facilities are developed in the midst of such activities. Human relations in intergenerational exchanges are based on horizontal and mutually beneficial relationships, rather than vertical and dominant relationships. In order to maintain a peaceful society, we sincerely hope for a community where all generations can be involved throughout their lives in building an inclusive and sustainable society, supporting people throughout their lives. And if this book is of any help to you, we will be more than happy.

Atsuko Kusano

References:

Bateson, M.C. (2010) Composing a further life. The age of active wisdom. New York: Knopf

Kaplan, M. & Sánchez, M. (2014). Intergenerational programs and policies in aging societies. In S. Harper & K. Hamblin (Eds.). International handbook on ageing and public policy (pp. 367-383). Cheltenham, UK: Edward Elgar Publishing.

Newman S., Creating an "International Consortium for Intergenerational Programs", pp. 263-272, Kaplan M., Henkin N., Kusano A., Linking Generations-A Global View of Intergenerational Exchange, 2002,University Press of America

Sally Newman, Creating an "International Consortium for Intergenerational Programs", Kaplan M., Henkin N., Kusano Atsuko, editors and supervisors, translated by Sumi Kato, Intergenerational Exchange in the Age of Globalization, 2008 Akashi Shoten (Japanese).

Sanchez, M. (2022). 12 reflections connecting my past, present and future in the intergenerational studies field, The annual conference of JSIS on Oct. 2, 2021.

United Nations (2007). First review and appraisal of the Madrid International Plan of Action on Ageing: preliminary assessment. Report of the Secretary-General. E/CN.5/2008/7, November 23.

United Nations (2011). Second review and appraisal of the Madrid International Plan of Action on Ageing, 2002. Report of the Secretary-General. E/CN.5/2012/5, November 6.

目　次

第２部　世代間交流：諸外国

Part 2 Intergenerational Exchange in the World; Several Countries

第３部　メッセージ
Part 3　Message

第1部

Part 1

世代間交流：日本

Intergenerational Exchange in the world; Japan

第1章　子ども食堂に見る世代間交流
―ケアリング[1]としての役割―

齋藤　美保子

1．はじめに

子ども食堂*は2022年現在、全国で6,000以上が存在し、2012年「子ども食堂」設立から比べると数十倍の勢いである。

子ども食堂がどこでいつ頃、誰が開店したのかは諸説あり、定かではないが「こども食堂」の名付け親は近藤博子だ。近藤は、地域のおばさん・おじさんたちが子どもの成長の役割を担っていたことや子どもたちの話をじっくり聞いてくれるところとして「こども食堂」を位置づけている[2]。そもそも、子ども食堂の設立は、その背景に「貧困」があったことは確かである。2008年の医療を受けられなかった子どもが３万人いた、という報道から、子ども及び大人の「貧困」が再認識されたからである。さらに現在、「貧困」の様相がより深刻化・広域に拡大し、かつ貧困格差が激しい。厚生労働省の発表によれば、今や子どもの７人に１人は、貧困である[3]。このような状況を問題解決する場として、子ども食堂の現在は、「食事」「ケア」を土台に、地域の「コミュニティ」としての役割を担ってきている。

このように、本稿は、直接に子ども食堂運営主体者の立場から、子ども食堂の役割について「世代間交流」という視点で、事例をもとに報告をしたい。

2．世代間交流実践

（1）子ども食堂利用者からの声

筆者は2016年から、鹿児島県の子ども食堂に携わってきて、なかす子ども食堂・ほのぼの食堂につぐ県内で３番目に子ども食堂を開設した。県内３番目の開設「森の玉里子ども食堂」で代表を務め、その様子は単行本として発行した[4]。

「森の玉里子ども食堂会報・もりもりだより」[5)]から、利用者の声を拾ってみた結果(2017年：子ども食堂に来てよかったこと N=152 複数回答)、利用者の方々が「ボランティアの人と話せた」が28人、という声が多かったことである。むろん、食事することは当然であるが、「子どもが無料」が33人から、「ゆったりとした時間」が38人、「他の親子さんと話せた」が15人というように、「交流」を望んでいることがわかった。

運営上ボランティアの人は必ず各テーブルに入り、利用者と話をする、というのを目標に掲げてきた結果もあるが、利用者の方々からこのような声があることは運営上も成果が出ていると考えられる。また、親同士がメール交換し、情報交換の場でもある。ボランティアではあるが、利用者との上下関係ではなく、平等で「食事」「コミュニケーション」「遊び」「ケア」などを一緒に行い事実上、地域社会としてのコミュニティを形成している。

写真1：子ども食堂の様子

利用者人数と利用者構成は、各子ども食堂によって異なり、平均してスタッフは15人前後で、おおよそ大人25人、子ども50人前後・「母と子」の利用者が多い。高齢者がほとんど、または子どもだけという子ども食堂もある。

子ども食堂で欠かせないのは、高齢者のボランティアである。活動主体として自分の力を生かそうとしていることである。

写真2：調理担当

(2) 高齢者と子ども食堂

写真2は開店当時から調理担当の

最も高齢の上久木田セツ子さんだ。夫の遺留品を新聞利用して整理しているときに、その新聞に子ども食堂が開店することを読んだことから始まっている。本人は「夫の導き」と称している(現在は引退。当時 85 歳)。

写真3：クリスマス会での手品

① ボランティアとして

写真３は子ども食堂でクリスマス会を行ったときに手品をご披露していただいた。後方に見えるのは高校生のボランティアである。彼らは子どもたちの良き遊び相手だ。

写真4：絵本の読み聞かせ

写真４は本の読み聞かせである。定年後、子どもたちの支援として、毎回「本の読み聞かせ」を行っているボランティアである。澄本禎子さんによる冊数は１年間で 100 冊以上である。他に娘さんのフルート演奏・夫さん(隣)のギターなどコンサートもある。

② 交流の場－抱っこからはじまった

「子どもから大人まで楽しめる」という利用者の声から、特に高齢者の利用の声をここでは述べていきたい。そこで利用について伺ったところ、全員が「子ども食堂は子どものもの、だから私のような高齢者が来てよいものとは思わなかった」と答える。他の理由は、「調理ができず難儀している」ということである。「それにひとりで食べるのも寂しい。だからこうして皆さんと食べたい」というのである。

ボランティア活動以外では、子ども食堂に食事利用をすることであるが、いわゆる「想定外」のことがあった。それは、全くの見ず知らずの関係であるにもかかわらず、「赤ちゃん」を通して、お互いが親密になることである。それは「抱っこ」からはじまった。

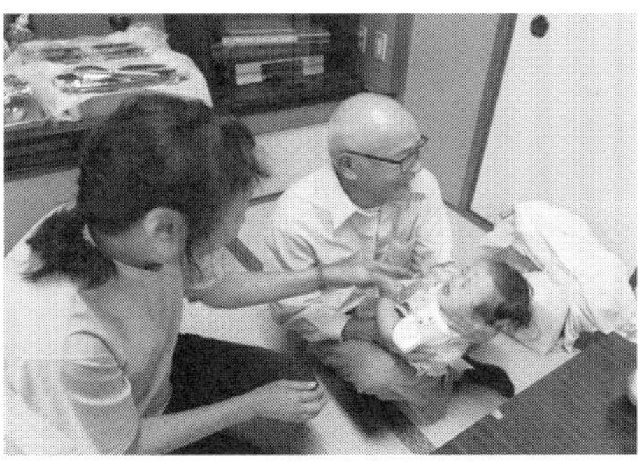

写真５　赤ちゃんをあやす？

写真５は、赤ちゃんを抱っこしていたところ、急に赤ちゃんが泣きだしたので、母親にバトンタッチしたところだ。

写真６　赤ちゃんと一緒にハイチーズ

高齢者７人にインタビューしました（下表）。

Q1. なぜ赤ちゃんを抱っこ・あやすのですか。

A1: 自分でできることはお母さんのお手伝いで、母親が食事するときには、子どもにかかりきりで自分が十分に食べられない時がある。その時抱っこして、母親が食事に専念させたい。

A2: 孫を十分抱けなかったので、抱きたい。孫と同様にかわいがりたい。

A3: 子育ての経験から子どもを抱きたい。

A4: 抱いたり、あやしたりすると気持ちがいいね。

A5: そうそう癒しだよね。母親も助かるしね。（みなさん、うなずく）

A6: 私たちがほっとすると・・・みんなもほっとする。ところだった。

Q2. 子ども食堂はどんなところでしたか。
A1: 高齢者がほっとできるところ。
A2: みんなが楽しいところ。
A3: 食事だけではなくて、いろいろな人が話している。
A4: 思っていたよりはるかに明るいところだった。
A5: 明るいところ。
A6: 高齢者だけでなく、あらゆる人たちが楽しく食事ができる場。
A7: こんなに多くの人が来ているとは思わなかった。

世代のケアもある事もわかった。このことは、子どもの親世代にとっても食事や時間的なゆとりを見出すこと、それがひいては高齢者も子どもの親世代も精神的な安心感につながることが散見された。他にも「子どもの発達」や「母親の調理技能・経済の軽減」があり、これらについては別に報告をしている[6)]。

③　**大学生のボランティア**

大学生のボランティアについては、写真７のように会のイベントを組織し多様な企画・アイデアを寄せ、かつ実践している。机や荷物の搬入・搬出、設定はもちろん、子ども食堂の運営上、欠かせない力である。さらに、子ども食堂としての学習支援のほか、将来社会人としての準備段階としての体験である。これから起こりうるいろいろな状況の重要な課題への挑戦と自身受け止め、「自分だけでなく、社会に役に立ちたい」という価値観を強固にするだけでなく、子どもたちに慕われ、実際このような理由で、卒業・就職を選択している。

写真７: クリスマス会で大学生によるクイズと地域の方のバルーンアート

④　高校生のボランティア

高校生のボランティアは、「良き子どもの遊び仲間・遊び相手」である。特に女子生徒より男子生徒が子どもたちの大の人気者である。詳細に観察すると、遊びの中でも「タカイ、タカイ」「肩車」「レスリング」「飛行機」、外遊びでは「縄とび」「鬼ごっこ」など体全身の運動がその中心である。これから見ると親子とは異なる、「きょうだい」という関係を結んでくれている。子どもたちは高校生を見つけると、駆け寄って－しかも体当たりしながらも、遊んでくれるようにせがんでいるのが毎回の光景である。保護者のみなさんたちは、高校生に子どもの面倒を見てもらい、安心して親同士の会話に夢中になっている。当の高校生の話は、ここに来るとやはり「ほっとする」「自分でできることが明確である」「貢献して、充実感がある」と楽しんで来ている。また、大学の進学や職業選択に大きな影響を与えている。

３．まとめ

以上から、子ども食堂は、老若男女、異世代から構成されている、ケアリング（食事・ケア）中心とした地域の実践コミュニティである。世代ごとに役割が分担されてはいるが、食材（モノ）・流通⇒調理（コト）・⇒食事・遊び・会話（ひと）という一連の流れの中で、人々が「ケア」や「食事」を通して交流発展してきている場所であるといえる。こうした意味では、子ども食堂の存在は「地域の力」だ[7]。

付記

本稿は、『世代間交流－老いも若きも子どもも－』2018年　19-26　通算第18号（特定非営利活動法人日本世代間交流協会第11号）を加筆・修正したものである。また、平成27年度文部科学省科学研究費補助金：基盤研究Ｃ「地域貢献としての「子ども食堂」の意義と役割」（研究代表：齋藤美保子、課題番号：17K01906）の助成を受けた研究に基づいている。

引用・参考文献

1） ノルディングス著 , 立山善康・清水重樹・新茂之・林泰成・宮崎宏志（訳）（1997）ケアリング－倫理と道徳の教育 女性の観点から , 晃洋書房

2） 近藤博子（2016）子どもの居場所を作り、孤立を防ぐ－「こども食堂」第１号店からの発信－ , 月刊保団連 , No.1225, pp.29-35.

3） 厚生労働省（2020）2019 年　国民生活基礎調査 , 最終閲覧 2021 年７月

4） 齋藤美保子編著（2017）森の玉里子ども食堂奮闘記－鹿児島発 , 南日本出版社

5） 森の玉里子ども食堂会報（2017）森の玉里子ども食堂発行ニュース・もりもりだより

6） 齋藤美保子（2019）子ども食堂の役割 , 自治研かごしま , No.211, pp.20-28.

7） 齋藤美保子　論点　子ども食堂は地域の力 , 南日本新聞（2018 年６月 18 日掲載）

＊　「子ども」の表記については「こども」や「子供」が見られるが、本稿では、「子ども」に統一し、「子ども食堂」と表記する。

要約

貧困対策として始まったといって過言でない「子ども食堂」は、今や日本で 6,000 か所ともいわれている。その子ども食堂の役割は今日、多様に富み、食事だけでなく、学習や文化の交流の場でもある。本稿は、鹿児島でも早くから立ち上げた子ども食堂の中でも、高校生から高齢者のボランティが多く、しかも利用者が多様な世代にわたる子ども食堂を事例としている。

高齢のボランティアは、子ども食堂の運営－会場の設営、食材の提供・運搬、調理、調理の配膳、読み聞かせやコンサート、あとかたづけ－など多岐にわたり中心的存在である。若い大学生は運営もし、子どもの学習支援をし、頼もしい存在である。高校生は、運営というよりは、よき子どもの遊び相手であり、自らの居場所をここに見出して通う場合が多い。一方、高齢者のインタビューからも、子ども食堂への期待と楽しみが伺えられた。特に孫世代の子どもの相手をすることで充実感が得られ、ケアを中心としたコミュニティを支えている。

以上のように、「子ども食堂」は、どの世代にも「ケアリング」が見られる場所となり、幼児から高齢者まで「食事」を通じてさまざまな文化交流が行われている。

齋藤美保子

神戸女子大学特任教授。埼玉・東京などの小・中・高校・大学（34 校）を経て、現職。専門は家庭科教育学、教育実践・教材開発等。

「子ども食堂」代表（2016 ～ 2018）、「かごしまこども食堂・地域食堂ネットワーク」顧問（2018 ～現在）。

Summary

Intergenerational Exchange as Seen in Children's Cafeterias - The Role of Caring

It is not an exaggeration to say that "children's cafeterias" started as a measure against poverty, and now there are about 5,000 of them in Japan. Today, the roles of these cafeterias are diverse and include not only meals, but also learning and cultural exchange.

This paper is a case study of a children's cafeteria that was established early in Kagoshima, which has many volunteers ranging from high school students to elderly people, and whose users are of various generations.

Elderly volunteers play a central role in the operation of the Children's Cafeteria by setting up the venue, providing and transporting food, cooking, serving food, reading stories and holding concerts, and cleaning up afterwards etc. The young university students are reliable in running the cafeteria and supporting the children's learning. High school students, rather than running the center, are good playmates for the children and often come to the center to find a place of their own.

On the other hand, the interviews with the elderly also revealed their expectations and enjoyment of the Children's Cafeteria. In particular, they feel a sense of fulfillment in the company of their grandchildren's children, which supports the care-centered community.

As mentioned above, the "children's cafeteria" has become a place where "caring" can be seen in every generation, and where various cultural exchanges take place through "meals" from infants to the elderly.

Mihoko Saito

Mihoko Saito is a specially appointed professor at Kobe Women's University. She has worked at 34 elementary, junior high, and high schools and universities in Saitama and Tokyo etc. before assuming her current position. She specializes in home economics pedagogy, educational practice, and development of teaching materials. She is a representative of "Children's Cafeteria" (2016-2018) and an advisor to "Kagoshima Children's Cafeteria and Community Cafeteria Network" (2018-present)

第２章　くわなの宿における幼老統合ケアの実践と成果

小林　久人

１．はじめに

「少子高齢化」が叫ばれて久しい。だが、状況は一向に改善せず、少子化、高齢化の流れは止まらない。核家族化が進み、一極集中による地域社会の高齢化による地盤沈下状態も進んでいる。核家族化は、世代間の相互扶助機能も低下させ、家庭は地域社会と切り離されている傾向が強くなっている。共同体意識が希薄なものになり、ただの「個」が社会の中で漂うようになってしまっている。挙句、自己責任がまん延し、子ども、障がいを持つ人々、高齢者を共同体全体で支えていくことが難しくなっている。そのような状況下で世代間の相互扶助機能を復元する試みも多く見られるようになった。幼老複合型施設もそのひとつであろう。

私たちの事業所「グループホームくわなの宿」は以前より、法人理事長多湖光宗の提唱する「幼老統合ケア」を実践する場として、併設の学童保育所「くわなっ子」とともに様々な世代間交流を行ってきた。高齢者や子どもたちにとって世代間の相互扶助機能がいかに重要なことであるか、私たちが行ってきた試みを通して得られた成果を報告したい。

世代間交流における相互作用

当事業所は、三重県桑名市に本拠をおく「ウエルネス医療クリニック」を母体とする医療法人「創健会」と社会福祉法人「自立共生会」からなるウエルネスグループの事業所である。グループ本体は、桑名市の中でも新興住宅地にあるが、グループホームくわなの宿と学童保育所くわなっ子は、本部から５キロほど離れた旧東海道に面した古い城下町の中にある。

当法人における幼老統合ケアはウエルネス医療クリニックの隣に建てられたグループホーム「ひかりの里」と併設の学童保育所「パンの木」での取り組みに端を発している。グループホームの利用者と放課後、学童に帰ってくる子どもたちが、宿題を見てもらったり、一緒に遊んだりして交流するうちに、スタッフの手を借りなければ身の回りのことができなかった利用者に顕著な変化が見られた。自分でトイレにいくことができず、たびたび失禁をしていた利用者が、子どもたちの前では当たり前のように自分からトイレに行き排尿ができたり、普段は意欲がなくスタッフに促されても字を書くこともしなかった利用者が子どもに漢字の書き取りを教えたり、ピアノで曲を弾いて聞かせたりできたのである。子どもたちの前では、スタッフが驚くほどいきいきとした豊かな表情を見せていた。

子どもたちの側にも変化が見られた。今までスタッフや指導員が叱っても言うことをきかなかった子どもたちが、お年寄りに叱られると言うことを聞く。スタッフや指導員が褒めるよりも、お年寄りから褒められると本当に嬉しそうな顔になる。認知症高齢者の記憶障害としてマイナスイメージで語られる同じことを繰り返し言うという問題点が逆に「何度も叱られ」「何度も褒められ」という中でうまく子どもたちの子育てにいかされるようになった。考えてみれば、不思議はなことではない。利用者はかつては父であり、母であり、祖母であり祖父であった。子どもたちによって眠っていた子育てのプロとしての能力が引き出されたのである。

２．くわなの宿とくわなっ子による共同調理

私たちの事業所、グループホームくわなの宿とくわなっ子は、前述したように桑名市の古い城下町の中にある。地域的にも、まだ地域社会ならではの人のつながりが残っている場所である。学童保育所くわなっ子はグループホームくわなの宿とともに、地域との交流、地域への貢献も担ってきた。江戸時代から続く地域の祭事、行事への参加、地域の人たちと町内の清掃、防犯パトロールへの参加、そして地域の老人会の人たちとの交流なども行っている。夏休みには、学童保育

所の子どもたちが中心になって地域の人たちも招いて夏祭りを行ったり、年末には昔ながらの餅つき大会を行ったりしている。くわなっ子の子どもたちはみな地域の子どもたちである。子どもたちを通して、地域の方たちと顔見知りになったり、関係づくりができたりすることも多かった。子どもたちがくわなっ子に向けて旧東海道を元気に帰ってくると近所から「おかえり」という声がかかる。子どももたちも「ただいま！」と元気に挨拶しているのが日常の風景になっている。そのような風景の中にくわなの宿とくわなっ子はある。

平成28年の改正社会福祉法によって「社会福祉法人の地域への公益的な取り組み」が責務規定となった。私たちの法人では、その取り組みの一環として平成29年より学童保育に通う子どもたちへの長期休暇における昼食の無償化を始めることになった。昼食の無償化はもちろん、学童保育を利用する家庭の負担軽減ということもあった。ただ目的はそれだけではなかった。学童保育を利用する子どもたちの家庭状況による「お弁当格差」の問題や子どもたちの「偏食」の深刻さも背景にはあった。当法人の学童保育所を利用する子どもたちの中には、家で味噌汁を飲んだことがない子どもや、お弁当の中身がそっくりコンビニのお弁当を利用したもの、中には市販のパンとジュースだけを買い与えられた子どももいた。野菜が一切食べられない子ども、夕食は兄弟でお金だけ渡されてコンビニのから揚げだけを毎日食べている子どももいた。

昼食の無償提供という取り組みを始めるにあたって、このような子どもたちの状況を何とか改善する一助になれば、ということもあった。それと同時に、この取り組みを単に子どもたちの「食」の問題へのアプローチだけではなく、長期休み、普段から行っている子どもとグループホームのお年寄りとの交流をさらに深めるためのものにできるのではないか、という考えもあった。何とかこの機会をうまく生かす方法はないか、できることはないか、グループホームのスタッフや学童保育の指導員と話し合った。そしてグループホームの高齢者と子どもたちと一緒にお昼ごはんをつくり、一緒に食べよう、ということになった。行事の際のおやつ作りなどは過去にも共同で行ってはいた。ただ、毎日のお昼ごはんを一緒につくる、となるとかなり大変な作業になるな、という不安がなかったわけではない。一過性の行事ならばなんとかなるが、毎日やり切れるだろうか、という思いと、でもやれたら楽しいだろうなあ、という思いがスタッフ・指導員の中で交錯していた。ただ、私たちはこれまでの子どもたちとお年寄りとの交流の中で、双方がいきいきとする場面を何度も目にしてきていた。介護の現場ではよく理想と現実の乖離が言われる。たしかに現実を見ずに理想だけが先行しても絵にかいた餅になってしまう。ただ、私たちは何の理念もなく介護や保育に携わっているわけではない。現実にひたすら拝跪するだけでは、何も生まれない。私たちの事業所は「幼老統合ケア」の実践の場である。その思いはスタッフ全員に強くあった。そして、やってみよう、挑戦してみようという思いでスタッフの意志は固まった。

子どもたちの親にも理解を得ることができた。平成 29 年の夏休みから、グループホームの高齢者と学童保育の子どもたちとの共同調理が始まった。実際に始めてみると、子どもたちも慣れない包丁の扱いにとまどったり、思ったような段取りで進まなかったりして、食事を始める時間が遅れてしまうこともあった。ただ、日を重ねるうちに、子どもたち、お年寄りの間で変化が見られてきた。

危なっかしい手つきで包丁を握る子どもたちにお年寄りが実際に手本になって食材を切って見せてくれ、子どもたちに包丁の扱い方や切り方を教えてくれ始めたのである。「そんな手つきじゃ指を切るよ、こうやって指を曲げてね、猫の手にするの」と子どもたちに手本を見せてくれる A さん。彼女は入居当初、強い帰宅願望と易怒性でスタッフが対応に苦慮することが多かった。認知症の進行により、自宅での独居生活ができない状態になり、市内に住む家族が食事を持っていくことができる日以外は毎日お菓子ばかりを食べていた。そんな A さんだが、もともとは調理師の資格を持ち、バリバリ働いていた人である。子どもたちを前にして鮮やかな包丁さばきを見せる姿は、私たちが対応に苦慮していた A さんとは別の人のようだった。この合同調理をきっかけに A さんの帰宅願望はほぼ解消され、笑顔を見せることが多くなった。

B さんは、ペンションを経営していた女性。認知症をきっかけに独居生活が営めなくなった。部屋はごみ屋敷と化し、家族が困り果て入居にいたった。世話焼きで行動的で活発なBさんは子どもを前にすると持ち前の活発さから、子どもたちを放っておけない様子で「ちょっとちょっとそのキャベツはそんな切り方ではダメだよ。キャベツはこうやって芯のところを切っておいてから切るんだよ」「あら、上手に切ったねえ。えらいね」。子どもたちはお年寄りの鮮やかな手つきを見て「僕もやってみる」「わたしにもやらせて」と目をキラキラさせている。

その姿を見ていた私たちは、考えさせられた。スタッフや指導員だけでは、あるいは子どもたちだけ、お年寄りだけでは作り出せない生き生きとした表情や笑顔、それは世代間交流でしか生み出せない相乗効果ではないだろうか。できるだろうか、と最初に思っていた不安は杞憂だった。

「ねえ、なんでそんなに早く切れるの？」とAさんやBさんに羨望の眼差しを向ける子どもたち。認知症によって家庭内での立場や役割を喪失した高齢者にとって、子どもたちから尊敬の眼差しや「すごい！」と称賛の声を受けることは久しくなかったことだろう。確かに一瞬一瞬、彼女たちの記憶は失われていく。しかしながらその瞬間、彼女たちが輝きを取り戻し、自信を取り戻すのは言葉の本来の意味でのリハビリテーション、「尊厳の回復」ではないだろうか。

一方の子どもたちの変化も顕著だった。好き嫌いが多かった子どもたちが「自分たちが作ったんだから食べないと」と言いながら残さず食べるようになった。食の細い子どももしっかりと食べられるようになった。最初は危なっかしくて見ていられないような手つきだった子どもたちが、夏が終わる頃にはすっかり包丁の扱いが上手くなっている。卵を割ることすらままならなかった子どもたちがお年寄りに教わりながら錦糸卵を作れるまでになった。家でも「今日は～を作ったんだよ」「AさんとかBさんはね、きゅうりをものすごく早いスピードで切るんだよ。ママよりずっと上手だよ」と母親によく話していると聞く。家でも自分もできるから何か切らせて、という子どももいると母親たちからよく聞く。

一年が過ぎ翌年になると、新入所の子どもたちに年長の子どもが共同調理のやり方を教えたり、ルールを教えたりしている。年長の子どもが年下の子どもたちに色々教えたり、年下の子どもどうしの揉め事を年上の子どもが間に入って折り合いをつかせたり、まるでかつて存在した子ども社会の再生のようだ。子どもたちは、認知症を学ばなくても「何回も同じ話をしている面白い誰々さん」と自然にまるごとお年寄りを受け止めているのも興味深い。

子どもたちとお年寄りがワイワイ盛り上がりながら、一緒にご飯を作って一緒に食べる。ただそれだけのことが私たちに多くの気づきと発見をもたらしてくれた。冒頭に触れたように少子化や核家族化、共同体意識の希薄化といった流れは、容易に変わることはないだろう。ただ、だとしたら、あえてそういう環境をつくり出していき、世代間の相互扶助や子育てと高齢者のケアの相乗効果を狙った取り組みがより必要になってくるのではないかと思う。

引用・参考文献

多湖　光宗（監修）幼老統合ケア研究会（編）（2006）幼老統合ケア　少子高齢化も安心！“高齢者福祉”と“子育て”をつなぐケアの実践と相乗効果，黎明書房．

要約

日本では少子高齢化と、核家族化、地域社会の崩壊により子どもとお年寄りが交流する機会が激減している。

私たちの事業所は認知症高齢者のグループホームと放課後児童クラブを併設し、長年にわたり世代間交流の試みを行ってきた。普段、職員の介助を受けなければトイレに行けず、失禁を繰り返してきた高齢者が子どもたちを前にすると一人でトイレに行けるようになったり、いつもより元気になったりした。また、認知症高齢者特有の何度も同じことを繰り返すという特性が、何度も叱り、何度も褒めるという形で子育てに活かされる効果を得た。

また、2017年から夏休み、春休みなどの長期休みの間、子どもたちとグループホームの高齢者が一緒にお昼ご飯を作り、一緒に食べるという試みを始めた。普段、食事作りをする機会のない子どもたちに、高齢者が手本を見せて食材の切り方や焼き方を教えてくれた。子どもたちも初めて使う包丁に緊張していたが、高齢者の鮮やかな手つきに感動して「私もやりたい」と目を輝かせて高齢者に教えてもらいながら毎日料理をするうちに上手に料理ができるようになった。野菜が嫌いな子どもや好き嫌いが多い子どもも「自分たちで作ったのだから」と残さずに食べられるようになった。一方の高齢者も子どもたちから尊敬の目で見られ、尊厳を取り戻している様子が見られた。擬似的な共同体ではあったとしても、多世代の交流が相互に良い効果をもたらすことを実感させられた取り組みであった。

小林　久人

社会福祉法人自立共生会グループホームくわなの宿施設長　介護支援専門員

三重県桑名市の認知症グループホームで認知症高齢者の支援に関わりながら、併設の学童保育所の子どもたちと高齢者の共同作業を通してケアの相乗効果を目指している。

Summary

Practice and Results of Integrated Care for the Elderly and Young at Kuwana-No-Yado

In Japan, children and elderly people have significantly fewer opportunities to interact with each other nowadays due to a declining birthrate, an aging population, an increase in the number of nuclear families, and the diminished role of neighborhood communities.

Our facility, which operates both a group home for elderly people with dementia and a hokago jido club (a lounge where elementary schoolchildren spend time after school until their parents come home from work), has been experimenting with intergenerational exchange for many years.

During one such experiment, elderly people suffering from urine incontinence, who used to wet themselves often as they could not go to the restroom unassisted, began using the restroom independently when around children. We also found them to be more energetic in front of children.

While observing another intergenerational interaction/In another experiment, we found that the habit of repeating the same remarks, a characteristic of elderly people with dementia, proved useful in child-rearing as they admonished or commended children over and over again.

In 2017, we started an experiment in which the children and the elderly people at the group home cooked and ate lunch together during long vacations such as summer and spring breaks. The elderly people taught the children, who usually did not have the opportunity to cook at home, how to chop and grill food. The children were initially nervous about using kitchen knives; however, impressed by the elderly people's knife skills, they became eager to try them. They began to cook enthusiastically everyday with the help of the elderly people, and eventually learned to cook independently. Children who initially did not like vegetables or were picky/fussy eaters now ate everything they cooked. The elderly people, for their part, seemed to have regained their sense of dignity because the children treated them with respect. While this may not have been a real community, the experiment has demonstrated that intergenerational communication benefits both children and elderly people.

Hisato Kobayashi

Facility Manager, Social Welfare Corporation Jiritsu Kyosei-kai.

While providing support for elderly people with dementia at a dementia group home in Kuwana City, Mie Prefecture, we aim to create a synergy of care through joint work between the elderly and children at the school nursery attached to the home.

第3章　小平西地区地域ネットワークづくりの取り組み

瀧口　優

1．はじめに

白梅学園は東京郊外の多摩地域、小平市の西の端にあり、立川市や東大和市、東村山市、国分寺市、国立市とも近い関係にある。創立は東京家庭学園として1942年となっており、現在は幼稚園、中学校（女子のみ）、高校（女子のみ）、短期大学、大学そして大学院（修士・博士）が開校され、まもなく80周年をむかえる。小平の地に移転してからも60年が経過している。小平市は東京都心から1時間以内ということで、ここの居住地に定める人も多くなり、現在ほぼ20万人の人々が住んでいる。一方で地域としてのつながりを示す自治会や町内会は減少の一途をたどり、現在では40％を割るところまで下がってしまっている。地域のつながりが弱くなっている現状がある。

短期大学の保育科、大学の子ども学部（こども学科、発達臨床学科、家族地域支援学科）ともにこどもや地域に関係する専門であり、研究としてもこうした分野が対象となっている。2005年からスタートした学内の「地域ネットワーク作り」では、内閣府の「ソーシャルキャピタルー豊かな人間関係と市民活動の好循環を求めて」（内閣府国民生活局市民活動促進課2002）をもとに、同じ内容の調査を大学周辺の小学校保護者にお願いし、国と同じような結論にいたった。

人間は知り合っている人間の数が多ければ、人間に対する信頼が高くなること、少なければ信頼を持ちにくいこと等が結論である。それをどのような形にしていくのか考えている矢先に2011年、東日本大震災があり、被災報道の中で日常的なつながりが大きな力を発揮していることが伝えられた。地域ネットワーク作りのメンバーはどのような地域ネットワークにするのか相談して1年後「小平西地区地域ネットワーク」(以下西ネット)を立ち上げた。個人的な知り合いをたどって民生委員やNPOの代表などを地域世話人にお願いし、大学内、とりわけ家族地域支援学科の先生方に参加してもらって結成にたどり着いた。

詳細については「白梅学園大学・短期大学の地域活動」(小平まちづくり研究のフロンティア)に触れているのでここではその後の経過と現状、とりわけ関わりの深い地域での取り組みについて報告したい。

2．西ネットの設立に関わって

西ネット設立の呼びかけにこたえて参加してくれた地域の人々は、民生委員をはじめとして自分たちも地域のつながりをどうしたらいいか気になっていたということで、大学が声をかけたことによって形になったというところである。設立集会では小平市長を含めて100人近い参加があり、地域づくりへの期待が寄せられた。

西ネットは小平市の西地区で広さも人口も4分の1程度(とはいっても人口3万人以上)で、それを更に4つのブロックに分けて、ブロックごとの集まりを基本としてきた。地域懇談会は3ヶ月に1回、地域世話人会は2ヶ月に1回、そして大学の世話人会はほぼ毎月行い、ブロックもほぼ月に1回行うということで10年間やってきたというのが現状である。

4つのうち3つのブロックは居場所としてのコミュニティサロンを確保し、週に1回～2回の集まりをもってきた。このコミュニティサロンは小平市の居場所作りのモデルになって広がってきている。なお少し遅れたが、公民館の協力を得て中学生勉強会「分かった会」がスタートして高校入学に向けて中学生の支援をしてきた。これは4つのブロックをまたぐ形になっている。毎年3月には修了式を行っているが、高校入学を実現してきている。

３．運営に関わって

（1）広報紙「小平西のきずな」の発行

「西ネット」の運営は、まず大学の運営委員会で案を考える。３ヶ月ごとの懇談会の内容とその懇談会に会わせて発行する情宣紙「小平西のきずな」の編集会議である。Ａ４で８頁の記事を集めるためには10人以上に記事を依頼しなければならない。その候補を出し合うのである。地域の世話人会があるときは世話人会にはかり、無いときはメーリングリストで流して意見をもらう。印刷は1,200部で地域内の公的な施設、医院、薬局、そして民生児童委員や今まで関わってきた人々に郵送する。コロナ禍の前は、懇談会に来た地域の人々が持ち帰ってくれたので郵送する数が少なくなった。現在は一部を除いて180通程度郵送している。2021年６月で38号になり、大学のHPで読めるようになっている。以下特徴的な内容を紹介したい。

号	年	月	日	巻頭記事タイトル・（執筆者）	内容（一部）
01	2012	06	01	「お互いの顔が見える地域づくり」にあなたも参加しませんか？（奈良勝行）	設立集会の様子：小平市長、白梅学園理事長講演、地域からの発言。
02	2012	09	17	高齢者と地域社会（渡辺穂積）	ブロック報告
03	2012	11	22	参加した多くの市民の皆さまに感謝－市民活動まちづくりシンポー（細江卓朗）	ほっとスペース「さつき」ミニバザー開催します！
09	2014	03	11	鎮守の境内を地域の方が集う場に（小平神明宮宮司 宮﨑和美）	「中学生勉強会――分かったかい（会）？」に参加して
14	2015	06	02	顔の見える地域への旗手（船頭）－西ネットの役割を考える－金田利子（元白梅学園大学教授）	ブロックだより【小平市役所の組織改革について】（担当者一覧）
17	2016	03	12	小平は関係づくりの宝庫　関谷榮子（家族・地域支援学科教授）	小平南西地区にコミュタクを走らせるには－塚本博子（走らせる会事務局）

20	2016	12	20	「西の風」第２ブロック（芳井正彦）	朝鮮大学校創立 60 周年記念学園祭　朝鮮大学校学生委員会
21	2017	03	11	白梅学園と大学まちづくりの実践－小平西地区ネットワークづくり３周年を迎えて（瀧口優）	白梅幼稚園作品展　高橋敬子（白梅幼稚園）
25	2018	03	10	これからも地域を見据えて、ともに集い・小平の地で－白梅学園の方向－（企画調整部長　本田百合子）	「きよか」のクリスマス会　宮本美子（きよかスタッフ）
30	2019	06	11	他人（ひと）の子も、正しく叱る、思いやり（白梅学園理事長 井原　徹）	３月地域懇談会報告映画『ケアニン』を観て
33	2020	03	09	白梅変わったもの（こと）・変わらないもの（こと）（白梅学園生活協同組合：理事　高祖亜希子）	「カフェ　なかじま」がオープン「西の風」（第２ブロック）
35	2020	09	29	コロナ禍での学生支援（白梅学園大学・白梅学園短期大学学生部長　松田佳尚）	コロナ禍の高齢者施設－小川ホームの取り組み－
37	2021	03	06	保育・子育てと地域性ということ（白梅学園大学・短期大学学長　近藤幹生）	西ネット第 38 回地域懇談会報告：地域包括から見えてくる現状

（２）地域懇談会

地域懇談会では３ヶ月に１回、地域に在住或いは在職する人々を中心に話をしてもらうが、火曜日の夜に設定し、最後の３月だけは土曜日の午後に設定している。３回に１回は学園の内部に依頼し、宣伝と同時に地域理解を広めることを目標にしている。懇談会は講演会の場合もあれば、上映会やワークショップなどにあてられることもある。時には行政に関係する人々に参加してもらうこともあり、30 人から 40 人程度の参加がある。地域懇談会の後半はブロックごとの集まりを行って、地域の顔と顔がつながるようにしてきた。世話人会の案内はメーリングリストで行っているが、懇談会は葉書や封書で行うことが多い。

（3）大学世話人会

８月を除いてほぼ毎月、大学の専任教員と協力者である嘱託研究員の会議を開いている。上述の「小平西のきずな」の原稿依頼対象者を出し合うことをはじめとして、地域懇談会や地域世話人会などの内容について相談する。更に各ブロックの動きを交流し、サポートやアドバイスを行う。この 10 年間でほぼ 100 回にのぼる。この１年半はコロナ禍のために基本的にオンラインで行わざるを得ず、細部の相談がしにくくなっているが、中断することなく続いている。

（4）ブロックの集まり

私が担当しているのは第一ブロックで小平市の障がい者センター、高齢者施設、市民などから世話人が出ている。月に１回の世話人会を障がい者センターを借りて開催し、地域での取り組みを話し合う。地域の小児科医に話をしてもらったり、小川西町の良いとこ探しのワークショップなどを行ってきたが、コロナ禍の中でオンラインの世話人会を開催し、その話合いの中で小川西町の良いこと紹介「地域ごころ通信」を発行することになった。５月に第１号を発行し、第２号の準備中である。

（5）大学・法人の支援体制

「西ネット」の活動を進めるにあたって、大学の研究助成制度に毎年応募して活動に必要な資金を確保してきた。また「小平西のきずな」の発行や研究年報に活動状況を報告することによって、学内での理解を進めることができ、大学の全面的な支援、法人の支援を得ることとなった。

４．今後の課題として

2021 年は結成 10 年目を迎えて今後の方向性について考えなければならないところに来ている。以下視点に沿って整理したい。

①　顔の見えるつながりを作ることについて

10年間の取り組みを通して、小平西地区において地域に関心のある人々の顔が見えてきた。しかし3万人を越える住民から考えるとまだまだ点にしか過ぎない。自治会のような身近なところでの「顔が見える関係」を作らないといざというときに役に立たない。コミュニティサロンとして7年近く取組んできた「さつき」や「きよか」は家主の都合で使えなくなり、せっかくできたつながりが続かなくなっている。新たな居場所作りが必要である。

②　行政を巻き込んだ制度作り

居場所作りは個人の力では限界があり、行政の制度として取り組めるようにしなければならない。そのためには行政に働きかけて政策に反映するような取り組みが求められている。

③　世代間交流から世代間連帯へ

世代間交流が叫ばれはじめてからかなりの時間が過ぎた。様々なところでこの言葉が使われるようになったが、次のステップとして世代間の連帯を考えて行く必要があるのではないだろうか。もちろん交流することが連帯につながるところもあるが、一緒になって何かを実現していくというような取り組みが求められているのではないか。高齢者から下の世代が学ぶこと、あるいは下の世代から高齢者が学ぶことを組み合わせて、社会や地域をどのようにしていくのか一緒に考える連帯の場を意識的に作ることが求められていると感じる。高齢者も子どももともに「参加」「参画」することがこれからの地域活動では必要になっていると思われる。

参考文献・資料等

稲葉洋一『ソーシャルキャピタル入門』中央公論社 2011

草野篤子・瀧口真央「人間への信頼とソーシャルキャピタル」白梅学園大学・短期大学教育福祉研究センター年報15号 2010

小松歩編著『遊び心でコミュニティの再生を』新読書社 2021

瀧口優・森山千賀子「地域ネットワークに関する調査研究」白梅学園大学・短期大学教育福祉研究センター年報13号 2008

内閣府「ソーシャルキャピタルー豊かな人間関係と市民活動の好循環を求めて」(国民生活局市民活動促進課 2002)
広井良典『コミュニティを問い直す』筑摩書房 2009

要約

「小平西地区地域ネットワーク（以下「西ネット」）づくりの取り組み」は白梅学園大学・短期大学で「地域ネットワーク作りの研究」を行なっていたグループが、研究のまとめとして地域のつながりをつくることがネットワーク作りに資するということでスタートしたことにはじまる。

大学が地域につながっていく必要性は叫ばれるものの、どうやって地域との関係をつくっていくのかが問われる。西ネットでは地域世話人を積極的に確保し、運営委員会（世話人会）を定期的に開くことになった。この地域世話人が地域に根を張って声がけや様々な配布を引き受け、その中からコミュニティ・サロンが３つも誕生している。

本稿では、西ネットの①広報紙の定期的な発行による地域交流、②地域の顔が見える懇談会の定期的な開催、③運営を支える大学世話人会の定期的な開催とリーダーシップ、④小さな単位での集まり、⑤そして、大学や法人の支援体制を背景に、４分割した地域の１つを視野に、更に日常的にどのような取り組みを行なっているのかを展開した。特に広報紙では地域で活躍する様々な人々に登場してもらうことを大事にしてきている。

また課題として３点あげている。１つは顔の見えるつながりをどのように作るのかということ、２つ目として、行政を巻き込んだ制度作りを進めること、そして３つ目として、世代間交流から世代間連帯へと発展させることである。

瀧口優

白梅学園短期大学保育科教授（2022 年３月 31 日まで）

新英語教育研究会、日本児童英語教育学会等、英語教育での研究をすすめる傍ら、大学において学生の子育て広場を指導し、地域ネットワーク作りに取組んでいる。小平西地区地域ネットワークは2022年３月で10年をむかえる。『遊び心でコミュニティの再生を』（新読書社、2021）、『ことばと教育の創造』（三学出版、2017）、『小学校英語授業バンク（全８巻）』（三友社出版、2020）いずれも共著。

Summary

Organizing the Regional People's Network in the Western Part of Kodaira City

The Regional People's Network in the Western Part of Kodaira City got started in 2012 a year after the Great Earthquake of Eastern Japan in 2011. Teachers of Shiraume Gakuen University and College called out to the people around the school. People who had interests to build comfortable region to live responded to this message from the university.

About 15 members took part in this project with 10 staff(teachers) in the school. These members did their best to organize the area. Three community salons were started up and one regional meeting has been started.

There are five points that these movements began to start with;

1. To publish the communication newspaper regularly
2. To have regional meetings regularly
3. The leadership of the university staff(teachers) by regular meetings
4. Meeting of small area with small members
5. The support system of university and school corporation

Especially we picked up the people who worked for other people through our communication newspaper.

However there are some subjects to control the problems.

6. How to organize the "face to face relation" among the people
7. How to organize the region with administrative supports
8. To develop the intergenerational exchange into intergenerational solidarity

Masaru Takiguchi

Professor of Shiraumegakuen Junior College (until the end of March, 2022)

A Member of New English Teachers Association, The Japan Association for the Study of Teaching English to Children(JASTEC) and the supporter of students who promote Children's Plaza in Shiraumegakuen, and also one of the promoters to organize Kodaira Western Community Network around the college since 2012. To Restore the Community by Playfulness(co) (Shindokushosha,2021), To Create the Language and Education(co) (Sangaku Publishing Co., 2017), The Instruction Materials for English Education in Elementary Schools:8 volumes(co) (Sanyusha Publishing Co.,2020)

第４章　幼老統合施設として
―社会福祉法人　江東園35年の歩みとこれから―

杉　啓以子

１．はじめに

社会福祉法人江東園は住むところのないお年寄りが安心して住める終の棲家を造るために、1962（昭和37）年に養護老人ホーム江東園を東京都江戸川区に設立した。法人名の江東園には「江戸川の東にお年寄りの楽園を創る」という思いが込められている。

その後、女性の社会進出が進み、保育所設立への地域の期待の声が高まり、1976（昭和51）年に江戸川保育園を設立。その後、1987（昭和62）年には養護老人ホーム・保育園・特別養護老人ホーム・高齢者在宅サービスの４施設を合わせた幼老複合施設を建設。念願であった「ひとつ屋根の下の大家族」となった。

その後も社会的ニーズの変化に合わせて、事業を拡大。2006（平成18）年には法人初となる障害者支援施設（旧：知的障害者通所更生施設）と高齢者の通所介護・訪問介護事業・地域住民向けカフェテリアの機能を持った江東園ケアセンター「つばき」を開設。2017（平成29）年には事業所内保育所を開設し、こども・高齢者・障害者・地域住民がひとつ屋根の下に集う「地域共生社会の中の幼老複合施設」となり、今日に至っている。

２．世代間交流実践の歴史、背景

「おじいちゃん汚い、臭い」

幼老複合施設建設へのきっかけとなった言葉である。養護老人ホームと保育所が同一敷地内別建物であった時代、保育園のある子どもが高齢者に放った言葉が、その後の幼老複合施設のきっかけとなった。高齢者が大切にされ、子どもたちに見守られる環境が作られ、かつ、子どもは高齢者から知恵と経験を学ぶ、そのような環境を目指して、この施設建設と本格的な世代間交流が始まった。

これはまさに古き良き日本の大家族の姿である。昔の農家の大家族は何世代もの家族が生活を共にし、助け合って生きてきた生活であり、「孤独な生活をしていたお年寄りには温もりを与え、少子化と核家族化のなかで人のふれあいが減っているこどもには、優しさと感謝の念を学ぶ場」となった。

3．プログラムの内容

（1）江東園で行われる世代間交流の分類

園で行われる世代間交流の分類

規模	内容
小規模	日常のあいさつ、同じ空間で過ごす、ラジオ体操、お芋を食べよう会など
中規模	居室訪問、オープン保育、サマーキャンプ、節分・こどもの日・ひなまつりウィークなど ※季節行事はふれあい促進委員会で企画・立案する
大規模	合同夏祭り盆踊り大会、合同すもう大会、クリスマスお遊戯会、合同もちつき大会など

（2）小規模プログラムの例

①ラジオ体操

・毎朝 09：40 から園庭またはホールにて行う。

・ラジオ体操のあとにふれあいの時間を設ける

・高齢者は自由参加。参加する高齢者が自主的にイスを並べるなどの役割がある。

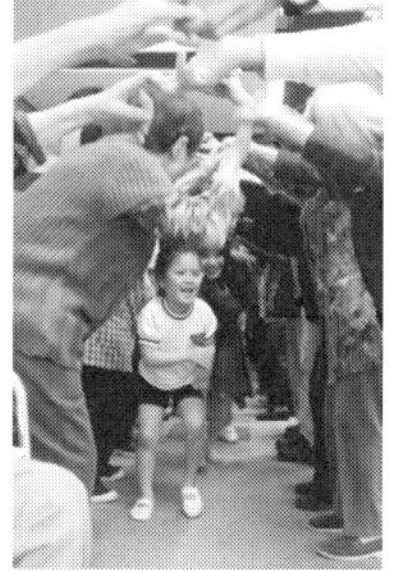

②卒園式

・お年寄りが保育園の卒園式に参列。

・お年寄り代表が壇上で送辞を読む。

・謝恩会後、アーチで最後のお見送り。
　コロナ禍のために、「ベランダからさようなら！」
・生活の節目を感じる行事。

（3）中規模プログラムの例

①オープン保育

・毎月第３木曜日に１日こどもと高齢者が遊んだり、食事を共にする。
・あそびのメニューはふれあい促進委員会で決定する。
※ふれあい促進委員会は介護・保育・看護・栄養など職種を越えたメンバーで構成されている。

②居室訪問

・保育園と介護（特養・養護・在宅等）と連絡を取りあいスケジュールに入れる。
・特養では、ベットサイドでの交流を行う。

（4）大規模プログラムの例

①合同相撲大会

・毎年６月実施。保護者とともにお年寄りが観戦。おとしよりと力士の交流プログラムもあり。
・その他、区内認可私立保育園11ヶ園対抗すもう大会あり。高齢者は応援参加する。

②合同運動会

・毎年10月実施。高齢者は応援団として参加する他、子どもと一緒に行う競技もある。
・会場の都合により、参加者を制限せざるを得ない課題もあり。

４．現在抱える問題

（１）高齢者の重度化と人手不足

高齢化の進展により、特別養護老人ホーム等への入居者は要介護度の高い高齢者が増加し、交流が困難になっている。特に、移動に際して人手を要するため、高齢者にとっては交流の機会が減少せざるを得ない。

（２）新型コロナウィルスによる交流制限

高齢者が重症化しやすい新型コロナウィルス感染症の拡大により、お年寄りとこどもの交流が制限された。例えば、それまで行っていた対面による交流が、放送による「声の交流」となり、また、子どもと一緒に作業をしていた装飾の作業が高齢者のみになったが、何らかの交流は続いている。

５．考察

日常的な世代間交流によりたくさんのふれあいが生まれてきた。たくさんの子どもたちが成長し、保育園を巣立っていった。その後成長し、親となって江東園に戻ってきている。また介護士や保育士となって戻ってくるケースも生まれた。また、この交流によってつちかわれた子どもとのつながりを受けて、多くの高齢者が見送られ旅だっている。この、一連の流れは、江東園が目指した「ひとつ屋根の下の家族」という世代間交流の姿であり、成果でもある。

しかし、今回の新型コロナウィルスのパンデミックは、人と人がふれあうことを分断した。江東園においても令和２年は対面での交流ができなくなった。それでも、ICT の活用を促進し ZOOM によるリモート交流など、新しい方法を取り入れる試行錯誤が進んだ。その結果、重度の高齢者にとっては移動することもなく交流を行うことが出来るようになり、物理的な距離を縮めることが可能になった。ZOOM の活用は幼老統合施設にとって、新たな成果を示すことになった。

6．結論

人間社会はいつの時代も分断と協調を繰り返してきた。新型コロナウィルスのパンデミックは、それまでの当たり前となるふれ合いを奪った。そのことであらためて人と人は関係をもちながら、成長したり、幸せを感じるものだということに気づいた。このことから、私たちは、このアフターコロナの時代に、新しい手法を取り入れ、私たちの実践としてさらなる世代間交流を進めたいと考えている。

＋＋＋新たな社会へのメッセージ～2022＋＋＋

コロナ後はどのような社会になるのでしょうか。

対面でマスク無しの当たり前の日常は訪れるのでしょうか。

眼だけの笑顔で本当の心が伝わるでしょうか。

インターネットで世界の様々な人々と知り合うことは容易になりますが、人の温もりは伝わるでしょうか。

コロナ禍で分断された「人と人の関わり」や「深くなってしまった差別の溝」を取り除くことが出来るでしょうか。私たちは、人のもつ人間らしさを信じて、世代間交流を進めます。

要約

社会福祉法人「江東園」は、1962年に東京都江戸川区に設立された養護老人ホームである。「江東園」の名前には「江戸川の東となる位置に高齢者の楽園を創る」との願いが込められている。この「江東園」は、その後1976年に、「女性の社会進出に応じた期待に応えるために江戸川保育園を併設して、「一つ屋根の下の大家族」を理念とする幼老複合施設となった。現在は、社会のニーズに対応した障害者支援施設と、高齢者通所介護、訪問介護事業、地域住民に向けたカフェテリア機能を併設する「地域共生幼老複合施設」になっている。

「江東園」は「一つ屋根の下の大家族」を理念としているが、これは古きよき日本の大家族の姿である。江東園は、「孤独な高齢者には温もりを与え、少子化・核家族の中に人と人のふれ合いの体験が少ない子どもには優しさと感謝の気持ちを学ぶ場」となることを目指して活動をしている。江東園のプログラムは3段階に分かれていて、参加者の形態に応じた活動の内容となっている。第1段階は、日常の生活にある挨拶や運動、食事といった人と人のふれ合いを主とする活動を行っている。第２の段階はふれあい委員会が行う企画を主とする子どもと高齢者のふれ合いの場の設定を行っている。第３段階は園の各施設が合同で行う盆踊りや相撲大会やクリスマスといった行事となっている。

この江東園の活動も順調に進んでいるが、入所する高齢者の高齢化にともない介護度が高くなっている。そのため移動に人手を必要とすることから交流の機会が減少している。さらに、2020年以降、新型コロナウイルス感染症による日常生活の制限が加わり、人と人が接する直接の交流が制限されたために、活動のプログラムも館内放送やZoomによるテレビ画面越しとなる間接的な活動になっている。

人間社会は、これまでも分断と協調を繰り返してきた。新型コロナウイルスによるパンデミックは、これまでの当たり前のふれ合いや日常の生活の場を奪い取った。このコロナウイルス収束を目指すアフターコロナの時代を見据えて、江東園は新たなる世代間交流を進化させたいと考えている。

杉　啓以子

社会福祉法人 江東園 江東園本部 経営企画管理本部（Total Quality Manager）本部長

特定非営利活動法人 日本世代間交流協会　会長（JIUA）

世代間交流協会では、「世代間交流コーディネーター養成」を行い現在までに100名を超える「世代間交流コーディネーター」（名称独占資格）を輩出。定期的に世代間交流実践例についてセミナーを開催し情報発信に努めている。

1987年　江東園内：保育園児と施設入所高齢者・認知症高齢者との世代間交流を実践

2006年　江東園ケアセンターつばき（新設）：知的障がい者とデイサービス高齢者との交流

2017年　事業所内保育所開設（９月）：幼児と高齢者と障がい者との共生型世代間交流を実践

＜主な著書＞

『世代間交流学の創造』あけび書房、2010年（共著）

『よみがえる笑顔　老人と子どもふれあいの記録』静山社、2012年（単著）

Summary

Looking back on 35 years of the intergenerational programs at Social welfare corporation, Kotoen, and what will await us for the future of the intergenerational society

The social welfare corporation "Kotoen" is a nursing home for the elderly established in 1962 in Edogawa-ku, Tokyo. "The name "Kotoen" means "to create a paradise for the elderly in the east of the Edogawa River". Later, in 1976, Kotoen added the Edogawa Nursery School to meet the expectations of women entering the workforce, and became a complex facility for children and the elderly based on the concept of "a big family under one roof". Currently, it is a "community living in harmony with facility for children and the elderly" with a support facility for people with disabilities that meets the needs of society, day-care services for the elderly, home care services, and cafeteria functions for local residents.

"The philosophy of Kotoen is "a big family under one roof", which is the image of a big family in old Japan. Kotoen aims to provide warmth to the elderly who are lonely and a place to learn kindness and gratitude to children who have few experiences of human interaction due to the declining birth rate and nuclear families. The program at Kotoen is divided into three stages, with the content of the activities depending on the form of the participants. The first stage consists of activities that focus on human interaction such as greetings, exercise, and meals in daily life. The second stage is to set up a place where children and the elderly can interact with each other, which is mainly planned by the Interaction Promotion Committee. In the third stage, all the facilities in Kotoen join together to hold events such as Bon Odori, Sumo wrestling tournament and Christmas.

The activities at Kotoen are progressing well, but the elderly residents are getting older and their level of care is getting higher. As a result, the number of opportunities to interact with the elderly is decreasing due to the fact that they need more manpower for transportation. In addition, after 2020, the new coronavirus infection has limited daily life, and direct person-to-person interaction has been restricted, so the program of activities has become indirect, such as through Zoom audio and TV screens.

Human society has been repeatedly divided and coordinated. The pandemic caused by the new coronavirus has deprived us of our normal interactions and daily life. In anticipation of the after-coronavirus era, which aims to bring the coronavirus to an end, Kotoen hopes to evolve a new intergenerational exchange.

Keiko Sugi

Social Welfare Corporation Kotoen

General Manager, Total Quality Manager

President, Japan Intergenerational Unity Association (JIUA), a non-profit organization

The Japan Intergenerational Unity Association has been training Intergenerational Exchange Coordinators, and to date has produced over 100 Intergenerational Exchange Coordinators (a title exclusive qualification). The association regularly holds seminars on practical examples of intergenerational exchange and works to disseminate information.

1987 In Kotoen: Practicing intergenerational exchange between nursery school children and elderly residents of facilities and elderly people with dementia

2006 Kotoen Care Center Tsubaki (newly established): Interaction between intellectually disabled people and day service elderly people

2017 Opened an in-office daycare center (September): Practiced symbiotic intergenerational exchange between infants, the elderly, and people with disabilities.

Books;

The Creation of Intergenerational Exchange Studies, Akebi Shobo, 2010 (co-author)

"Reviving Smiles: Records of Interaction of the Elderly and Children",Seizansha, 2012 (Sole author)

第５章　囲碁を活用した世代間交流プログラムの開発と実践

飯塚　あい

１．はじめに

世代間交流プログラム (Intergenerational program, 以降IGPと呼ぶ) の効果は、社会科学や老年学など多方面で検証され、総論として万人に推奨されている。しかしながら、IGP を具体的に普及・継続することは難しいと言われている[1)]。その理由として、世代によって積極的に参加したいプログラムが異なり、万人に受け入れられるプログラムの構築が難しいこと、青少年の学年が上がるにつれて IGP への参加希望者が減ることなどが挙げられる[2)]。この問題を解決し、IGP の普及・継続に向けてより多くの参加者を得るためには、多世代の心をつかみ、長期に継続したいという気持ちが自然と芽生えるような、魅力的なツールを用いたプログラムを開発する必要がある。そこで筆者らは、そのようなツールとして卓上ゲームの囲碁に注目し、囲碁を用いた IGP を開発、実践したので報告する。

２．囲碁を活用した世代間プログラムの可能性について

囲碁はおよそ 1,500 年前に中国から日本に伝播したと言われ[3)]、日本の囲碁人口は約 400 万人と[4)]、現在も多くの人に楽しまれる日本の歴史と文化に根付いたゲームである。数ある遊び、卓上ゲームの中から筆者らが囲碁に注目したのは、①子どもの教育に有用であること ②高齢者の健康増進に効果的であること ③ルールがシンプルで誰もが楽しむことができ、奥が深く学習に終わりがないこと ④自然と世代間交流ができる環境が整っていること、以上の４点が IGP を開発、実践する上で利点になると考えたからである。

子どもの教育への有用性（利点①）については、囲碁は子どもや青少年の集中力、忍耐力、抑制力を高めると考えられており、近年では大学の授業に採用されるなど[5)]、教育現場での展開が期待されている。また、囲碁は対局の開始前に一礼をし、挨拶を交わす等、礼儀を重んじる傾向がある。対局の際のマナーを守ることにより礼儀作法が身に着くことからも、囲碁は単なる遊戯・ゲームではなく、社会教育的ツールとみなされている。このように、IGP に囲碁を用いることで、子どもや青少年の教育的効果が期待できる。

高齢者の健康増進効果（利点②）については、囲碁は高齢者の認知機能低下を抑制し[6) 7)]、安静時の脳活動を増加させること[8)]、心身症の予防に効果的であることなど[9)]、様々な研究によって有効性が示されている。さらに、囲碁の技術や礼儀作法を子どもに教えることで、自己肯定感の向上や役割の獲得などの相乗効果も期待できる。

また、囲碁は他の卓上ゲームに比べてルールがシンプルで初心者でも気軽に楽しむことができ、上達するほどに奥深く多様な戦術を習得する必要があり、飽きることなく継続できる生涯学習といえる（利点③）。さらに、碁会所や囲碁サロンと呼ばれる対局場が各都市に存在し、幅広い世代が集まり真剣勝負をしている。このような場で特別にセッティングされなくとも自然と世代間の交流が発生し（利点④）、それが日常的な風景であることも囲碁の特徴である。

このような理由から、我々は囲碁による世代間交流プログラムは実行可能性が高く、全世代に魅力的かつ子どもと高齢者に互恵的なプログラムになり得ると考え、囲碁を活用した IGP「iGO こち」を開発した。

3．プログラムの概要

「iGO こち」は、囲碁未経験の子どもと高齢者がともに囲碁を学ぶことを通じて、子どもの教育・文化的環境づくりと高齢者の健康増進を目指した IGP である。囲碁未経験者を対象とした理由は、参加者同士に上下関係がないところで、ともに「新しいことを学ぶ」ことが IGP として魅力的な要素になり得ると考えたからである。なお、本プログラムはIGPの効果を検証する研究の一環として2015年～2016年に実施した事業である。

（1）参加者の募集

東京都板橋区内Ａ小学校の学童保育スタッフの協力を得て、学童保育利用児童にチラシを配布し、児童の募集を行った。また、小学校周辺の自治会や地域包括支援センターなどの職員の協力を得て、近隣に住む高齢者にチラシを配布する、公共施設の掲示板にポスターを掲示するなどの方法で高齢者を募集した。募集の結果、小学校１～３年生の児童14名、高齢者14名の参加が得られた。

（2）プログラムの内容

参加者である児童と高齢者は、日本棋院プロ棋士による囲碁入門教室を週１回１時間、合計12回受講した。各回は、①基本的なルールの講義、②高齢者と児童がペアを組み協力し合う練習問題、③１対１の個人対局、④チーム戦（高齢者と児童混合のペア碁）で構成され（図１）、プログラム終了時には入門用の碁盤で対局ができるようになることを最終目標とした。学習内容に沿ったオリジナルの教材を作成し、各回で配布した。プログラムの運営は、講師１名、囲碁アシスタント２名、研究スタッフ２名、学童保育スタッフ１名で行った。

プログラムの開始前（初回の囲碁教室の前）に、児童と高齢者がトラブルなく円滑に交流できるよう、学童スタッフ協力のもと、高齢者に対し児童への接し方についての研修を行った。内容は、現代の児童の傾向（高齢者との触れ合いに慣れていないこと等）や、児童と接する際の注意点（不必要に叱らない、児童を抱っこしたり、頭を撫でるなど接触は控える等）、服装や身なりの注意点（動きやすい服装、香水を控える等）、児童とトラブル

講義

練習問題

個人対局

チーム戦

図1 プログラムの構成

が発生した際は学童スタッフに指示を仰ぐ等である。この研修は、児童の安全を確保することに加え、高齢者自身のトラブルを回避するために実施した。

（3）IGP としての工夫

囲碁教室を実施する中で、児童と高齢者の交流を促す工夫を行った。まず、座席表を作成し、同世代同士で固まらないよう席の配置を工夫した。座席は固定ではなく、児童と高齢者の相性をみながら毎回座席を変更し、児童と高齢者が満遍なく交流できるようにした。

児童と高齢者はペアになり、練習問題や対局に取り組んだ。練習問題や対局を行う際はペアの参加者同士が積極的に会話できるように、「相談しながら取り組んでください」と説明した。チーム戦は、児童と高齢者が交互に着手するように対局を進めた。参加者自身がいつ、誰と対局したかわかるよう、対局記録カードを作成した。また、囲碁以外の部分、たとえば碁盤・碁石など物品の準備や片付けなども、参加者同士で協力し合えるように工夫した（児童が碁盤を回収し、高齢者がそれを受け取って戸棚にしまうなど）。

さらに、囲碁教室への出席率を維持するために、教室に出席した対象者には囲碁の戦術に関する格言を基にしたオリジナルカルタ（図２）を配布した。毎回異なる種類のカルタを配布し、教室に出席して多種のカルタを集めることで様々な戦術を理解できるという仕掛けを作り、出席することへの動機づけとした。また、教室の最終回では修了証を授け、囲碁の継続意欲の向上を図った。

図２　オリジナルカルタ

（4）プログラムの効果、プログラム中にみられた児童の変化

プログラムへの平均出席率は 87％、離脱者は高齢者１名と少なく、アンケートでは高い満足度が得られた。糸井らの開発した世代間交流プログラムの評価

である Community Intergenerational observation Scale for Elderly（CIOS - E）/ for Children（CIOS - C）[10] を実施したところ、CIOS - C の 第Ⅱ因子「尊重」において、プログラム後半で得点が向上する傾向がみられ（$p < .1$）、プログラムを通じて児童は高齢者への尊敬と思いやりの心を養い、主体的に行動するという変化が示唆された[11]。実際に、教室の後半になるにつれて、高齢者が石を打ちやすいように児童が座席の位置を調節したり、対局のスピードを高齢者に合わせるなどの気遣いがみられた。また、児童が高齢者に「ここはこう打った方が良いよ」と教える場面が頻繁にみられ、本プログラムの特徴と考えられた。

（5）実践者が気をつけること

プログラムの運営にあたり注意すべき点がいくつかある。まず、囲碁のような対戦型ゲームの場合、対戦相手との相性を考慮する必要がある。ペアとなった児童と高齢者の相性が悪い場合、特に児童には「囲碁教室＝嫌な場所」というイメージが生まれ、プログラムの離脱につながる可能性がある。スタッフは常に教室全体を注意深く観察し、相性を見極めることが重要である。

今回、小学校低学年の児童が多く参加しており、教室の途中で騒がしくなったり、寝転がるなどの行動がみられ、高齢者から「もっとおとなしくしていてほしい」「礼儀がなっておらず驚いた」などの感想もみられた。それは、児童に緊張感がみられる前半にはあまりみられず、場に対する「慣れ」が生じる５回目以降からみられる傾向にあった。「慣れ」は良いことでもあるが、場の空気が緩みすぎるとプログラムとして成立しなくなる可能性がある。運営の際には、開始と終了の挨拶、練習問題や対局にかける時間を定めるなど、要所にメリハリを持たせ、ある程度の緊張感を保つことも大切と考えられた。

また、基本的なことではあるが、参加者の体調管理にも気を配るべきである。本プログラムは秋季～冬季のインフルエンザ流行期に実施したため、マスク着用や予防接種を促すなど対策を講じた。夏季に実施する際には、熱中症対策としてこまめな水分補給を勧めるなど、アナウンスすることも重要であろう。

4．おわりに

今回、全世代に魅力的かつ子どもと高齢者に互恵的なIGPを目指し、囲碁を活用したプログラムを開発・実践した。結果として参加者から高い満足度が得られ、児童の行動に変化が生じるなどポジティブな効果がみられた。世代間交流は通常、「高齢者からこどもへの教育」や「こどもから高齢者へのボランティア」という一方向性のプログラムが多い。一方、本プログラムでは「高齢者が子どもに教える」だけでなく、「子どもが高齢者に教える」という双方向性の関係を構築できた。「子どもが高齢者に教える」ことについてはIGPの評価項目に含まれていないが、高齢者からは「小さいのに頭の回転が速く、将来が楽しみ」など肯定的な意見が多く、子どもに教えられることを喜んでいる様子がみられた。よって「高齢者が子どもに教える」ばかりが世代間交流として望ましいわけではなく、「子どもが高齢者に教える」こともひとつのIGPの形であることがわかった。今後、本プログラムを実践する中でみられた利点と注意点を考慮し、より多くの人に受け入れられるIGPを開発・展開していきたい。

引用・参考文献

1） 藤原佳典、大場宏美、野中久美子、村山陽、鄭恵元、小池高史、桜井良太、鈴木宏幸 (2012)、学校教育における世代間交流プログラムの現状と課題 (会議録)、日本健康教育学会誌 ,(20)80

2） 高山緑 (2003)、青少年と高齢者の世代間交流プログラムに関する一考察、武蔵工業大学環境情報学部紀要、(5)121-131.

3） 西沢よしお (2001)、新たな地域文化の創造－囲碁によるまちづくり、都市問題 92(6):49-59

4） 公益財団法人 日本生産性本部 (2013)、2012 年度版 レジャー白書

5） 石倉昇、梅沢由香里、黒瀧正憲、兵頭俊夫 (2007)、東大教養囲碁講座 ゼロからわかりやすく、光文社新書

6） Iizuka A, Suzuki H, Ogawa S, Kobayashi-Cuya KE, Kobayashi M, Takebayashi T, Fujiwara Y. Pilot Randomized Controlled Trial of the GO Game Intervention on Cognitive Function. American Journal of Alzheimer's Disease and Other Dementias, 33(3), pp. 192-198. 2018.

7） Iizuka A, Suzuki H, Ogawa S, Kobayashi-Cuya KE, Kobayashi M, Inagaki H, Sugiyama M, Awata S, Takebayashi T, Fujiwara Y. Does social interaction influence cognitive intervention programs? A randomized controlled trial using Go Game. International Journal of Geriatric Psychiatry, 34, pp. 324-332. 2019.

８）Iizuka A, Ishii K, Wagatsuma K, Ishibashi K, Onishi A, Tanaka M, Suzuki H, Awata S, Fujiwara Y. Neural substrate of a cognitive intervention program using Go game: a positron emission tomography study. Aging Clinical and Experimental Research, 2020 Jan 17.

９）石川中、心身症の予防－囲碁、将棋、麻雀の効用－、自由と正義 31(8):25-29.2008.

10）糸井和佳 , 亀井智子 , 田髙悦子 , 梶井文子 , 山本由子 , 廣瀬清人 . 地域における高齢者と子どもの世代間交流観察スケールの開発 : CIOS-E,CIOS-C の信頼性と妥当性の検討 . 日本地域看護学会誌 , 17(3),pp.14-22.2015.

11）飯塚あい , 倉岡正高 , 鈴木宏幸 , 小川将 , 村山幸子 , 安永正史 , 藤原佳典 . 囲碁を活用した世代間交流プログラムの開発と評価－世代間交流観察スケール「CIOS-E,CIOS-C」を用いて－ . 日本世代間交流学会誌 , 7(1), pp. 61-68. 2018.

要約

全世代に魅力的かつ子どもと高齢者に互恵的なプログラムを目指し、卓上ゲームの囲碁を用いた世代間交流プログラム「iGO こち」を開発、実践したので、ここに報告する。

「iGO こち」は、囲碁未経験の子どもと高齢者がともに囲碁を学ぶことを通じ、子どもの教育・文化的環境づくりと高齢者の健康増進を目指した IGP である。参加者は学童保育利用児童と 65 歳以上の高齢者であり、週１回１時間、合計 12 回、日本棋院プロ棋士による囲碁入門教室を受講した。各回は、①基本的なルールの講義、②高齢者と児童がペアを組み協力し合う練習問題、③個人対局、④チーム戦で構成され、プログラム終了時には入門用の碁盤で対局ができるようになることを目標とした。

囲碁教室を実施する中で、同世代で固まらないような席の配置にする、練習問題やチーム戦の際に児童と高齢者が話し合えるよう声掛けをするなど、児童と高齢者の交流を促す様々な工夫を行った。その結果、プログラム後半では、児童が高齢者を気遣う行動や発言が見られるようになったほか、児童が高齢者に囲碁の技術を教える場面が頻繁にみられ、本プログラムの特徴と考えられた。

このように、本プログラムでは「高齢者が子どもに教える」だけでなく、「子どもが高齢者に教える」という双方向性の関係を構築できた。参加した高齢者の満足度は高く、「子どもが高齢者に教える」こともひとつの IGP の形として重要な要素であると考えられた。

飯塚　あい

東京都健康長寿医療センター研究所　社会参加と地域保健研究チーム

〒173-0015 東京都板橋区栄町 35-2

東京都健康長寿医療センター研究所非常勤研究員。日本内科学会認定内科医、日本老年医学会認定老年科専門医。埼玉医科大学医学部を卒業後、慶應義塾大学医学部大学院にて博士（医学）を取得。現在は東京都健康長寿医療センター研究所にて、主にボードゲーム等の知的活動を活用した世代間交流プログラムや、認知機能低下抑制プログラムの開発と効果評価に従事している。

Summary

Development and Practice of Intergenerational Exchange Programs Using Go

To create a program that all generations find attractive and that mutually benefits children and older people, we developed and conducted an intergenerational program called "iGO-Kochi", using the board game, go.

IGO-Kochi is an intergenerational program aimed at creating an educational environment for children and at promoting the health the older people by enabling children and older people how to play the go game together. The participants were children attending after-school care and older people aged 65 years and over; they attended an introductory class of the go game, taught by a Nihon Ki-in, a professional go player, once a week for one hour, 12 times in total. In the go-game class, various measures were taken to encourage the children and the older people to interact. Consequently, in the latter half of the program, the children began to act and speak in a manner that demonstrated that they cared for the older people. Furthermore, on frequent occasions, the children taught go skills to the older people. We considered this a unique characteristic of this program.

In this manner, this program could to establish a bidirectional relationship in which not only the older people taught the children but the children also taught the older people. The satisfaction level of the older people was high; therefore, the children teaching the older people was an crucial element of this form of intergenerational program.

Ai Iizuka

Dr. Ai Iizuka is a part-time researcher of Tokyo Metropolitan Institute of Gerontology. She received PhD in Medicine in 2019 from Keio University, Japan. She has engaged in developing intergenerational programs and cognitive intervention programs using board games.

第６章　地域に共生・協働意識が継続する世代間交流プログラム

－四半世紀続いているＡ小学校の「里孫制度」－

佐々木　剛、草野　篤子

１．「里孫制度」を巡る背景と日米の考え方の違い

日本における世代間交流は草野らによる日本世代間交流協会の設立や日本世代間交流学会の創立により、社会的に認知されるようになり体系的に論じられるようになった。ここでは、世代間交流概念の黎明期の時代から実践されて来たＡ小学校の実践「里孫制度」を通して、小学校教育と世代間交流プログラムの可能性を考えたい。

「里孫制度」を想起させる概念の一つに、1965年に米国連邦政府によって公的に開始され体系的になった「里祖父母プログラム」(THE FOSTER GRANDPARENTS PROGRAM)がある(草野、2004)。NEWMAN S.によると、「米国における世代間交流プログラムには二つの局面があり、1960年代後半から70年代にかけての世代間分離(GENERATIONS SEPARATION)と、1980年代及び1990年代にかけての社会問題に取り組んだもの」があり、「里祖父母プログラム」は前者に当たる(NEWMAN S. 2004)。ここで取り上げる「里孫制度」は、この米国での高齢者と子どもを結び付ける「里祖父母プログラム」との共通性を持っている。しかし、米国の世代間交流プログラム(INTERGENERATIONAL PROGRAMS)が、高齢者を社会的に差別するエイジズムに対する介入プログラムとしてスタートしている歴史的経緯があることによって、子どもの側からではなく、高齢者の側からの「里祖父母プログラム」となっている。米国における「里祖父母プログラム」は、連邦政府による国家的な事業として教育分野を中心に普及・発展し現在に至っている(SALTS R., 1987、PEACOCK, J.R. et al, 2006,

ROBIN A.J. et al.1981, SCHIRM V. et al., 1995, LANE P. J. et al.,1980, TEH L et al., 2005, MUIR, K.B.,2006）。一方、日本における世代間交流プログラムは、1960 年代から、老人会、保育園、小学校などでの世代間交流事業など、産業構造の変化に伴う人口の都市集中、地方の過疎化に伴う自然発生的なもので、その数はまだそれほど多くなかった（草野、2004）。

小学校の長期的な世代間交流の取り組み例としては、内田（2012）が進める兵庫県姫路市の小学校で 2007 年から取り組んだ例や、藤原ら（2010）が開発し 2014 年から今日まで、東京都・川崎市・高浜市などを中心に継続研究を進める「高齢者による世代間交流型ヘルスプロモーション“REPRINTS”；絵本の読み聞かせ」や、山田（2011）らの「児童と高齢者の世代間交流効果－児童と高齢者のコミュニティフレンド事業の場合－」等がある。

ここで取り上げる「里孫制度」とは、この活動を実践する小学校によれば、「里親をもじった高齢者と小学生の交流活動の名称」である（佐々木・草野、2015）。具体的には、保護者の同意のもとに学校の教育の一環として行う高齢者施設との交流活動であり、小学生が施設入所高齢者と「擬似的な孫関係」となる交流プログラムである。この「里孫制度」について、永島（2011）は、同様の名称は「全国の９都道府県の自治体の福祉活動に見られる」と指摘しているが、計画性や継続性からすると、この A 小学校の活動は四半世紀以上も続いており、世代間交流プログラムとして特筆される活動の一つであると言える。

２．世代間交流プログラムと教育計画・地域・高齢者施設の関係性

「里孫制度」に関して聞き取り調査を行った。その結果、この「里孫制度」は、学校が地域との連携・協働の意識を大切にして、その活動を継続してきたことが分かった。プログラムは教科として位置付けするため、学習指導要領改訂の都度、実施する教科が若干変化している。特に、1997 年代には、福祉教育の考え方が浸透している時期であったことから、特別活動に関連付けている。しかし、授業時数の確保が難しいとの理由から家庭科に一部を充てるなどの工夫をしている。

活動する教育計画も学習指導要領が1998年には生活科が、2008年には総合的な学習の時間が創設されたことを受けて、A小学校では、小学校低学年（1・2年生）は生活科、中学年以上では総合的な学習の時間と特別活動、高学年では、さらに家庭科・社会科を加え、全学年を通した発達段階に応じた体系的プログラムとなるように工夫している。

この取り組みを長年支えてきた高齢者施設側は、福祉の側面の経緯を次のように述べている。「里孫制度」は、「1972年に財団から委託された実験的地域福祉サービスを市（当時は、町）が受け取ることから始まった」。その時に「三つの町が事業の対象になったが、受け取りを担当する地域人口の関係や中心となる保健師の活動範囲との関係で、小学校を有する町として当市が受け皿になった」。また、背景には1981年の国際障害者年で「障害者がB園（国

表1　学習指導要領改訂と取組変化

月/年代	1997年	2002年	2010年
5月	ホーム訪問	ホーム訪問 子どもまつり招待 散策解除訪問	
6月	運動会招待	移動教室の報告訪問	
7月	ホーム納涼大会参加	ホーム納涼大会参加	事前学習 ホーム訪問（1） 有志によるホーム納涼会参加
9月	移動教室の報告訪問	運動会招待	ホーム訪問（2） 事前・事後学習 運動会招待
10月	子どもまつり招待	招待給食	招待給食
11月	学習発表会招待 ホーム焼き芋大会参加	学習発表会招待	事前・事後学習 ホーム訪問（3） 書き初め展招待
1月	招待給食 書き初め展招待	書き初め展招待	事前・事後学習 ホーム訪問（4） 書き初め展招待
2月		ホーム訪問 給食会	事前・事後学習
3月		4年生への引継ぎ 卒業式招待	ホーム訪問（5） 4年生への引継ぎ 卒業式招待
特色と変化	**福祉教育概念による実施** 教科：家庭科 訪問時：特別活動	**全学年取組へ** 3・4年が中心 保護者参加あり。	**事前・事後学習を重視** 年間を通した訪問 **系統的**、かつ、行事との関連性・関係性重視

立療養所）へ行う支援活動がそのエネルギーでもあった」と言う。さらに、地域の子ども会にとっても「子ども会活動の縮小の時代変化に伴い、子どもとお年寄りとの接点が少なくなった時代に、お年寄りが多数いる特養（特別養護老人ホーム）との連携の必要性が関係者に分かり始めた」ことが、学校・施設・地域という三者の関係が強まるきっかけであったと話している。すなわち、学校は教育活動の一環として計画を進めているが、小学生を受け入れる高齢者施設や地域との関係は、教育や福祉だけでは語り尽くせない深い歴史がある。この「里孫制度」はその意味で、「地域との共生・協働」関係に効果をもたらした活動であったと言える。運営も、当初は高齢者施設と、地域による協働活動であったが、その後、学校とPTA、さらにPTAのOBや地域福祉の関係者、高齢者施設・病院のコーディネーターが加わり「里孫制度」運営委員会による活動となっている（図１）。

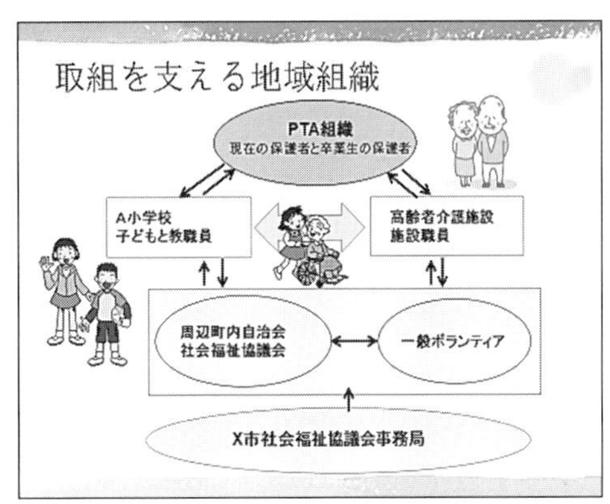

図１　里孫制度の運営組織概要

３．「里孫制度」がもたらす地域共生・協働意識の効果

この小学校の資料によると、地域での自治会活動と福祉活動、福祉教育としての学校の施設訪問が資料から読み取れる。この背景には、この地域周辺に転地療養のための病院や施設が多くあったことや、行政の福祉施策が大きく関与している。この考え方は、比較調査した近隣Ｙ市の事例からも同様の結果を得ている。例えば、近隣Ｙ市の元小学校長は、「2001年頃に、当時の教育委員会から要請があって、学校の空き教室の活用による高齢者交流室を校内に設置した（佐々木・草野、2015）」と述べている。

この施策時期は、当時の厚生省が、高齢化社会への対応として実施したゴールドプラン(1993)、新ゴールドプラン(1994)、ゴールドプラン21(1999)に相当する。つまり、文部省が全国の小中学校の空き教室の活用による福祉教育の充実を推進したことに符合する。しかし、保存資料には行政サイドからの働きかけを示すものは残っていない。唯一、当時の社会福祉協議会が関与している例として、1984(昭和59)年1月13日の読売新聞多摩版に、「市医師会(後に社会福祉協議会が実施主体)の提唱で始まった老人保健福祉事業のボランティアグループと小学校の交流」として、この学校の「まゆだまづくり」による小学生と地域の交流の様子を報道した資料が残っている。また、年度は不詳であるが、「ミニコミ誌『まつかさ』20年活動記録」には、上記に示すボランティア活動について、「1976(昭和51)年10月にX市の社会福祉協議会と老人保健福祉事業事務局の呼びかけによるモデル事業として同自治会が選ばれたことから始まる」と記載されている。このことから、初期の福祉教育は行政主導であったことが伺える。

新たま風土記

伝統行事継承にも力

主婦ら老人介護と交流

図2「1984年読売新聞多摩版」

図2　1984年読売新聞多摩版

4．活動を継続する上で乗り超えなければならない課題

初期の「里孫制度」教育の位置づけには家庭科と特別活動が示されていた。現存する資料には、手書きで、「道具の持ち込みは社協に依頼する」、「集合時間、お年寄り○○」「準備はボランティア～」と記載されていた。すなわち、当時の教育計画では活動を地域との関係構築に求めている。このことは、「里孫制度」10年の節目の記念として発行された記念誌『虹のかけはし』に、校長であったE氏が寄せた文書に、「この活動が始まった背景に、協力的な教職員と地域古老の

濃い想いと、それを支える地域があった」との苦労話が紹介されている。また、E氏によると「この高齢者施設と学校が交流するいきさつは、1988年12月19日の音楽クラブが同施設を訪問したこと」が直接的な始まりだったと言う。そして、その活動に地域の有力者と教員の相互の関係が「“まゆだまづくり”の開催につながり、急斜面を転がる雪だるまのように大きくなり1991年の『里孫制度』へ発展した」と証言している。

活動も長きに渡ってくると、学校を取り巻く環境も変化してくる。幸いなことにこの制度はまだ現存している。これはこの学校の誇りでもあり、地域との共生・協働意識の高さだと言える。しかし、学校は授業時間の確保と同時に活動存続に苦心している。また、住宅環境の変化に伴い地域との関係にも変化が出てきている。この活動が継続するために乗り越えなければならない課題は、教育では教育計画、人的な側面ではボランティアとしての参加者の確保、活動内容では、「自分の家族ではない高齢者と子どもの関係という認識上の問題」がある。

このA小学校は、この2018年に、学校の基本的な取り組みを、「国際交流」・「特別支援学級との交流」・「学校内の相互交流」とする表記に、「里孫制度」を福祉ボランティアの活動と併記した。

5．おわりに

世代間交流に関して学習指導要領の記述を調べて見ると、世代間交流の概念が各所に分散していることが分かる。特に、総合的な学習の時間や、生活科の中に支援との言葉が取り入れられたことにより、世代間交流概念が進展したといえるが、教科として学習指導に具体的な内容が提供されているとは言えない。A小学校の「里孫制度」は、その意味で、子どもの

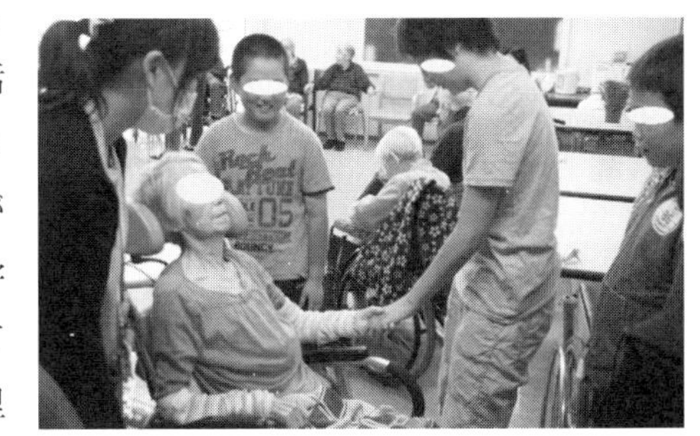

写真1　「里孫制度」での行事例

成長過程で小学校が果たす縦断的な実践と教科内容の横断的な把握と関連する重要な課題を提言していると言える。A小学校と高齢者施設の記録には、「施設に在籍した45名の高齢者が小学生訪問により生活意欲が変化した」ことが1993年の記録に残っていた。また、1997年の記録には「高齢者は小学生の訪問を待ち望み、交流によって高齢者の生活が改善された」と記載されていた。また、参加者の声として「地域の人の力も大きいと思う」や、「この地域の人は障害者の問題にも熱心に取り組んでいる」。また、「地域の意見の中には子どもがそのようなお年寄りと接することに否定的な意見の人もいるが、子どもが学校を卒業すると、ただでさえ学校に行く意味もないのに、この活動で学校に行く用事があれこれと続いている。これが重要だ」との声も残っていた。

現在、我が国は具体的な世代間交流プログラムが必要とされる超高齢社会に突入している。この喫緊の課題を乗り越えるためには、より具体的な施策が必要なのであるが、その実践や計画が生涯学習に頼っている現状がある。その意味で、このA小学校の例が、世代間交流プログラムの見直しにつながることを期待するのである。

引用・参考文献等

藤原佳典(2010)、プロダクティビティの視点からみた高齢者の次世代支援、世代間交流学の創造－無縁社会から多世代間交流型社会実現のために－、あけび書房、東京、pp.60-68

厚生労働省(2010)、新高齢者保健福祉推進10か年戦略(新ゴールドプラン、ゴールドプラン21) www1.mhlw.go.jp/topics/h10-kyoku/roujin-h/t0120-10e.html

草野篤子(2009)、世代間交流とソーシャル・キャピタルを考える－スウェーデン、アメリカ、日本を例として－、世代間交流学の創造－無縁社会から多世代間交流型社会実現のために－、あけび書房、東京、pp.22-35

草野篤子(2004)、インタージェネレーションの歴史、現代のエスプリ444、インタージェネレーション、東京、pp.33-41

LANE P. J. et.al.(1980) Training Volunteer Foster Grandparents as Behavior Rates, Child Behavior Therapy, vol.2, No.2,pp:5-78

MUIR K.B. (2006) Measuring the Benefits of Mentoring for Foster Grandparents: A Research Note, Gerontology, Vol.32, No.5, pp.79-387

永嶋昌樹 (2011)、世代間交流における「里孫」活動・制度の現状に関する調査研究、聖徳大学児童学研究紀要 13、pp.9-16

NEWMAN S. (2004) アメリカのインタージェネレーション、現代のエスプリ 444、インタージェネレーション、東京、pp.116-123

PEACOCK J. R., O' QUIN J. A. (2006), Higher Education and Foster Grandparents Programs : Exploring Mutual Benefits, Educational Gerontology, Vol.32, No.5, pp.367-378

ROBIN A.J. et al. (1981) Use of Critical Incidents for Planning, Implementing and Evaluating a Training Program for Foster Grandparents, Educational Gerontology, vol.7, No.2-3, pp.111-155

SALTS ROSALYN (1987)、Research Evaluation of a Foster Grandparents Program, Journal of Children in Contemporary Societies, Vol.20, No.3-4, pp.205-216

佐々木剛・草野篤子 (2015)、ソーシャル・キャピタルとしての世代間交流プログラムー持続可能な開発のための教育 (ESD) の実践との関連を通して、日本世代間交流学会誌 Vol.5(1)、pp.65-72

佐々木剛・草野篤子 (2017)、地域の共生・協働意識に支えられた世代間交流プログラムー東京都A 小学校が独自に実践する「里孫制度」からの検討ー、日本世代間交流学会誌 Vol.6(1)、pp.37-47

SCHIRM V., ROSS-ALAOLMOLKI, K., et al (1995), Collaborative Education through a Foster Grandparents Program: Enhancing Intergenerational Relations, Gerontology and Geriatrics Education, vol.15, No.3, pp.85-94

TEH L., TERRY D. (2005), Foster Grandparents Program, Journal of Intergenerational Relationships, vol.3, No.1, pp.79-84

内田勇人 (2012)、シニアボランティアによる小学校教育支援活動、多様化社会をつむぐ世代間交流、三学出版、京都、pp.134-145

山田和廣 (2011)、児童と高齢者の世代間交流効果ー児童と高齢者のコミュニティフレンド事業の場合ー、日本世代間交流学会誌、Vol.1(1)、pp.89-97

要約

東京都多摩地区にあるA小学校は、1991年から現在までおよそ25年の長期に渡り、小学生と高齢者の間で「里孫制度」と名付けた世代間交流プログラムを実施して来た。「里孫制度」を想起させる概念の一つに、1965年に米国連邦政府によって公的に開始され体系的になった「里祖父母プログラム」(THE FOSTER GRANDPARENTS PROGRAM) がある (草野 2004)。米国の「里祖父母プログラム」と違って、日本の世代間交流プログラムは1960年代から老人会、保育所、小学校などで自然発生的に始まったもので、その数はそれほど多くはない(草野 2004)。「里祖父母プログラム」と「里孫制度」の違いは、子どもが家族である祖父・祖母と交流するのではなく、保護者の理解と同意を受けた小学生が介護施設に入所している高齢者と疑似的な祖父・祖母の関係となって、学校教育や行事の中の世代間交流としての体験を行うことである。

その活動も、初期は単なる高齢者施設訪問であったが、運営する介護施設と地域を包括する社会福祉協議会と地域ボランティアが中心となって、疑似体験活動プログラムを作り上げてきた。この研究では、この活動の始まりを知る人への聞き取り調査により、このプログラムに含まれる活動理念と活動者のボランティア意識を明らかにした。その結果、この小学校の活動は、学校教育のカリキュラムに「総合的な学習の時間」が取り入れられる前から独自に、地域と一体化した福祉教育を進めていたことが分かった。この事例は、地域を好循環化する数少ない事例の一つである。ただし、この活動にも課題がある。幸いなことにこの活動は継続しているが、教育においては教科へ組み込む授業時間の確保、地域においては「自分の家族ではない高齢者と子どもの関係」を理解することの難しさ、支援する協力者の確保などの課題が残る。我が国も人口構成において、高齢者が若い世代を上回る超高齢社会になった。この時代の中にあって世代間交流プログラムのあり方が問われることになる。この小学校の事例が、これからの世代間交流の見直しのための事例につながることを期待するものである。

佐々木　剛

星槎大学共生科学部　非常勤講師　Email: t_sasaki@kyosei.seisa.ac.jp
元都築教育学園　第一幼児教育専門学校副校長
専門は、学校教育相談、特別支援教育、障害者福祉研究、子ども学。

草野　篤子 (編著者紹介欄 p.275 参照)

Summary

Intergenerational exchange programs that continue to create a sense of coexistence and cooperation in the community: The "Foster-Grandchildren System" has continued for a quarter of a century in A primary School

Primary School A, located in the Tama district of Tokyo, has been running an intergenerational exchange program between Primary School children and senior citizens for about 25 years, since 1991. "One of the concepts reminiscent of the "foster grandparent system" is THE FOSTER GRANDPARENTS PROGRAM, which was officially initiated and systematized by the U.S. federal government in 1965 (Kusano, 2004). Unlike the U.S. Foster Grandparents Program, Japan's intergenerational exchange programs began spontaneously in the 1960s at senior citizen associations, nursery schools, and primary schools, and there are not many of them (Kusano, 2004).

The difference between the "Foster Grandparents Program" and the "Foster Grandchild System" is that instead of children interacting with their family grandparents, Primary School children, with the understanding and consent of their parents, become pseudo-grandparents to elderly people residing in nursing homes, and experience this as an intergenerational exchange during school education and events.

In the early days, these activities were simply visits to elderly people's homes, but the nursing home, the local social welfare council, and local volunteers have taken the lead in creating a simulated experience activity program.

In this study, we clarified the activity philosophy contained in this program and the volunteer awareness of the participants through interviews with people who knew the beginning of this activity. As a result, we found that the activities of this primary school had been independently promoting welfare education integrated with the local community even before hours for "The Period for Integrated Studies " was incorporated into the school curriculum. This case is one of the few examples of creating a virtuous cycle in the community. However, this activity also has its challenges. Fortunately, this activity has been continuing, but there are still issues to be solved, such as securing enough class time to incorporate it into the curriculum in education, the difficulty of understanding the "relationships between elderly people and children who are not their own family members" in the community, and securing collaborators to provide support.

Japan has become a super-aged society with the elderly outnumbering the younger generation in terms of population composition. In this age, the nature of intergenerational exchange programs will be questioned. It is hoped that this elementary school case study will serve as an example of how to review intergenerational exchange in the future.

Tsuyoshi Sasaki

Part-time Lecturer of Seisa University. Faculty of Life Network Science.

Former Vice Principal of Daiichi Nursery Teachers College: Tsuzuki Education Group.

He specializes in school education counseling, special needs education, welfare research on the disabled, and child studies.

Email: t_sasaki@kyosei.seisa.ac.jp

Atsuko Kusano (See p.275)

第７章　高校生とシニア健康ボランティアによる食を伝える世代間地域ネットワークづくりのための活動

廣田　直子

１．はじめに

WHO（世界保健機関）から発表された「世界保健統計報告書 2021 年版（World Health Statistics 2021）」で、日本の平均寿命は WHO 加盟国である 194 の国と地域の中で、男性が 81.5 歳で第２位、女性は 86.9 歳で第１位となっている。さらに、平均健康寿命は男性 72.6 歳、女性 75.5 歳で男女とも１位であり[1]、日本は、世界の中で最も良好な状態にある国の一つである。このような状況には、様々な要因が関連している。日本人の食事のあり方もその要因の一つであると考えられる。2013 年に「和食；日本人の伝統的な食文化」がユネスコの無形文化遺産に登録され、「多様で新鮮な食材とその持ち味の尊重」、「自然の美しさや季節の移ろいの表現」、「正月などの年中行事との密接な関わり」とともに、「健康的な食生活を支える栄養バランス」が「和食」の特徴として挙げられた[2]。「健康的な食生活を支える栄養バランス」に関しては、一汁三菜を基本とする日本の食事スタイルが理想的な栄養バランスである、うま味を上手に使い動物性脂質の少ない食生活を実現し、日本人の長寿や肥満防止に役立っていると説明され、日本人の食事と健康との関連にも視点が置かれた。日本において継承されてきた食事のあり方が、現在の日本における良好な健康寿命の状況に寄与していると考えられる。

（1）高校生とシニア健康ボランティアによる世代間交流の意義

本稿で紹介する活動は、長野県において実施した事例である。長野県は、健康寿命が世界一となっている日本の中で、2015 年の都道府県別生命表において男性は全国で２位、女性は１位であり[3]、（公社）国民健康保険中央会が公表した都道府県別の平均自立期間（2019 年統計情報分）でも、男女ともに全国１位であった[4]。食生活改善推進員や長野県農村生活マイスターなどの食や健康に関するボランティアの活動が活発に行われており、2015 年に公表された長野県健康長寿プロジェクト・研究チームの分析では、積極的な社会活動・ボランティア参加率が高く、こうした活動の成果でもある健康に対する意識の高さと健康づくり活動が長寿要因の一つとして挙げられている[5)]。こうした活動を担っているのは、主としてシニア世代である。

このような背景を踏まえて世代の相違に着目すると、長野県民の野菜の平均摂取量は男女ともに全国 1 位であるが[6)]、2019 年度の長野県県民健康・栄養調査結果では、20 歳代・30 歳代の平均野菜摂取量は少なく、野菜摂取に気をつけている人の割合も、年代が若いほど低くなる傾向にあり、20 歳代では 40% 未満であることが報告されている[7)]。こうした世代間にみられる相違から、筆者らは、長野県民の健康に結びついていたと考えられる食習慣が、若い世代に受け継がれていない状況にあると推察した。本来は、家庭の中で伝承されていた健康につながる食習慣、食文化等の継承がなされにくくなっているのは、長野県のみならず、日本の多くの地域で生じている状況であると考えられる。筆者らは、地域内における家庭の枠を外したライフステージをつなぐネットワークの構築をめざし、そのねらいを達成するための取組が必要であると考え、そのターゲットとして高校生期に働きかけることとした。具体的には、高校生の食に対する意識向上や行動改善のために食生活改善推進協議会と連携した取組を推進したいと考えた。高校生期とした理由は、現在、日本においては栄養教諭制度が整備され、小・中学校では学校給食を通じた食育の推進が図られているが、高校生を対象とした食育や栄養教育の充実のための対策は十分ではないと考えたからである。

（2）高校生と食生活改善推進員とのネットワークづくりのための活動

食生活改善推進員は、“私達の健康は私達の手で”をスローガンに、家族の健康管理はもとより、食を通した健康づくりのボランティアとして、自分たちの市町村等の地域住民に対して、健康づくりのための食生活改善を中心とした実践活動を推進している。食生活改善推進員が伝統的な食事を踏まえた上で、現在の食事の課題を学び、適切な食生活のあり方について伝えてきた地域内における横のネットワークの功績は大きい。

長野県内の食生活改善推進員の活動として、若年層の野菜摂取量不足という課題の解決や、高校生向けに進学や独立等のライフイベントに先立つ食習慣の形成を目的として、「食支援講座」を実施した先行事例はあるが、これは単発の取組みとして実施されたものであった[8)]。筆者らは、世代間交流を主眼とした活動により、地域内のネットワークの構築につながる食を題材とした体系的なプログラムが必要であると考えた。そのための実践として、長野県内において、食生活改善推進員が健康に結びついていた食生活の在り方を高校生に伝えることを目的として、異世代の食生活改善推進員と高校生が共同で活動する健康づくりのための食生活講座を３回シリーズで展開した。その結果から、高校生と食生活改善推進員という異世代交流の場としての講座が、高校生にとって新たな発見を生み、食生活を見直す機会や、理想とする食習慣を学び、意識変化につながる機会になっていたこと、また、この講座で実施した異世代交流活動が、シニア世代が受け継いできた「健康に結びついていたと考えられる食をめぐる営み」を高校生に伝えるための「食を伝える新しい世代間地域ネットワークづくり」の活動モデルになり得ると判断することができた[9) 10)]。本稿ではこの実践事例について紹介する。

２．プログラムの概要

「食を伝える新しい世代間地域ネットワークづくり」の活動は高校の授業で実施することとし、３回シリーズ（夏休み前の７月、夏休み後の９月、10月）とした。食生活改善推進員は市町村の「食生活改善推進員養成講座」を修了した後、「市町村食生活改善推進協議会」に入会して活動することから、食生活改善推進員との活動にあたっては、当該市町村の関連課担当者との連携が不可欠である。このような体制を整えた上で、食生活改善推進員の参加メンバーには、これまで継承されてきた「健康に結びついていたと考えられる食」を、高校生にも受け入れやすいメニュー構成で「食事の形」として伝えてほしいと依頼した。それを受けて、参加する食生活改善推進員と市町村担当者は、講座の実施日までに献立検討のための事前打ち合わせ、当日の役割分担に関する会議、高校調理室の下見などを行った。

（1）1回目の食生活講座：食事の基本形を伝えてもらうために、食生活改善推進員がみそ汁を基本とした「主食＋主菜＋副菜２品」(具体的には、主食：発芽玄米ごはん、副菜：具だくさんみそ汁、主菜＋副菜：添え野菜付き和風ハンバーグ、副菜：小松菜の辛子酢和え、デザート：トマトかん)の献立を作成し、高校生４～５人の調理実習グループに食生活改善推進員が１～２人混じって、その献立による調理実習を一緒に行った。

（2）食生活講座1回目の事後学習と２回目の事前学習：１回目の食生活講座実施後、高校生のみを対象として授業１回分を使い、１回目の食生活講座の振り返りの事後学習と２回目の食生活講座に向けての事前学習を行った。その内容は、筆者による異世代への理解を深めるための高齢期の栄養特性に関する講義、低栄養と骨粗鬆症の予防という観点でテーマとして設定した牛乳・乳製品を使った料理を紹介するためのデモンストレーションとした。その後、高校生は事前・事後学習での学びに基づいて、夏休み中に各自で牛乳・乳製品を用いたメニュー考案を行った。この指導は高校の家庭科教諭が担当した。

（3）２回目の食生活講座：高校生が上記（2）の学習を踏まえて検討した牛乳・乳製品を用いた献立により、１回目の講座と同一メンバーで食生活改善推進員とともに調理実習を行った。

（4）３回目の食生活講座：３回目の食生活講座では、異世代間の交流を図るため、これまで同一グループで活動した高校生と食生活改善推進員によるグループディスカッション等を実施した。その内容は、① ２回の食生活講座の活動について振り返るグループディスカッション(講座２回を通しての感想、学んだこと等についてブレインストーミングを行い、KJ法に準じた方法でまとめる)、② グループでまとめた結果の発表、③ 食生活改善推進員、高校生ともに、個人ワークシートを記入、④ 全体での講座のまとめ、とした。この活動では、地域内の異世代ネットワークづくりをめざしていたことから、３回とも同一グループで実施して世代間の交流を深めてもらうことに力点を置いた。３回シリーズの食生活講座は、その実施後も、食生活改善推進員が高校の授業等に協力する、地域のイベント等で交流する、といった活動につながった。

この活動事例を踏まえて、筆者らは、長野県内の高校教員を対象として、シニアボランティアによる食育活動について郵送法調査を実施した。回収率は59.4％であったが、活動を実施した高校の回答では、活動内容としては調理実習が最多で、普段の食生活の見直しや食文化、一汁三菜のバランスのよい食事、調理のコツ等の学びになったとの回答が多く、学外者との活動を通し積極的に授業に取組む生徒の姿勢が見られ、食に関してより深く学ぶことができたと評価されていた。さらに、異世代の交流によって社会性の成長がみられた等の成果も認められた。未実施の高校がその理由として挙げた項目では、シニアボランティアと共同で行う実習時間の確保が難しい等の実施面での課題があることが明らかとなった[11)]。また、食生活改善推進員など地域のボランティア活動に関する認識がない高校もあった。今後、本稿で事例としてとりあげたような異世代間の食を通した活動を推進していくためには、高校に対して、地域交流を組み入れた調理実習の授業としての実施について年度計画の作成前に働きかけることや、課外活動としての実施を検討してもらうなどの方途が有効であると推察される。また、実施された食育活動事例の成果等を学校関係者に向けて発信することも必要であると考える。

引用・参考文献

1）World Health Organization　2021　World Health Statistics 2021, https://apps.who.int/iris/bitstream/handle/10665/342703/9789240027053-eng.pdf　(閲覧日：2021年7月15日)

2）農林水産省　「和食」がユネスコ無形文化遺産に登録されています https://www.maff.go.jp/j/keikaku/ syokubunka/ich/index.html　(閲覧日：2021年7月15日)

3）厚生労働省「厚生労働統計一覧」　平成27年都道府県別生命表の概況, https://www.mhlw.go.jp/toukei/saikin/hw/life/tdfk15/dl/tdfk15-02.pdf　(閲覧日：2021年7月15日)

4）公益社団法人国民健康保険中央会　2021　平均自立期間・平均余命 都道府県一覧（令和元年統計情報分）, https://www.kokuho.or.jp/statistics/heikinjiritukikan.html　(閲覧日：2021年7月15日)

5）長野県健康福祉部　2016　健康長寿プロジェクト・研究事業, https: //www.pref.nagano.

lg.jp/kenko-fukushi/kenko/kenko/ kenkochojupj.html （閲覧日：2021 年 7 月 15 日）
6）厚生労働省　平成 28 年国民健康・栄養調査結果の概要　野菜摂取量の平均，https://www.mhlw.go.jp/file/04-Houdouhappyou-10904750-Kenkoukyoku-Gantaisakukenkouzoushinka/kekkagaiyou_7.pdf （閲覧日：2021 年 7 月 15 日）
7）長野健康福祉部　2021　令和元年度県民健康・栄養調査，https://www.pref.nagano.lg.jp/kenkochoju/kenko/kenko/kenko/chosa/chousa-r1.html （閲覧日：2021 年 7 月 15 日）
8）原田直樹，白井祐二，山崎宗廣　2008　地区組織活動との連携による健康づくり・食育推進活動について「健康の“きそ”いきいき健康づくり発信事業」について（実施報告），信州公衆衛生雑誌 3：58-59
9）熊谷麻紀，廣田直子　2018　食を伝える異世代間地域ネットワークづくりの試み 食生活講座による高校生の意識変化に関するテキストマイニング分析．ヘルスプロモーション・リサーチ 11：39-46
10）廣田直子，熊谷麻紀　2018　高校生とシニア健康ボランティアによる食を伝える新しい異世代間地域ネットワークづくりのための活動，日本異世代交流学会誌 8：41-49
11）熊谷麻紀，廣田直子　2022　長野県の高等学校におけるシニアボランティアによる食育活動　－実施状況と高等学校担当教員のとらえ方－，信州公衆衛生雑誌 16：107-119

要約

平均寿命、健康寿命が世界トップレベルの日本の中でも、長野県の両指標は良好な状態にある。食や健康に関するシニアボランティアの活動が活発であることがその要因の一つと推察されている。しかし、従来、家庭の中で継承されていた適切な食習慣は、若い世代には受け継がれなくなっている。

筆者らは、家庭の枠を外したライフステージをつなぐ地域内ネットワークの構築をめざした食を題材とする世代間交流の体系的なプログラムが必要であると考えた。その実践として、適切な食生活の在り方を高校生に伝えることを目的として、食生活改善推進員と高校生が共同で活動する健康づくりのための３回シリーズの食生活講座を企画し、展開した。その結果、この講座が高校生にとって新たな発見を生み、食生活を見直す機会や、理想とする食習慣を学び、意識変化につながる機会になっていたこと、また、この講座で実施した異世代交流活動は、シニア世代が継承してきた「健康に結びついていたと考えられる食をめぐる営み」を高校生に伝えるための「食を伝える新しい世代間地域ネットワークづくり」の活動モデルになり得ると判断することができた。

廣田　直子

松本大学大学院健康科学研究科・人間健康学部健康栄養学科教授／博士（学術）。長野県短期大学助手、講師、助教授を経て、現職。現在の研究分野は、食育および栄養・健康教育、栄養調査、栄養疫学等。

Summary

High School Students and Senior Health Volunteers' Activities for Intergenerational Community Networking to Pass on Food Culture

Japan's average life expectancy and healthy life expectancy are among the highest in the world. Especially in Nagano prefecture, these indicators are very good. It has been speculated that one of the factors is the activities related to diet and health by senior volunteers. However, currently, it is difficult for the younger generation to inherit such proper eating habits at home.

We aimed to create a regional intergenerational network outside the home. Therefore, we designed and conducted a three-part dietary workshop series for health promotion involving regional older and younger generations. Through these activities, we wanted to build an intra-regional network that connects life stages outside the home.

As a result, we have obtained that this course was an opportunity for high school students to make new discoveries, to review their eating habits, to learn their ideal eating habits, and to lead to a change in their consciousness. In addition, we found that the cross-generational exchange activities are beneficial to convey to high school students the "food-related activities that are considered to have been linked to health" that the senior generation has inherited. We consider that this program could be a model for building intra-regional network regarding dietary life.

Naoko Hirota, Ph.D.

Professor, Matsumoto University Graduate School of Health Science and Department of Health and Nutritional Science, Faculty of Human Health and Science after working as an assistant, lecturer, and associate professor at Nagano Prefectural College.

Current research fields: Dietary Education (Syokuiku) and Nutrition / Health Education, Surveys of Dietary Intake, Nutrition Epidemiology, and Others

第８章　学童保育における地域特性に合わせた世代間交流プログラム

森田　久美子・青木　利江子・小林　美奈子
山本　晴美・呂　暁衛・永嶺　仁美・佐々木　明子

１．はじめに

女性の社会進出、家族構造の変化、子育て環境の安全を守る必要性といった背景の下、子どもを家庭だけでなく地域社会で育てることが求められている。平成26年、厚生労働省・文部科学省の放課後子ども総合プラン[1)]において、すべての就学の児童の安心・安全な居場所作りが実施されるようになった。また少子高齢化の中、放課後の子どもたちの居場所である学童保育において、地域の子育て支援の中で高齢者の果たす役割は大きい。高齢者が地域で他の世代と交流する機会や場所は次第に少なくなっているが､小学校の空き教室や公民館､児童館といった既存の施設で実施されている学童保育は、多世代が利用しやすい場所であり、世代間交流プログラムを開催しやすい。

そこで、学童保育の子どもと高齢者に対し、地域特性に合わせた世代間交流プログラムを学童保育担当者らと共に作成・実施した事例をここで紹介する。

２．プログラムの概要

本プログラムは、森田ほか[2)]が全国学童保育を対象に行った世代間交流の実施状況調査結果をもとに開発したものである（表１）。事前に実施地域の学童保育担当者（放課後児童支援員）より、世代間交流の現状、地域のつながり、文化・歴史・自然等に関する情報収集を行い、地域特性に合わせた回想法（昔話）や、影絵による昔遊びを考案した。プログラム実施時間は約１時間、実施場所は学童保育施設や学童保育に隣接した公民館で実施した。また、ファシリテーターとして研究者（看護職）６名がプログラムに一緒に参加した。

表１　世代間交流プログラムの詳細

プログラム項目	プログラム内容	時間配分
①歩み寄り交流を促すプログラム	構成的グループエンカウンター[注)] 出会いのゲーム：ふれあい・共通点を探す	10 分
②地域特性を生かした共有プログラム	地域の昔話（文化・自然・生き物等）の回想法：過去と現在の写真、絵などを使った回想法	10 分
③地域特性を生かした共同プログラム	地域の昔話に関連する昔遊び（影絵）：影絵人形制作、上演	30 分
④交流を深めるプログラム	構成的グループエンカウンター 承認のゲーム：高齢者・子ども双方向の承認	10 分

写真１　歩み寄り交流

写真２　地域の写真を用いた回想

写真３　影絵制作と上演

写真４　お互いの承認

※写真は新型コロナ感染症流行前に撮影したものである。

注）構成的グループエンカウンター：リーダーが用意したプログラムによって作業・ゲーム・討議をしながら、こころのふれあいを深めていく方法（國分ほか 2014）。

３．プログラムの実施

今回は、世代間交流を継続して実施している２箇所（地域特性の異なる都市部A 地区・郊外 B 地区）の学童保育で世代間交流プログラムを実施した。参加者は、A 地区の子ども 23 名（低学年 23 名）、B 地区の子ども 23 名（低学年 14 名、高学年９名）、高齢者は両地区 10 名（67 ～ 81 歳）であった。参加した高齢者は、地域の学校活動支援者（行事支援）や敬老会によって選ばれた者であった。

（1）事前打ち合わせ・関係者との情報共有

事前に学童保育担当者と行政の高齢課担当者より、対象地域における子ども・高齢者の交流の様子、地域の文化・祭事等についてヒアリングを行い、回想法に用いる写真や影絵の題材などを一緒に考えた。

子ども、高齢者ともに興味を持ってもらえるような内容、そして地域の良いところをみんなで共感できるような内容になるようにしっかりと情報収集することが重要である。

（2）歩み寄り交流を促すプログラム

今回は構成的グループエンカウンターとして、グループ作り→じゃんけんゲーム→同じところ探しゲームという流れで実施した。グループ作りでは、子ども達の学年や高齢者が均等に分かれるように、子ども達（学年別）と高齢者それぞれで早く起きた順に並んでもらい、時間が早い人から１グループ、２グループ…というようにグループ分けを行った。１グループあたりの人数は６～７人とした。じゃんけんゲームでは、相手が何を出すかを考えて、“あいこ”になるように各グループで挑戦してもらった。同じところ探しゲームでは、１人１回は発言するというルールでグループ対抗戦とした。最初は緊張気味だった参加者も歩み寄り交流を通して一気に和やかな雰囲気になった。

（3）地域特性を生かした共有プログラム（回想法）

地域の自然・文化に関する過去・現在の写真、地域に残る文化・歴史・自然を題材にした話を高齢者と子どもが語り合った。A 地区では近くの公園の江戸時代から続くお花見の様子や神社の伝統行事、昔の洗濯機やアイロンなどの日常生活品についての話で盛り上がった。B 地区では近くの天然記念物の話や、昔の小学校の写真、地元の食材や植物の話などであった。高齢者の話を子ども達はとても興味深く聞き、また高齢者は子ども達が昔、自分達が遊んだ場所で今はどのような遊びをしているのかを聞いたりして楽しそうに参加していた。

（4）地域特性を生かした共同プログラム（影絵遊び）

事前のヒアリングを元に学童保育関係者・高齢者とともに地域に馴染みのある場所や動植物などを題材にした５分程度の話を作成し、高齢者と子どもが共同して影絵人形を作成･上演した。影絵人形は厚紙、割りばし、セロファン、両面テープを用いて、小学校低学年でも作成できるように事前に下準備を行った。上演では高齢者がナレーターになり、子ども達が人形をスクリーンの裏で動かした。

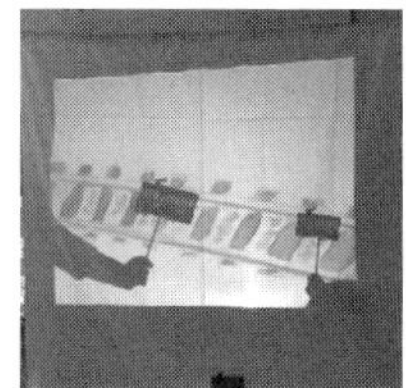

写真５　影絵上演時の様子　左：きつね　中央：桜　右：都電

（5）交流を深めるプログラム

最後に高齢者は子ども達の、子ども達は高齢者の良かったところをお互いに褒め合った。参加者全員がこの日一番の笑顔になった。

（6）世代間交流プログラム実施後の感想

参加者の実施後の感想をいくつか紹介する。

【小学生】

- 地域の人が優しくしてくれた。もっと遊んでみたい。（小１男子）
- おじいちゃんやおばあちゃんはいつも（僕たちのことを）見守っているんだなーと思った。（小２男子）
- 一緒に食べたり遊んだりしてすごく楽しいし、今度もおじいちゃんおばあちゃんと遊びたいなと思いました。（小２女子）
- 褒め褒めゲームではほめられてうれしかったしいろいろなことを知ってるし、勉強になりました。（小２女子）
- またおじいちゃんとおばあちゃんに昔のことを教えてもらいたい。（小３女子）
- じゃんけんや同じところ探しゲームは、人の気持ちがわかるようなゲームで楽しかったです。（小３女子）
- 影絵で遊んだのが楽しかったです。（小５男子）

【高齢者】

- 今日はとても楽しいひと時を過ごしました。子どもと遊ぶのはなんと楽しいのでしょう。周りの方々が準備をしてくださり、ただ参加するだけでしたが、お手伝いをしたいくらいでした。出来ればもっとたくさんの方が参加出来れば良かったです。（67 歳女性）
- 楽しい交流会でした。特に参加型の進め方が良かった。地域の事例なので親しみを感じ、参加意欲が出やすかった。（78 歳男性）

４．まとめ

プログラムの実施において、世代間の交流を深めるためには、交流・関係性を深める構成的グループエンカウンターなどの手法を用いて、出会いの緊張感から少しずつ馴染んでいけるように、プログラムを構成する必要がある。地域特性に合わせた回想法による共有プログラムは、地域の昔と現在の様子を対比させながら回想することにより、高齢者・子ども共に、地域の歴史や文化、自然、地域とのつながりなどの地域特性を共有、共感することができる。岡[3]による地域と連携した世代間交流プログラムでは、地域社会に対する理解を深めるなどの効果があった。CHUNG[4]は、回想法における世代間交流で高齢者の認知や若者の自尊心等、双方の心身の状態に効果のあることを示している。またMERCKEN[5]は近隣の学校、公園、レストラン、図書館などで多世代で話し、地域や住民相互の理解を深めることが地域の住民活動に発展する場合もあると述べている。本プログラムでも、地域の同じ話題を話し合うことにより、共感や地域への思いを醸成する交流につながったと考える。地域特性を生かした共同プログラムは、参加者の身体能力を観察し、高齢者と子どもが共に支援しあい、それぞれの身体的能力に応じた参加の仕方を自由に選択できるように順応なプログラムを用意する必要がある。また共同作業になるため、高齢者・子ども共に、年齢・発達を考慮し、デモンストレーションの実施や、理解度を確認しながら実施していく必要がある。

付記　本プログラムは科学研究費助成事業：基盤研究(C)（課題番号25463617　研究代表：森田久美子）（平成26～28年度）の助成を受けて実施した。また、本稿は2018年日本世代間交流学会誌Vol.7 (1) pp.23-32「学童保育における地域特性に合わせた世代間交流プログラムの実施と課題」（青木他）の論文に加筆修正を加えたものである。

引用・参考文献

1）厚生労働省「放課後子ども総合プランについて」

2）森田久美子,青木利江子,小林美奈子,他　2017　全国の学童保育における高齢者との世代間交流の実施状況と実施に関わる要因，日本世代間交流学会誌　6(1)　27-36.

3）岡和子,太湯好子,木村麻紀，　他　2016　地域高齢者と看護学生及び児童との世代間交流プログラムの実践報告～看護学生の交流会への参加と高齢観の視点から,吉備国際大学研究紀要　26　51-62.

4）CHUNG, J. C. 2009　An intergenerational reminiscence programme for older adults with early dementia and youth volunteers: values and challenges, Scandinavian journal of caring sciences, 23(2) 259-264.

5）MERCKEN, C. 2002 Neighborhood reminiscence integrating generations and　cultures in the Netherlands, Journal of Intergenerational Relationships, 1(1) 81-94.

要約

女性の社会進出、家族構造の変化、子育て環境の安全を守る必要性といった背景の下、子どもを家庭だけでなく地域社会で育てることが求められている。学童保育の子どもと高齢者に対し、地域特性に合わせた世代間交流プログラムを学童保育担当者らと共に作成・実施した事例をここで紹介する。

本プログラムは、森田らが全国学童保育を対象に行った世代間交流の実施状況調査結果をもとに開発したものである。事前に実施地域の学童保育担当者より、世代間交流の現状、地域のつながり、文化・歴史・自然等に関する情報収集を行い、地域特性に合わせた回想法（昔話）や、影絵による昔遊びを考案した。プログラム実施時間は約１時間、実施場所は学童保育施設や学童保育に隣接した公民館で実施した。また、ファシリテーターとして研究者（看護職）６名がプログラムに一緒に参加した。

今回は、世代間交流を継続して実施している２箇所の学童保育で世代間交流プログラムを実施した。プログラムは１．歩み寄り交流を促すプログラム、２．地域特性を生かした共有プログラム（回想法）、３．地域特性を生かした共同プログラム（影絵遊び）、４．交流を深めるプログラムで構成された。

プログラムの実施において、初めに交流・関係性を深める構成的グループエンカウンターなどの手法を用いて、出会いの緊張感から少しずつ馴染んでいけるように工夫した。地域特性に合わせた回想法による共有プログラムは、地域の昔と現在の様子を対比させながら回想することにより、高齢者・子ども共に、地域の歴史や文化、自然、地域とのつながりなどの地域特性を共有、共感することができた。また、共同プログラムは参加者の身体能力を観察し、高齢者と子どもが共に支援しあい、それぞれの身体的能力に応じた参加の仕方を自由に選択できるような内容を用意する必要がある。年齢・発達を考慮し、デモンストレーションの実施や、理解度を確認しながら実施していくことが大切である。

森田　久美子

東京医科歯科大学大学院保健衛生学研究科地域健康増進看護学分野

〒113-8519　東京都文京区湯島 1-5-45

東京医科歯科大学大学院　教育教授。博士（看護学）（東京医科歯科大学）。専門は地域保健、公衆衛生看護学。現在は世代間交流に関する研究のほか、介護予防に関する研究等に従事している。

青木　利江子

城西国際大学看護学部母性看護学分野

〒283-8555 千葉県東金市求名１番地

城西国際大学看護学部　准教授。専門は地域母子保健、母性看護学。現在は世代間交流

研究、多文化間精神医学研究に従事し、地域に残る昔話を再話、影絵を通して多世代間交流を実践している。

小林　美奈子

学校法人 誠広学園 平成医療短期大学看護学科

〒 501-1131　岐阜県岐阜市黒野 180 番地

平成医療短期大学看護学科　教授。博士（心身健康科学）（人間総合科学大学）。専門は在宅看護と老年看護学。現在は世代間交流に関する研究のほか、在宅看護に関する研究等に従事している。

山本　晴美

東京医科歯科大学大学院保健衛生学研究科地域健康増進看護学分野

〒 113-8519　東京都文京区湯島 1-5-45

東京医科歯科大学大学院　研究生。修士（看護学）（東京医科歯科大学）。専門は地域保健、看護ケア実践。現在は世代間交流に関する研究のほか、新たな看護ケアの開拓に関する研究等に従事している。

呂　暁衛

中国湖南科技大学体育学院理論教育研究室

〒 411201 中国湖南省湘潭市桃園路

中国湖南科技大学体育学院　理論教育研究室講師。博士（看護学）（東京医科歯科大学）

専門は健康教育学、運動医学など。現在の研究は世代間交流に関する研究のほか、運動健康に関する研究に従事している。

永嶺　仁美

和洋女子大学 看護学部 成人看護学

〒 272-0827　千葉県市川市国府台 2-1-18

和洋女子大学 看護学部 成人看護学助教。博士（看護学）（東京医科歯科大学）。専門は成人看護学、健康増進。現在は世代間交流に関する研究のほか、糖尿病予防における健康教育に関する研究に従事している。

佐々木　明子

東北文化学園大学医療福祉学部看護学科

〒 981-8551　仙台市青葉区国見 6 丁目 45-1

東北文化学園大学　教授。東京医科歯科大学　名誉教授。博士（医学）。専門は公衆衛生看護学、地域保健看護学。現在は高齢者の介護予防に関する研究、世代間交流に関する研究等を行っている。

Summary

Intergenerational exchange program in after-school care optimized for regional characteristics

There has been an increasing demand for local communities to support child-rearing. Woman's participation in society, changes in the conventional family structure and the safety issues in educational environment are a few examples of the driving factors in this over the recent years. In the current paper, we introduce a case of an intergenerational exchange program in after-school care optimized for regional characteristics.

The program was developed from a survey on the status of implementation of intergenerational exchange programs in after-school care across Japan (Morita et al.). Two subject areas (one urban and one rural area) with ongoing intergenerational activities were selected for the program. We also conducted interviews with persons in charge of after-school care of each area. The interviews were conducted regarding the recent status of intergenerational exchange, the level of the community network, and cultural, historical and environmental aspects of the subject areas and the data was used to produce contents of the program, such as folk tales and shadow plays. Duration of the program was one hour and it was performed at an after-school care facility and a city hall. Six researchers participated in the program as facilitators.

The program focused on 1) Facilitation of intergenerational exchange 2) Reminiscence activity on the history of the subject area 3) Participatory activity (i.e. shadow play) 4) Facilitation of further interaction among participants.

At the beginning of the program, ice-breaking activities such as a structural encounter group were implemented. Reminiscence activity was centered on the comparison of the past and present status of the subject areas, which encouraged the participants of both young and elderly generations to share details about the regional characteristics. It is noted that participatory activity should be organized taking into consideration of physical capacity of participants to provide freedom of choice of the way they participate in the activity, and this facilitates supportive interaction between the generations. Age and development of participants should also be considered and the program should proceed with demonstration and comprehension assessment at each stage.

Kumiko Morita

Department of Community Health Promotion Nursing, Graduate School of Health Care Sciences, Tokyo Medical and Dental University

1-5-45 Yushima, Bunkyo-ku, Tokyo, 113-8519 JAPAN

Tel&Fax: +81-3-5803-5337 E-mail: morita.phn@tmd.ac.jp

Dr. Kumiko Morita is a Teaching Professor of the Graduate School of Health Care Sciences at the Tokyo Medical and Dental University, Japan. Her Major is Community Health Nursing. Her latest researches are about the intergenerational exchange and preventive care for older adults.

Rieko Aoki

Department of Maternity Nursing, Faculty of Nursing, Josai International University

1 Gumyo, Togane-shi, Chiba 283-8555 Japan

Rieko Aoki is an Associate Professor of Faculty of Nursing at Josai International University. Her field of research is Community-based Maternal and Child Health Care and Maternity Nursing. Her latest work focuses on intergenerational exchange and cross-cultural psychiatry. She is an active practitioner of multigenerational exchange programs via folktale and shadow play.

Minako Kobayashi

Department of Nursing, Heisei College of Health Sciences.

180 Kurono, Gifu City, Gifu Prefecture ,501-1131 JAPAN

E-mail: m.kobayashi@heisei-iryou.ac.jp

Dr. Minako Kobayashi is a Teaching Professor of the Department of Nursing, at the Heisei College of Health Sciences, Japan. Her Major is Home Care Nursing and Gerontological Nursing . Her latest researches are about the intergenerational exchange ,as well as study on Home Care Nursing.

Harumi Yamamoto

Department of Community Health Promotion Nursing, Graduate School of Health Care Sciences, Tokyo Medical and Dental University

1-5-45 Yushima, Bunkyo-ku, Tokyo, 113-8519 JAPAN

Tel&Fax: +81-3-5803-5337 E-mail: morita.phn@tmd.ac.jp

Harumi Yamamoto is a student of the Graduate School of Health Care Sciences at the Tokyo Medical and Dental University, Japan. Her Major is Community Health Nursing. Her latest researches are about the intergenerational exchange and the development of new nursing care.

Xiaowei Lyu

Laboratory of Theoretical Education, School of Physical Education, Hunan University of Science and Technology

Taoyuan Road, Xiangtan, Hunan Province 411201 CHINA .

E-mail: xwlyu@hnust.edu.cn

Dr. Xiaowei Lyu is a Lecturer of the School of Physical Education, Hunan University of Science and Technology, China. Her Major is Community Health Nursing, and current studies focus on intergenerational exchange, as well as research on exercise health.

Hitomi Nagamine

Department of Adult Nursing, Faculty of Nursing, Wayo Women's University

2-1-18 Kohnodai, Ichikawa City, Chiba Pref. 272-0827, JAPAN

Tel: +81-47-371-1344 E-mail: h-nagamine@wayo.ac.jp

Dr. Hitomi Nagamine is an Assistant Professor of the Wayo Women's University, Japan. Her Major is Adult Nursing and Health Promotion. Her latest researches are about the intergenerational exchange and the health education for diabetes prevention.

Akiko Sasaki

Department of Nursing, Faculty of Medical Science and Welfare, Tohoku Bunka Gakuen University

6-45-1, Kunimi, Aoba-ku, Sendai, 980-8551 JAPAN

Tel: +81-22-233-3683 E-mail: sasaki.phn@ns.tbgu.ac.jp

Dr. Akiko Sasaki is a Professor of Department of Nursing, Faculty of Medical Science and Welfare at the Tohoku Bunka Gakuen University and Emeritus Professor of Tokyo Medical and Dental University, Japan. Her Major is Public Health Nursing. Her latest researches are about the health aging for the elderly people and the intergenerational exchange.

第９章　地域子育て支援への参加開始・継続動機と世代性

田渕　恵・小西　順子

１．はじめに

地域コミュニティの崩壊による人間関係の希薄化や、家庭内での伝統的な世代間関係の消失は、子育ての孤立という深刻な問題を引き起こしている。退職後の高齢者による地域子育て支援は、こうした問題の解決策として提唱されている枠組みのひとつである。1980 年以降の欧米における急激な社会環境変化の中で注目され始め、わが国においても、「子ども・子育て応援プラン」(内閣府 , 2004) の具体的施策である「高齢者活用子育て支援事業の推進」を背景に、高齢者の子育て支援が推奨されるようになった。

しかし、高齢者による地域の子育て支援が親世代に認知されるに伴い、親世代の参加者は増加するものの、支援者側の継続的活動が困難になるケースが報告され始めている (e.g 田渕・権藤 , 2011) 。ここでは、そうした問題解決の糸口を見つけるべく、ある１グループを対象として行った研究をご紹介したい。

子育て支援の開始・継続動機と世代性

高齢期に、子育て支援といった次世代に対する利他的関心や行動が増す背景には、世代性 (generativity) の発達があると考えられる。世代性とは、ERIKSON (1950, 仁科訳 1977) が「次世代を確立させて導くことへの関心」と第一義的に定義し、後に「新しい存在や新しい政策物や新しい概念を生み出すこと」(ERIKSON & ERIKSON 1997, 村瀬・近藤訳 2001) と拡張して再定義した概念であり、心理社会的生涯発達論の第７段階 (壮年期) の発達課題とされている。長寿化や晩婚化等の社会的背景の変化に伴い、世代性は壮年期のみならず、高齢期においても重要な発達課題となっている (CHENG, 2009) 。

では、子育て支援に関わる全ての高齢者が、次世代への利他性や世代性の高まりによって活動を開始、あるいは継続しているのだろうか。片桐(2012)の社会参加位相モデルによれば、退職後の社会参加を促進する要因は3種類の志向性に区分される。社会参加によって自身が楽しみたいという「利己的志向」、人と関わりたい、人とのつながりを作りたいという「ネットワーク志向」、そして、地域や社会のために役に立ちたいという利他性、世代性を背景とする「社会貢献志向」である。そして、子育て支援等の社会貢献活動の参加者は、これら3種類の志向性がいずれも高いとされている。子育て支援に関わる高齢者を対象に、参加・継続動機を調べた研究(田渕, 2008)でも、「自己へのメリット」「人間関係の充実感」「他者への貢献」といった、社会参加位相モデルと対応する動機が報告されているが、そこに個人差がどの程度存在するのかについての研究はない。実際に子育て支援に参加している高齢者全員が、活動の開始動機として3側面いずれも高いわけではなく、そこに個人差があり、その差によって継続動機も異なる可能性がある。また、参加開始動機の種類や強さによって、世代性の高低にも差が認められる可能性がある。そうした個人差に着目せず、子育て支援活動に参加する高齢者を一様に捉えていることが、活動の継続を困難にしている可能性はないだろうか。

そこで著者らは、退職後に子育て支援を行う1グループに着目し、メンバーの参加開始動機を明らかにした上で、開始動機の個人差によって継続動機や世代性の高さが異なるかを検討した。

2．研究の概要

(1) 調査対象グループおよび調査手続き

地域の子育て支援を行うAグループに所属する9名(平均年齢61.56±4.16歳、全員女性、幼稚園教諭を退職)を対象とした。子育て支援Aグループは、2016年に幼稚園教諭の退職者が中心となって地域の子育て支援講座を開設し、2018年にNPO法人として登記されたグループである。活動内容は、週5日間の託児事業を中心に、毎月約４回、子育て中の親子を対象としたイベント（親子体操、リズム遊び、英語教室等）を主催している。

調査では、まず子育て支援Ａグループのメンバーに、本研究の概要を説明し、質問紙を用いた調査への協力を依頼した。研究への参加が任意であることや個人情報の取り扱い等、倫理的配慮について、質問紙の表紙に記載した上で、口頭にて説明を行い、回答をもって研究参加への同意を得たものとした。質問紙を配布した１週間後に、９名すべての回答を回収した。

（2）調査内容

世代性を測定する尺度としては、田渕ほか（2012）の Generativity 尺度 20 項目（５件法）を用いた。項目は、「自分の経験や知識を人に伝えようとしている」、「私が人のためにしてきたことは、後世にも残ると思う」等であった。子育て支援への参加開始動機を測定する尺度としては、田渕（2008）で抽出された「高齢者の地域子育て支援活動開始動機カテゴリー」を参考に、17 項目（７件法）を設定した。項目は、「地域に貢献したいと思った」「子どもが好きで、子どもと接していたかった」「自分の専門性を活かしたかった」「知り合いから活動への参加を誘われた」などであった。子育て支援活動の継続動機を測定する尺度としては、田渕（2008）で抽出された「高齢者の地域子育て支援活動継続動機カテゴリー」を参考に、14 項目（７件法）を設定した。項目は、「子育て中の親の役に立っていると感じる」「自分の子や孫の役に立っていると感じる」「自分自身の健康維持になっている」「地域社会の役に立っていると感じる」などであった。

（3）結果

まず、子育て支援への参加開始動機の類似性によって対象者を分類するため、階層的クラスター分析（ウォード法、距離の計算はローデータによるユークリッド距離）を行った。その結果、子育て支援への参加開始動機項目「知り合いから活動への参加を誘われた」において、標準化得点が正の値（0.25）であり、その他の参加開始動機項目では全て標準化得点が負の値となるクラスター（６名）と、反対に「知り合いから活動への参加を誘われた」において、標準化得点が負の値 (-0.50) であり、その他の参加開始動機項目では標準化得点が正の値となるクラスター（３名）に分けられた。そこで、「知り合いから活動への参加を誘われた」において標準化得点が高いクラスターを「受動型」、もう一方のクラスターを「能動型」と命名した。さらに、

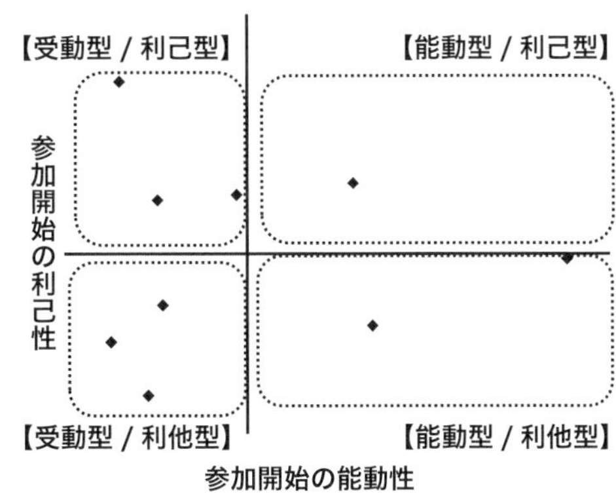

図１　参加開始動機による対象者 (n=9) のマッピング

多次元尺度法によって対象者をマッピングしたところ、水平方向の次元では「能動型」がプラスの方向、「受動型」がマイナスの方向に布置されたため、水平方向を「参加開始の能動性」とした。垂直方向の次元を調べるため、垂直方向を基準にプラスに布置された参加者と、マイナスに布置された参加者に分類し、子育て支援活動の参加開始動機を調べた。マンホイットニーの検定を行ったところ、「自分自身の健康につながると思った」において２群間で有意差が認められ、プラス方向に布置された群の方がマイナス方向に布置された群よりも有意に得点が高かった (U = 15.50, p = .04, r = .76) 。そこで、垂直方向を、自分自身にとってメリットがあるか否かが参加動機の背景となる「参加開始の利己性」とし、プラス方向に布置された群を「利己型」、マイナス方向に布置された群を「非利己型」とした (図１) 。

次に、「参加開始の能動性」(「受動型」/「能動型」) によって継続動機が異なるかを検討するため、継続動機 14 項目についてマンホイットニーの検定を行ったところ、「地域社会の役に立っていると感じる」(「受動型」平均値 = 4.71, 「能動型」平均値 = 5.33) (U = 1.00, p = .03, r = .77) 、「子育て中の親との触れ合いが楽しい」(「受動型」平均値 = 4.66, 「能動型」平均値 = 6.00) (U = 16.00, p = .03, r = -.76) の２項目において、「能動型」の方が「受動型」よりも有意に得点が高かった。その他 12 項目については、「参加開始の能動性」による違いは認められな

かった。「参加開始の利己性」(「利己型」/「利他型」)によって継続動機が異なるかを検討するため、継続動機14項目についてマンホイットニーの検定を行ったところ、14項目全てにおいて、「参加開始の利己性」による違いは認められなかった。また、「参加開始の能動性」(「受動型」/「能動型」)によって世代性が異なるかを検討したところ、「コミュニティや次世代への貢献」側面において、「能動型」(平均値 = 14.00)の方が「受動型」(平均値 = 13.67)よりも有意に得点が高い傾向が認められた($U = 16.00$, $p = .09$, $r = .59$)。「参加開始の利己性」(「利己型」/「利他型」)による世代性の違いは認められなかった。

(4) 考察

本研究により、子育て支援グループAのメンバーは「参加開始の能動性」と「参加開始の利己性」によって分類され、それによって継続動機や世代性が異なることが示された。開始動機の「能動型」は9名中3名であり、1/3のメンバーが残りのメンバーを牽引していると考えられる。

開始動機による継続動機の違いを検討した結果、「受動型」は「能動型」と比べて、地域社会や親への貢献感が継続動機とはなっていないことが示された。この結果から、「受動型」にとっては、活動を通して地域や次世代へ貢献できているという実感よりも、他の要因、例えば他のメンバーとの人間関係や責任感といった別の要因が、活動を継続する動機となっている可能性が考えられる。開始動機による世代性の違いを検討した結果においても、「受動型」は「能動型」よりも「コミュニティや次世代への貢献」という側面が低いことが示された。本研究の対象者は幼稚園教諭を退職後の女性であり、世代性が比較的高いグループであったが、その中でも個人差があり、活動を開始する際のきっかけや動機によって、その差をある程度予測できると考えられる。

本研究で示された通り、1つのグループ内で開始・継続動機の個人差が存在するため、子育て支援を行う高齢者を一様に「次世代への貢献感が高く、世代性が高い集団」としてみなすことが、かえって活動継続を困難にさせている可能性が考えられる。例えば、グループのリーダーが他のメンバーの継続動機を高めようとする試みが、必ずしも全メンバーに効果を発揮していない可能性が考えられる。メンバーの継続動機や世代性の高さは、開始動機に関連することが分かったため、メンバーの開始動機をまず把握し、介入方法をそれによって個々に変化させることで、より継続的な支援参加を促進できるかもしれない。

※本研究は、「田渕恵・小西順子 (2019)．女性退職者の地域子育て支援への参加・継続動機．日本世代間交流学会誌．8 (2)，13-19.」として発表されたものです。

引用・参考文献

CHENG, S. T. (2009) Generativity in later life: Perceived respect from younger generations as a determinant of goal disengagement and psychological well-being. Journal of Gerontology, 64B(1), 45-54.

ERIKSON, E. H. (1950) Childhood and society. New York: W. W. Norton.（仁科弥生（訳）1977　幼児期と社会Ｉ　みすず書房）

ERIKSON, E. H., & ERIKSON, J. M. (1997) The life cycle completed. Expanded ed. N.Y.: W. W. Norton.（村瀬孝雄・近藤邦夫（訳）(2001)　ライフサイクルその完結　増補版　みすず書房 pp.88）

片桐恵子　(2012)　退職シニアと社会参加　東京大学出版会

内閣府　(2004)　「少子化社会対策大綱に基づく重点施策の具体的実施計画について」（子ども・子育て応援プラン）の決定について

田渕恵　(2008)　地域の祖父母世代の子育て支援動機に関する質的研究　生老病死の行動科学，13, 33-44.

田渕恵・権藤恭之 (2011)　高齢世代が若年世代からポジティブなフィードバックを受け取る場面に関する研究　日本世代間交流学会誌，1, 81-87.

田渕恵、中川威、権藤恭之、小森昌彦　(2012) 高齢者における短縮版 Generativity 尺度の作成と信頼性・妥当性の検討 厚生の指標，59(3), 1-7.

要約

本研究では、退職後に地域の子育て支援を行う中・高齢女性の継続的な支援参加を目指し、参加開始動機を明らかにすること、そして開始動機によって継続動機や心理発達が異なるのかを明らかにすることを目的とした。地域の子育て支援を行う1グループに所属する女性9名(61.56 ± 4.16歳)を対象とし、質問紙を用いて、「子育て支援の参加開始・継続動機」、「世代性(generativity)」について尋ねた。開始動機の類似性により対象者を分類したところ、「知り合いから誘われた」において得点が高い受動型と、「育児中の親の助けになりたい」「経験を活かしたい」等において得点が高い能動型に分類された。また、能動型は「社会の役に立っている」、「親との触れ合いが楽しい」という継続動機や、世代性の「コミュニティや次世代への貢献」が受動型よりも有意に高い結果となった。メンバーの継続動機や世代性の高さは、開始動機に関連することが分かったため、メンバーの開始動機をまず把握し、介入方法をそれによって個々に変化させることで、より継続的な支援参加を促進できるかもしれない。

田渕　恵

安田女子大学心理学部
〒731-0153　広島県広島市安佐南区安東6丁目13番1号
安田女子大学心理学部講師。博士(人間科学)(大阪大学)。
専門は、発達心理学、社会心理学、老年学。

小西　順子

NPO法人子育て応援隊スマイルキッズ。
専門は、社会福祉学。

Summary

Motivation for starting and continuing participation in childcare support and ‘generativity'

The purpose of this study was to investigate the motives for beginning participation and whether the motives for continuing participation and psychological development differed depending on the motives for beginning participation, with the aim of ensuring the continued participation of middle-aged and elderly women who provide local child-rearing support. The data about beginning and continuing motivation and generativity derived from the questionnaires focused on 9 members in one child-support group (M=61.56, SD=4.16; all female). The members were classified into active or passive cluster depending on their beginning motivation. The members in active cluster had higher continuing motivation about “helping their society” and “enjoying the relationship with mothers” and had higher altruistic motivation about contribution to community and next generation (one of the aspects of generativity) than the members in passive cluster. Since the high level of continuity motivation and generativity of the members was found to be related to their initiation motivation, it may be possible to promote more continuous participation in support by first understanding the initiation motivation of the members and then changing the intervention methods accordingly.

Megumi Tabuchi

Department of Social-Psychology, Yasuda Women's University
6-13-1, Yasuhigashi, Asaminami-ku, Hiroshima, Hiroshima, 731-0153
Dr. Megumi Tabuchi is Assistant Professor of the Department of Social-Psychology, Yasuda Women's University Japan. Her majors are Developmental Psychology, Social Psychology and Gerontology.

Junko Konishi

NPO Childcare Support Group Smile Kids.
Her major is Social Welfare.

第10章　これからの日本における世代間交流の展望

－米国テンプル大学世代間交流学習センターの実践からの検討－

草野　篤子

1．はじめに

1997年から98年にかけて、米国ペンシルヴァニア州フィラデルフィア市にあるテンプル大学世代間交流学習センターで、上席研究員として研究・研修を行う機会を得た。20年余りの歳月を経ているので、必ずしも現在の日本の現状に合致するといえない部分があるかもしれないが、それを踏まえても、米国テンプル大学世代間交流学習センターで行われていた16のプログラムは、現在の日本においても、何らかの示唆を与える可能性を持ちあわせていると考えられるので、ここに紹介する[1)]。

当時、テンプル大学世代間交流学習センター(CIL)は、ピッツバーグ大学のGenerations Together(所長：Dr. Sally Newman)と並んで、主要な世代間交流センターと、考えられていた。両者共、多くのプログラム、財団からの豊富な資金、多くのスタッフを抱えていた。

本論文で扱う世代間交流とは、主に高齢者と子ども、青年、中年世代といった世代を超えた交流をいう。世代間交流プログラムとは、一定のシステムが構築された実践について使用している。ちなみに、国際世代間交流協会(The Intergenerational Consortium for Intergenerational Programs ICIP)は、世代間交流プログラムを、「高齢者と若者世代の間に、意図的・継続的な、資源の交換と学習を創りだす社会的媒体」と、定義している[2) 3)]。

2．米国テンプル大学世代間交流学習センターの実践

(1) 米国テンプル大学世代間交流学習センターについて

米国テンプル大学世代間交流学習センター(CIL 所長：Dr.Nancy Henkin)は、

世代間の協力と交流を促進するために、1980年に創立され、革新的な異年齢間のプログラム、訓練や研修の技術的な支援提供、資料などの普及・流布などを通じて、ペンシルヴァニア州フィラデルフィア市のみならず、世代間交流プログラムの全国的な供給源としての役割を果たした[3)]。そのカリキュラムやプログラムなどは、Generations United に引き継がれ、現在、Generations United のウエッブサイト[4)]で、見ることができる。

（2）1997年に行われていた16のプログラムについて

1) Across Ages（年齢を超えて）

これはハイリスクの小・中学生のための麻薬防止のプログラムである。このプログラムには、生徒たちのメンターとして、高齢者がかかわっている。地域サービスに生徒たちを関わらせ、教室で、生活の技術の訓練を与え、磨くものである。このプログラムは、青年時代に罪を犯し、少年院や刑務所に収監された経験がある高齢者なども、関わっている。

2) ECHO（Elders and Children Helping Each Other）（高齢者と子どもの相互支援）

保育領域で有償の仕事につくことに関心がある高齢者に向けての職業訓練プログラム。中年・高齢者で保育の研修を117時間受けることができる。参加者にはこの領域の仕事を斡旋する。

3) Experience Corps（エクスペリエンス・コア）

Experience Corps は RSVP（Retired Senior Volunteer Program：退職高齢者ボランティア・プログラム）と、フィラデルフィア学校区と協力関係にある。高齢者が、幼稚園、小・中学校の生徒たちに対して個人指導、地域サービスを教授し、中学生では、高齢者から今までの人生について聞き取りをし、レポートを作成。高齢者の生活史として毎年、学校ごとに編集し、ワシントン D.C. にある国立国会図書館に、寄贈している。

4) Family Friends (家族のお友達)

高齢者が、フィラデルフィア市の、障がいがあったり、慢性的な病気にかかっている子どもを抱えている家族に対して、家庭内での支援を行うプロジェクトである。ボランティアは、少なくとも週1回、その子どもを訪ね、面白く教育的な活動を行う。

5) Full Circle Theater Troupe (満転劇場一座)

ティンエージャーと高齢者による世代間交流劇団。一座のダイナミックなパフォーマンスは、個人や家族などが遭遇する典型的な状況を団員が寸劇として展開し、学校、高齢者センター、地域の団体、会合、行政団体などで演じられる。

6) Grandma's Kids (おばあちゃんの子ども)

祖父母や他の代わりの保育者によって育てられている子どもに対する広範囲なサービスを提供している。麻薬防止の教育、保育者支援グループ、資源の紹介を行う。

7) Health LINK (健康の輪)

高齢者の職業訓練プログラム。7週間の講習は高齢者に、高齢者や障がい者に対してどのようにケアを提供するかについて、教授する。参加者は、援助サービスと雇用が保障される支援を受けられる。

8) Learning Retreat (学びの場)

年齢を超えたコミュニケーションを促進するために、毎年、14歳から100歳の75人の参加者が5日間、一緒に合宿するプログラム。

9) Our Elders, Our Roots (わが高齢者、われらのルーツ)

テンプル大学、ニュー・メキシコ大学、ノースイースタン大学、サンフランシスコ州立大学のバイリンガルの学生が、彼らの地域に居住する限られた英語しか話せない高齢者に様々なサービスを、行なうプログラム。

10）Home friends（家庭のお友達）

Supportive Child /Adult Network（SCAN）と、協力・提携している。このプロジェクトは、SCANが取り扱っている特別なニーズを抱えている子どもと家族を、家庭内で支援する高齢者を、新たに補充・訓練・監督する。またこのプロジェクトは、両親に対する両親サポートを提供する。

11）Project LEIF（Learning English through Intergenerational Friendship 世代間交流を通じた英語学習）

高齢の難民や移民に英語を教える大学生を補充し、訓練を行う。レッスンは、１対１で行われ、各学習者の個人の目標に見合うようにデザインされている。

12）Project OPEN（Opportunities for Productivity, Empowerment and Nurturing 生産性、エンパワーメント、そして養育の機会）

テンプル大学学生、在住者、近辺にある養老院職員が、周辺環境をよくするためのサービス・プロジェクトを、一緒に行う。

13）Project W.R.I.T.E.（Writing and Reading through Intergenerational Teaching Experience 世代間交流教授体験を通しての読み書き）

高齢者の読み書き能力を高めるために大学生を補充し訓練するプロジェクト。レッスンは、１対１で行われ、各学習者の個人の目標に見合うようにデザインされている。

14）Sisters in Science（科学への関心を持つマイノリティー（少数者、すなわち黒人、ヒスパニック、アジア系など）の女子を支援する）

フィラデルフィア学校区と、科学のバックグラウンドを持つ高齢女性と、教育実習中の大学生が、小学４年生女子マイノリティーの、科学への関心を増進させる支援をし、環境コミュニティーサービス・プロジェクトと、カリキュラム増強を図る地域の団体との連携プロジェクト。

15) Tele Friends(電話のお友達)

高校生によるペンシルヴァニア州デラウエア郡に住む孤立して家に閉じこもっている高齢者に対する電話による安全確認をするサービス・ラーニング・プログラム

16) Time Out(中休み)

虚弱または健康を害した高齢者を世話している介護者に、必要な息抜きを提供するために、大学生を補充し訓練する。学生は、介護者のいない間、高齢者と親密な交流を持ち多様な活動に高齢者と携わり、食事を準備し、介護者に支援を与える。

3. 米国の世代間交流プログラムの実践や活動が、日本の世代間交流にどのように繋がったのか

1990年代の終わりごろから、米国ペンシルヴァニア州立大学のDr. Matt Kaplanが、フルブライト招請研究費を得て、東北大学医学部公衆衛生学研究室に客員研究員として訪日し、著者と日本の世代間交流についての共同研究を行なった[5)]。その後、著者が、Temple大学世代間交流学習センターの上席研究員として、米国の世代間交流プログラムについて研究および実践活動に従事する機会を得た。1998年にDr. Nancy Henkinが訪日し、2003年には、世界の世代間交流をリードするピッツバーグ大学のDr. Sally Newmanが、東京に立ち寄り、同年11月には、実践女子大学の招待で再来日し、信州大学、実践女子大学などで、世代間交流とは何か、地域の再構築とは、といった内容について議論をすすめ、日本世代間交流協会の創設に向けて、Joyful Generationsという研究会が組織

され、任意団体日本世代間交流協会（Japan Intergenerational Unity Association: JIUA）が2004年５月に設立された。その後、2006年５月には、特定非営利活動法人日本世代間交流協会が創立された。同年８月初めの３日間、「世代間交流国際フォーラム－世代をつなぎ地域を再生するため－」と、研究者向けの「世代間交流についての国際研究集会」が早稲田大学国際会議場において行われた[6)7)]。

4．日本における世代間交流の実践

日本で行われている世代間交流の実践は、この21年間、著者が編集に関わっている日本世代間交流学会の姉妹団体であるNPO法人日本世代間交流協会から出版されている『世代間交流－老いも若きも子どもも』第18号[8)]、及び19号[9)]を研究対象とした。

5．まとめ

米国テンプル大学世代間交流学習センターで行われていた世代間交流プログラムは、それぞれ、地域のニーズに基づいた多様な内容である。エクスピリエンス・コア・プログラムは、アメリカの５都市で、1995年から実験的に行われ、1960年代から行われている既存のプログラムやアイデアに触発されて、成立したプログラムである。プログラムの創設者の一人であるマーク・フリードマン（Mark Freedman）は、インスピレーションの鍵となったのは、里祖父母プログラム（Foster Grandparents Program）であると述べている[10)]。

例えば、Experience Corps（エクスピリエンス・コア）プログラムは、太平洋を越えて、東京都健康長寿医療センター研究所の藤原佳典氏を中心に、Johns Hopkins Universityで行われていた地域高齢者による学校支援活動ボランティアExperience Corpsをモデルに、REPRINTSプログラムとして実施されている[11)]。

日本における世代間交流については、26例のうち３件が子ども食堂、フードバンクなど、食環境に関わるもの、同じく３例が味噌づくり、お囃子、けん玉など、伝統継承に関わるもの、同じく3例が、大学が中心になったコミュニティネットワークや大学の授業を利用したプログラム、2例が紙芝居や絵本の読み聞かせをする中年・高齢者によるプログラムとなっている。その他は、高齢男性が中心になって運営するNPO法人など、多様である。

日本における世代間交流プログラムは、現在、まさに日本で実施されている世代間交流プログラムである。日本で唯一のかけがえのない実践例であるが、例えば、長野県長野市鬼無里地域で行われている世代間交流は、当時の鬼無里村で平成17(2006)年に始まった。介護保険制度の要介護・要支援認定の有無に関わらず、高齢者と保育園児が同じ屋根の下で、ほとんど毎日交流が行われていた[12)]。引き続き、日本で実施され取り上げられていない実践を、継続して掘り起こし、その実践がますます発展していくように、日本世代間交流学会やNPO法人日本世代間交流協会で、バックアップしていけることを願っている。

本来、現代社会においては、福祉社会の構築が切に求められている。超少子高齢化、核家族化を経て、単独世帯化、そして本来なら国家、行政、地域社会が責任を持って一人一人の生命、生活の質(QOL)を重視し、保障していくことが望まれるが、公的保障はますます自己責任に委ねる方向に進んでいる。女性の就業率の増加、高学歴化の中で、かつては女性の役割とされていた子育てや介護に関連した諸課題が大きな社会問題になっている。現代社会における社会経済的格差をはじめ、性差、年齢差をも超えた、一人の人間をも積み残すことのない、インクルーシブな社会を基礎とした「共生」が求められている[13) 14) 15) 16) 17) 18) 19) 20)]。これらのニーズに的確に応えられる多様なプログラムを開発し、今後も、実行に移していくことが、現在、切に望まれる。

引用・参考文献

1) CENTER FOR INTERGENERATIONAL LEARNING (1997), Temple University, Temple University, Philadelphia

2) KAPLAN, M., HENKIN, N. and KUSANO, A. (2002), Linking Lifetime: A Globql View of Intergenerational Exchange, University Press of America

3）マシュー・カプラン、ナンシー・ヘンケン、草野篤子（編著・監修）、加藤澄（訳）、(2008) グローバル化時代を生きる世代間交流、明石書店

4）GENERATIONS UNITED (2020), generations united, https://www.gu.org/the-intergenerational-center-resources/（参照日 2020 年 3 月 23 日）

5）KAPLAN, M., KUSANO、A.TSUJI、I.HISAMICHI,S. (1998) Intergenerational Program: Support for Children, Youth, and Elders in Japan, State University of New York

6）矢島さとる、草野篤子、倉岡正高、斎藤嘉孝、マット・カプラン（編）(2007)、世代間交流国際フォーラム－世代をつなぎ地域を再生するために－、世代間交流についての国際研究集会発表原稿集、Proceedings : Uniting the Generations : Japan Conference to Promote Intergenerational Programs and Initiatives, and Post Conference, International Academic Meetings on Intergenerational Issues and Initiatives、聖徳大学生涯学習研究所

7）Saito Y. Yajima S., Kusano A., Kaplan M., Special Issue: Intergenerational Pursuits in Japan A Mosaic of Practice and Inquiry, (2009) Journal of Intergenerational Relationships, 7 (1)

8）草野篤子、金田利子、水野宗一（編）(2018)、世代間交流－老いも若きも子どもも－ 第 18 号、NPO 法人日本世代間交流協会、東京

9）草野篤子、金田利子、水野宗一（編）(2019)、世代間交流－老いも若きも子どもも－ 第 19 号、NPO 法人日本世代間交流協会、東京

10）PUTTNAM, R.D., FELDSTEIN, L.M. and COHEN, D.J. (2003), Better Together : Restoring the American Community, Simon & Schuster, 186-205

11）藤原佳典（2020）、高齢者のプロダクティビティと世代間交流、草野篤子、金田利子、間野百子、柿沼幸雄（編著）、世代間交流効果―人間発達と共生社会づくりの視点から、三学出版、pp.59-71

12）田中慶子、角間陽子、角尾晋、草野篤子（2007）、超高齢社会における世代間交流の在り方－長野県鬼無里地域での実践を通して、信州大学教育学部紀要、119：147-156

13）草野篤子、秋山博介（編著）(2004)、現代のエスプリ、インタージェネレーション：コミュニティを育てる世代間交流　至文堂

14）草野篤子（2006）、日本における世代間交流の歩みと今後の展望、社会教育、61 (3)：8-11

15）草野篤子、金田利子、間野百子、柿沼幸雄（編著）(2007)、世代間交流効果－人間発達と共生社会づくりの視点から、三学出版

16）草野篤子、柿沼幸男、金田利子、藤原佳典、間野百子（編著）(2010)、世代間交流学の創造：無縁社会から多世代間交流型社会実現のために、あけび書房

17）草野篤子、内田勇人、溝邊和成、吉津晶子（編著）(2012)、多様化社会をつむぐ世代間交流－次世代への『いのち』の連鎖をつなぐ、三学出版

18) 草野篤子、溝邊和成、内田勇人、安永正史、山之口俊子（編著）（2015）、世代間交流の理論と実践1、人を結び、未来を拓く世代間交流、三学出版

19) 草野篤子、溝邊和成、内田勇人、安永正史（編著）（2017）、世代間交流の理論と実践2　世界標準としての世代間交流のこれから、三学出版

20) 倉岡正高（編著）、草野篤子、藤原佳典、村山陽（著）（2013）、地域を元気にする世代間交流、公益財団法人社会教育協会

要約

これからの日本における世代間交流を考えるにあたって、かつて米国テンプル大学世代間交流学習センター（所長：Dr. Nancy Henkin）で実践されていた16のプロジェクトを紹介するとともに、日本の最近の実践例を、合わせて考えてみたい。テンプル大学世代間交流学習センターは、世代間の協力と交流を促進するために、1980年に創立され、革新的な異年齢間のプログラム、訓練や研修の技術的な支援提供、資料などの普及・流布などを通じて、ペンシルヴァニア州フィラデルフィア市のみならず、世代間交流プログラムの全国的な供給源としての役割を果たした。今後の日本での世代間交流の実践において、各地域のニーズに基づいた、草の根からのプログラムが開発され、実行に移されることが、望まれる。

なお紹介プログラムのタイトルは以下の通りである。

1）Across Ages：麻薬防止のプログラム

2）ECHO（Elders and Children Helping Each Other）：職業訓練プログラム

3）Experience Corps：退職高齢者ボランティアとフィラデルフィア学校区との活動

4）Family Friends：高齢者による家庭内支援プロジェクト

5）Full Circle Theater Troupe：ティーンエイジャーと高齢者による劇団

6）Grandma's Kids：子どもに対する広範囲なサービス

7）Health LINK：高齢者の職業訓練プログラム

8）Learning Retreat：5日間、異年齢集団合宿プログラム

9）Our Elders, Our Roots：バイリンガルの学生による英語しか話せない高齢者向けサービス

10) Home friends：Supportive Child /Adult Network（SCAN）と協力・提携したプロジェクト

11) Project LEIF：大学生による高齢の難民・移民への英語レッスン

12) Project OPEN（Opportunities for Productivity, Empowerment and Nurturing）：周辺環境をよくするためのサービス・プロジェクト

13) Project W.R.I.T.E.（Writing and Reading through Intergenerational Teaching Experience）：

高齢者の読み書き能力を高める訓練プロジェクト

14) Sisters in Science：科学への関心を持つマイノリティー（女子）支援

15) Tele Friends：高校生による高齢者への電話サービス

16) Time Out：介護者の代役サービス

草野篤子（編著者紹介欄 p.275 参照）

Summary

The Future Prospects for Intergenerational Exchange in Japan; Drawing Upon the Innovation and Lessons Learned from the Center for Intergenerational Learning at Temple University, in the U.S.A.

In considering the future of intergenerational exchange in Japan, I would like to introduce 16 projects that were once implemented at the Center for Intergenerational Learning at Temple University (Director: Dr. Nancy Henkin) in the U.S., as well as some recent examples in Japan. The Center for Intergenerational Learning at Temple University, founded in 1980 to promote intergenerational cooperation and exchange, serves as a national source of intergenerational exchange programs, not only in Philadelphia, PA, but also in the United States, through innovative intergenerational programs, technical assistance for training and development, and dissemination of materials. In addition to the city of Philadelphia, Pennsylvania, it has served as a nationwide source of intergenerational exchange programs. It is hoped that future intergenerational exchange programs in Japan will be developed and implemented from the grassroots up, based on the needs of each community.

The titles of the introductory programs are as follows:

- Across Ages: Drug prevention program
- ECHO (Elders and Children Helping Each Other): Job training program
- Experience Corps: Activities of retired elderly volunteers with the School District of Philadelphia
- Family Friends: In-home support project by senior citizens
- Full Circle Theater Troupe: A theater troupe of teenagers and senior citizens
- Grandma's Kids: Extensive services for children
- Health LINK: Vocational training program for the elderly.
- Learning Retreat: 5-day, cross-age group camp program.
- Our Elders, Our Roots: Services for English-speaking seniors by bilingual students.
- Home friends: A project in cooperation and partnership with the Supportive Child / Adult Network (SCAN).
- Project LEIF: English lessons by university students for elderly refugees and

immigrants

- Project OPEN (Opportunities for Productivity, Empowerment and Nurturing): A service project to improve the surrounding environment.
- Project W.R.I.T.E. (Writing and Reading through Intergenerational Teaching Experience): A training project to improve the reading and writing skills of the elderly.
- Sisters in Science: Support for minorities (girls) with an interest in science
- Tele Friends: Telephone service for the elderly by high school students
- Time Out: Substitute service for caregivers

Atsuko Kusano (See p.275)

第11章　剣道を通した世代間交流の可能性

松本　大佑・濱口　雅行
濱口　郁枝・内田　勇人

1．はじめに

近年、我が国は世界に例を見ない速さで社会の少子高齢化が進行している。2020年の総務省統計局[1)]による人口推計結果をみると、日本人の人口は1億2565万人に対して、15歳未満の人口は1499万人で、前年に比べ18万人の減少となり、65歳以上の高齢者人口は過去最多の3617万人であった。また、日本の高齢者人口の割合は、世界で最も高い28.7%であった。こうした人口構成の変化は、我が国の子どもをとりまく環境に多大な影響を与えており、具体的には①核家族化や少子化の進展にともなう地域社会での対人交流の減少、②物質的な豊かさ、③価値観の多様化、④知育偏重の学歴社会、⑤親の過保護・過干渉、あるいは放任などの歪んだ養育態度といった問題が危惧されている[2)]。現代社会における少子高齢化の影響は様々な場面においてみられるが、世代と世代の結びつきの欠如は我が国の社会保障の基盤となる世代間の相互扶助が成す精神の醸成、より豊かな日常生活の背景を創造する文化の伝承・伝達の機会の喪失につながりかねず、喫緊の課題として認識されている。

内閣府[3)]の世代間交流に関する調査結果においても、子どもと高齢者の交流機会は著しく減少していることが指摘されている。異世代と交流することについて、草野・秋山[4)]は、子どもにとって親とは違った世代の考え方や生き方に触れることで、同世代の子どもとの関係から得られない社会性を育む良い機会になると述べている。このように世代間交流の機会が減少していることは、現代社会の課題となっている。

こうした社会的動向を背景として、世代間交流に関する研究が数多く実施されるようになってきている。船津・辻[5]は、高齢者と高齢者以外の世代との交流によって高齢者以外の世代が高齢者世代に対する偏見を低減し、相互理解が促進することを指摘しており、堀野・濱口[6]は、高齢者と高齢者以外の世代との交流が両者の人格発達に好影響を与えることを指摘している。また、世代間交流の手段として絵本の読み聞かせを主体とする“REPRINTS”研究や伝承遊び等における交流効果を検証した報告がみられ、世代間交流効果として子ども、高齢者の心身の健康度に良い影響を及ぼすことが指摘されている[7]。

ところで、スポーツ庁の体力･運動調査結果[8]をみると、高齢者の体力は年々、向上傾向にあり、運動・スポーツを介した世代間交流についても研究が行われるようになってきている。栗山[9]は家庭用ゲーム機を用いた疑似スポーツによる世代間交流の研究を実施し、初対面の異世代同士が疑似スポーツを通したゲームプレイにより、相互で印象が良くなったことを認めている。花井[10]は水中運動を活用した多世代間交流プログラムにより、参加者のプログラムに対する満足度や世代間交流が促進されたことに対する実感はそれぞれ有意に向上したことを報告している。その一方で、運動・スポーツを介した世代間交流についてはこれまでに必ずしも多くなく、その実態については不明な点が多い。

ところで、運動・スポーツを通した世代間交流を考えた場合、異世代同士が共に実施できることが必須条件になる。その観点において濱口ほか[11]は生涯を通じて、老若男女が世代を超えて実施できるスポーツのひとつとして「剣道」の重要性を指摘している。また、老若男女がともに稽古する環境としては部活動のOB 稽古会や主に小学校の体育館などで行われる町道場、多くの老若男女が集う暑中稽古、寒稽古といった伝統行事が挙げられる。さらに剣道の稽古内容に関する研究[12]では、高校生の場合も高段者の場合も、互角稽古は試合のシミュレーションとして位置づけられていないことを示唆しており、高校生レベルの剣道実践者においても互角稽古の際にはその実践内容を剣道の伝統的な価値観あるいは美意識に則った理念的な活動内容に近接させようとしていると指摘されている。また、丹羽[13]は高段者において、大学生との稽古のほうが高段者同士の稽古より運動強度が低いことを報告している。これらのことから剣道は生涯にわたって行うことができる武道であるといえる。

そこで本稿では、高齢者と稽古経験があり、日本の伝統文化である剣道を大学で実践している大学剣道部員を対象として、剣道に関わる高齢者イメージや特性を検討した研究について紹介する。

2．方法

（1）調査期間

2018年10月～11月。

（2）調査対象者

大学剣道部員102名（年齢18～22歳、関西地域の国公私立の5大学に在籍）を選択した。対象の中から高齢者と稽古経験がない者7名を除外したため、最終的な研究参加者は95名であった。

（3）調査項目

性別、学年などの他に、高齢者イメージに関する質問として、「あなたが思う総括的な高齢者イメージについて、次の各項目の最も当てはまる数字に○をつけて回答してください。」と尋ね、保坂・袖井[14]によって開発された高齢者イメージの尺度を用いた。これは50項目の形容詞からなる尺度（SD法）である。「高齢者イメージ」の50項目は－3～3段階で回答を求めた。項目得点は回答の数値を素点とし、点数が低くなるほど否定的なイメージが強く、高くなるほど肯定的なイメージが強くなるように得点化した。

（4）分析方法

高齢者イメージの構造を明らかにするために因子分析（主因子法、プロマックス回転）を行った。大学剣道部員が高齢者イメージに及ぼす因果関係を把握するために、仮説をもとにモデルを構築し、共分散構造分析を行った。

3．結果

（1）因子分析

高齢者イメージ尺度 48 項目について、探索的因子分析（重みなし最小２乗法・プロマックス回転）を行った（表１）。なお、“内向的－外向的”、“受動的－能動的”の２項目は、共分散構造分析において、従属変数に用いるため、あらかじめ、因子分析から除いた。

また、固有値の変化と解釈の可能性を考慮した上で、因子負荷量が 0.40 未満の項目を削除した結果、「身体性因子」、「充実性因子」、「徳性因子」の３つの因子が抽出された。

（2）相関分析

大学剣道部員の高齢者イメージ尺度における下位尺度間の関係性を明らかにするため、各下位尺度得点間の相関係数を算出し、表２に示した。下位尺度間において、「身体性因子」と「充実性因子」、「徳性因子」、および「充実性因子」と「徳性因子」に正の相関が認められた。

（3）共分散構造分析

つぎに大学剣道部員はどのようにして高齢者イメージを形成しているのかについて詳細に検討するため、因子分析で抽出された「身体性因子」、「充実性因子」、「徳性因子」を観測変数として用いた。また、「接しやすさ」を潜在変数とし、その変数から影響を受ける項目として、因子分析から除いた“内向的－外向的”、“受動的－能動的”を自己開示の観点から観測変数として用いた。その理由としては、榎本[15]によると自己開示は、自分はどういう人間かを他者に知ってもらうために自分自身をあらわにする行動であると述べている。また、JOURARD & FRIEDMAN[16]、WORTHY et al.[17]によると、開示された相手は開示者の大切な情報が伝えられることで、開示者は自分に対して心を開いていると認識し、被開示者も開示者に心を開き、自己に関する情報を徐々に開示していくと報告して

表1　高齢者イメージ尺度の分析結果

	因子負荷量		
	1	2	3
身体性因子　Cronbach の α =0.881			
弱い－強い	**0.746**	0.213	-0.244
小さい－大きい	**0.680**	-0.208	0.067
無能な－有能な	**0.677**	-0.070	0.087
だらしない－きちんとした	**0.633**	-0.063	-0.052
劣った－優れた	**0.616**	-0.098	0.135
小さい－大きい	**0.596**	0.023	0.086
低俗な－高尚な	**0.596**	-0.076	-0.088
弱々しい－たくましい	**0.584**	0.343	0.072
きたない－きれい	**0.577**	-0.191	0.238
感情的－理想的	**0.534**	-0.022	0.083
魅力のない－魅力のある	**0.511**	0.164	0.158
粗い－細かい	**0.493**	-0.270	-0.117
貧弱な－立派な	**0.479**	0.276	0.123
充実性因子　Cronbach の α =0.796			
静的－動的	0.091	**0.677**	0.054
地味な－派手な	-0.159	**0.635**	-0.062
閉鎖的－開放的	0.014	**0.559**	0.333
保守的－進歩的	0.099	**0.549**	-0.039
固い－やわらかい	-0.217	**0.539**	-0.048
消極的－積極的	0.063	**0.513**	-0.055
不自由な－自由な	-0.114	**0.500**	0.210
静かな－騒がしい	-0.393	**0.497**	-0.021
遅い－速い	0.356	**0.474**	-0.171
鈍い－鋭い	0.397	**0.401**	-0.291
徳性因子　Cronbach の α =0.739			
つめたい－あたたかい	0.162	-0.271	**0.695**
疎遠な－親密な	0.062	0.137	**0.602**
不幸な－幸福な	0.169	-0.049	**0.587**
悲観的－楽観的	-0.216	0.274	**0.541**
厳しい－優しい	0.006	-0.093	**0.494**
孤立－連帯	-0.105	0.352	**0.433**

因子抽出法：重みなし最小二乗法　プロマックス回転（n=95）

表 2　下位尺度間の関係性

(n=95)

	身体性因子	充実性因子
充実性因子	0.360**	-
徳性因子	0.343**	0.330**

Pearson の相関関係 , **p<0.01

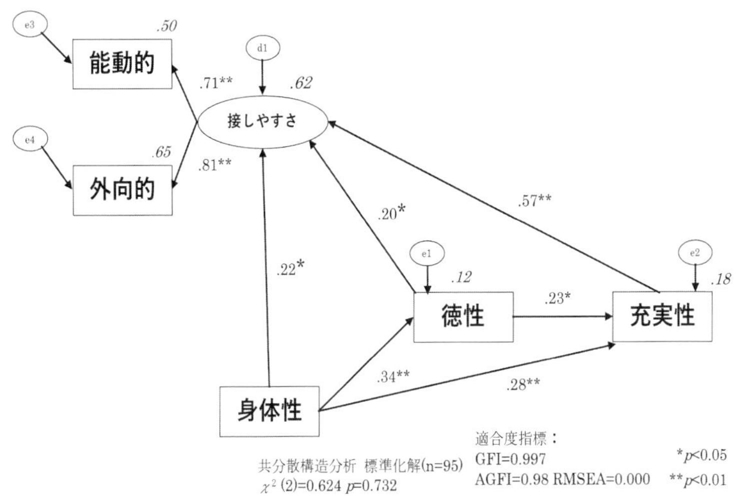

図 1　剣道部員が高齢者イメージに及ぼす因果関係

いる。これらのことから、「接しやすさ」には自己開示が重要であり、自己開示には“外向的”、“能動的”的な高齢者イメージがあると考えたからである。

そこで、「接しやすさ」、「身体性因子」、「充実性因子」、「徳性因子」を用いて、仮説モデルを構築し、共分散構造分析を行った（図 1）。仮説モデルとしては、剣道には異世代同士で身体を通した交流ができるといった特性がある。したがって、「身体性因子」から「充実性因子」、「徳性因子」に影響を及ぼし、最終的には「接しやすさ」に結びつき、異世代同士の人間関係を豊かにすることができるとした。

その結果、「身体性因子」から「徳性因子」と「充実性因子」に影響を与え、「接しやすさ」につながった。さらに「身体性因子」が直接的に「接しやすさ」を促進することも確認された。したがって、「身体性因子」は直接的にも間接的にも正の因果関係を示していることが明らかになった。

4．考察

本節では、高齢者と稽古経験がある大学剣道部員において、高齢者との稽古経験が高齢者イメージや特性にどのような影響を及ぼしているのかについて紹介してきた。その結果、「身体性因子」が直接的、間接的にも「接しやすさ」を促進することが確認された。

武道のひとつである剣道は怪我の危険性等が高いと予測されるが、実際には他競技に比べ、比較的低い[18)]。また、剣道には「打って反省、打たれて感謝」という言葉があり、お互いが尊重し合い、稽古に取り組む必要がある。元嶋ほか[19)]は剣道の特性である「人を打つこと・打たれること」によって相手への配慮が喚起されることを報告している。高校剣道部員と成人の高段者との互角稽古および試合に関する研究[12)]において、高校生の試合では勝利に対するこだわりから自ら攻撃を仕掛ける行為を減らして対戦の攻撃ミスを待つ場合が多い。一方、互角稽古では高校生、高段者ともに積極的に攻める姿勢がみられ、剣道の伝統的な価値観あるいは美意識に則った理念的な活動内容に近接させようとしていることが確認されている。

したがって、異世代同士が尊重し合いながら身体を通した交流が行えるといった剣道の特性により、「身体性因子」が強く印象付けられ、様々な因子に影響を与え、最終的には「接しやすさ」が促進されたと考えられた。

5．課題と展望

現代剣道には、大きく分けて、試合での勝敗といった「競技的要素」と、我が国の伝統文化としての「文化的要素」があり、それらが包含され、成立している（図2）。本節では、十分に剣道経験を積んだ大学生の剣道実践者は、相手となる高齢者を尊重するといった伝統的な考え方を理解し、異世代同士でも相互作用のある稽古を実践していることが伺えた。

しかし、小学生と指導者の剣道観に着目した研究[20]において、小学生は試合で勝つことや上の級を目指す技能向上への意欲が最も高く、剣道の先生の憧れや伝統様式などに対しては消極的・否定的であった。指導者においては高段者の指導者ほど日本剣道形といった文化的要素を重要視しており、小学生と指導者の剣道観に相違があると報告されている。高校生と大学生からなる青年を対象とした全国規模の剣道に対する意識調査[21]では、剣道授業の受講前の学生よりも受講後の学生の方が剣道に対してネガティブなイメージを抱いており、授業内容によっては剣道に対して、嫌悪感を抱きかねないと指摘されている。

したがって、今後は剣道を実践している子どもの成長段階と高齢者イメージとの関連について詳細に明らかにすること、日本の伝統文化に存在する師弟関係や地域や生活場面における指導者と指導される側との関係などの交流効果について質問紙調査、およびインタビュー調査を用いて明らかにしていきたい。

今後も少子高齢化が進行する我が国において、子どもが高齢者と接する機会は顕著に減少している。剣道に関わらず、伝統文化の伝承・継承の場においては、子どもから高齢者といった異なる世代間での交流が求められる。そこで、子どもに対して、文化的要素である伝統文化の魅力をわかりやすく伝えることが重要であり、そのような工夫が少子高齢化、国際社会といった時代における伝統文化の伝承・継承の発展に繋がるだろう。

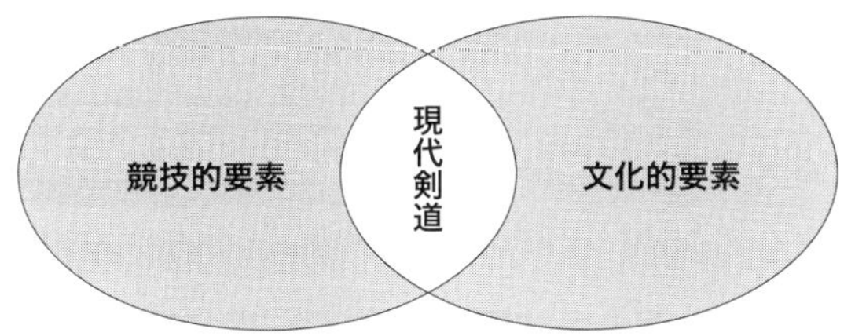

図 2　現代剣道のイメージ図（筆者作成）

引用・参考文献

1） 総務省統計局:高齢者の人口(2020), http://www.stat.go.jp/data/topics/topi1261.html,（参照日 2021 年 5 月 20 日）.

2） 堀野緑, 濱口佳和, 宮下一博(2006), 子どものパーソナリティと社会性の発達, 北大路書房, 京都 ,117-118.

3） 内閣府:「平成 26 年度高齢者の日常生活に関する意識　調査結果」, 2018 年, https://www8.cao.go.jp/kourei/ishiki/h26/sougou/zentai/index.html,（参照日 2020 年 10 月 20 日）.

4） 草野篤子 , 秋山博介 (2004) , 現代のエスプリ , 至文堂 , 東京 , 7-8.

5） 船津衛 , 辻正二 (2003) , エイジングの社会心理学 , 北樹出版 , 東京 , 53-54.

6） 堀野緑 , 濱口佳和 , 宮下一博 (2006) , 子どものパーソナリティと社会性の発達 , 北大路書房 , 京都 , 117-118.

7） 藤原佳典 , 渡辺直紀 , 西真理子 , 李相侖 , 大場宏美 , 吉田裕人 , 佐久間尚子 , 深谷太郎 , 小宇佐陽子 , 井上かず子 , 天野秀紀 , 内田勇人 , 角野文彦 , 新開省二 (2007) , 児童の高齢者イメージに影響をおよぼす要因“REPRINTS”高齢者ボランティアとの交流頻度の多寡による推多分析から , 日本公衛誌、54(9), 615-625.

8） スポーツ庁 (2018) , 平成 30 年度体力・運動能力調査結果の概要及び報告書について , http://www.mext.go.jp/sports/b_menu/toukei/chousa04/tairyoku/kekka/k_detail/1421920.htm (参照日 2019 年 5 月 10 日) .

9） 栗山裕 , 橋下友茂 , 園山和夫 , 山下利之 (2011) , 疑似スポーツが世代間交流に果たす効果、人間工学 , 47(2), 61-64

10） 花井篤子 (2014) , 水中運動を活用した多世代間交流プログラムの開発とその有用性 , 北翔大学北方圏生涯スポーツ研究センター年報 , 5, 95-100.

11） 濱口雅行 , 濱口郁枝 , 内田勇人 (2014) , 剣道における世代間交流についての一考察 , 第５回日本世代間交流学会全国大会要旨集 , 56.

12） 大澤一樹 , 池川茂樹 , 直原幹 (2017) , 剣道の互角稽古及び試合における競技的要素の比較研究 , 上越教育大学紀要 , 36(2), 625-631.

13） 丹羽昇 (1980) , 剣道中高年者の試合稽古における運動強度について , 武道学研究 , 12(2), 29-34.

14） 保坂久美子 , 袖井孝子 (1988) , 大学生の老人イメージ -SD 法による分析 -, 社会老年学 , (27) , 22-33.

15） 榎本博明 (1997) , 自己開示の心理学研究 , 北大路書房 , 京都 .

16） JOURARD, S. M., & FRIEDMAN, R. (1970) , Experimenter-sub- ject “distance” and self-disclosure. Journal of Personality and Social Psychology, 15, 278-282.

17) WORTHY, M., Gary, A. L., & KAHN G. M. (1969) , Self-disclosure as an exchange process. Journal of Personality and Social Psychology, 13, 59-63.

18) 全日本剣道連盟 (2012) , 剣道稽古・試合中におこる外傷と障害 , https://www.kendo.or.jp/knowledge/medicine- science/injury/ (参照日 2019 年 6 月 2 日) .

19) 元嶋菜美香、村嶋恒徳、鍋山隆弘 (2014) , 剣道授業による中学生及び大学生のイメージの変化ースポーツツーリズムにおける武道プログラムの検討ー , 長崎国際大学国際観光学会・観光学論集 , 9, 73-84.

20) 境英俊 , 山神眞一 , 石川雄一 , 藤原章司 , 長野智香 (2007) , 小学生と指導者の剣道観に関する一考察 , 武道学研究 , 40(1), 9-25.

21) 浅見裕 (2002) , カテゴリー分析法とエスノグラフィー法の併用による剣道の授業分析研究 , 平成 12 年度～平成 13 年度科学研究費補助金研究成果報告書 .

要約

本稿では、高齢者と稽古経験があり、日本の伝統文化である剣道を大学で実践している大学剣道部員を対象として、剣道に関わる高齢者イメージや特性を検討した研究について紹介した。研究参加者は関西地域の国公私立の 5 大学に在籍する剣道部員 95 名 (年齢 18 ～ 22 歳) であり、調査項目として、性別・学年・年齢・高齢者との稽古経験の有無、高齢者イメージを選択した。分析の結果、探索的因子分析では「身体性因子」、「充実性因子」、「徳性因子」の 3 因子が確認された。共分散構造分析を実施した結果、「身体性因子」から「充実性因子」、「徳性因子」に影響を与え、最終的には「接しやすさ」が促進されたことが確認された。したがって、剣道が有する異世代同士での身体を通した交流が「接しやすさ」を促進させる一助になっていることが推察された。剣道に関わらず、伝統文化の伝承・継承の場においては、子どもから高齢者といった異なる世代間での交流が求められる。そこで、子どもに対して、文化的要素である伝統文化の魅力をわかりやすく伝えることが重要であり、そのような工夫が少子高齢化、国際社会といった時代における伝統文化の伝承・継承の発展に繋がると考えられた。

松本　大佑

兵庫県立大学（〒 670-0092 兵庫県姫路市新在家本町 1-1-12）。
兵庫県立大学大学院環境人間学研究科博士後期課程所属。
修士（教育学）
専門：健康教育学、教育学
日本世代間交流学会会員（2019-）

濵口　雅行

大阪府立大学（〒 599-8531　大阪府堺市中区学園町 1-1）
大阪府立大学名誉教授　博士（体育学）専門：運動生理学、武道論
全日本剣道連盟 理事（2021-）　全日本学生剣道連盟 理事長（2021-）

濵口　郁枝

甲南女子大学（〒 658-0001 兵庫県神戸市東灘区森北町 6-2-23）
甲南女子大学　人間科学部 教授、大学院人文科学総合研究科　教授　博士（環境人間学）
専門：食生活学、調理学
日本栄養改善学会　評議員（2012-）

内田　勇人（編著者紹介欄 p.276 参照）

Summary

Possibility of intergenerational exchange through Kendo

In this paper, we introduced a study that examined the image and characteristics of the elderly related to Kendo, targeting university Kendo members who have practiced with the elderly and are practicing Kendo, which is a traditional Japanese culture, at the university. The participants in the study were 95 members of the Kendo club (ages 18 to 22 years old) enrolled in five national, public and private universities in the Kansai region. Gender, grade, age, experience of practice with the elderly, and image of the elderly were selected as survey items. As a result of the analysis, three factors, "physical factor", "repletion factor", and "virtuous factor", were confirmed in the exploratory factor analysis. As a result of covariance structure analysis, it was confirmed that "physical factor" influenced "repletion factor" and "virtuous factor", and finally "accessibility" was promoted. Therefore, it was inferred that the interaction between different generations of Kendo through the body helps to promote "accessibility". Not limited to Kendo, in the place of handing down and inheriting traditional culture, interaction between different generations is required. Thereby it is important to intelligibly convey to children the charm of traditional culture, which is a cultural element. It was thought that such ingenuity would lead to the development of tradition and inheritance of traditional culture in times such as the declining birthrate and aging population and the international community.

Daisuke Matsumoto

School of Human Science and Environment, University of Hyogo, 1-1-12, Shinzaike-honcho,

Himeji, Hyogo, 670-0092, JAPAN Tel&Fax +81-79-292-9367

Graduate student in the doctoral program at the School of Human Science and Environment, University of Hyogo.

E-mail: matsudai18@icloud.com

Master (Education)

Major Research: Health Education and Education

Member of Japan Society for Intergenerational Studies (JSIS) (2019-).

Masayuki Hamaguchi

Osaka Prefecture University (1-1 Gakuen-cho, Naka-ku, Sakai, Osaka, 599-8531, JAPAN)

Emeritus Professor of Osaka Prefecture University.

E-mail: hamaguti@las.osakafu-u.ac.jp

Doctor (Health and Sports Science)

Major Research: Exercise and Sports Sciences, Theory of Budo (Martial Arts)

All Japan Kendo Federation, Director (2021-)

University Kendo Federation of Japan, Chairman (2021-)

Ikue Hamaguchi

Konan Women's University (6-2-23, Morikita-machi, Higashinada-ku, Kobe, Hyogo, 658-0001, JAPAN)

Professor (Faculty of Human Sciences, Konan Women's University) (Graduate School of Humanities and Human Sciences, Konan Women's University) Doctor (Human Science and Environment)

Major Research: Dietary Science, Cookery Science

The Japanese Society of Nutrition and Dietetics, Councilor (2012-)

Hayato Uchida (See p.276)

第 12 章　地域の子育て世代と中高年の多世代交流型水引講座

糸井　和佳

1．はじめに

世帯における核家族の増加に加え、地域社会が希薄化している現代において、初めて育児をする母親は、育児に関する不安やとまどいを持ちながらも、日中は乳児と二人きりで過ごす生活となり、孤立感を感じている[1)]。一方、高齢者も、かつては三世代世帯の中で自らの知恵や経験を次世代に伝えることができていたが、現代では日常的に多世代との交流を持つ機会は減少している。地域の中で世代の異なる人々が交流する機会を作ることは、相互の理解や助け合い（互助）、地域の活性化につながり、各自治体における重要課題である。文部科学省は、「家庭における世代間のかかわりが減少する現代では、意図的に若者と高齢者との世代間交流の場を設けることが重要であり、ただし一過性で終わらせないよう、高齢者が気軽に集える居場所を作り、子育て中の親や子どもたちも気軽に遊びに訪れることができる居心地のよい場所にすることにより、世代間交流を日常化するための仕組みづくりも必要である」と述べている[2)]。本稿では、大学で創設した地域の子育て世代と中高年の多世代交流型水引講座[3)]について紹介する。

（1）世代間交流における世代の設定と活動の方向性

世代間交流は、その目的や実施者に応じ、様々な方法で行われている。子育て世代が対象である世代間交流実践例では内田ら[4)]は地域の高齢ボランティアによる母親への育児支援行動の効果として、高齢者のLOC尺度点数や学習活動点数の増加、ファンクショナルリーチなどの身体機能の向上を示している。母親への効果として、子どもの特徴に関するストレスの抑制効果を報告している。筆者も、出産育児のため仕事から離れていた時期に、徒歩圏に通える居場所がなく、孤立感を感じたことがあった。そんなときに商店街のお店のおばさんからの「お子さん大きくなったわねえ」という一言がとても嬉しく、育児中の母親が気軽に訪れることができる居場所としての世代間交流プログラムがあるとよいと思った。その思いから、復職したときに、平成27～29年度文部科学省研究費補助金（基盤研究C：「地域における世代間交流を用いたコミュニティ・ビルディング支援プログラムの開発」研究代表者：糸井和佳、課題番号15K11871）を得てプログラム開発を行った。

MCCREAら[5)]は、交流の方向性からみた世代間交流プログラムの類型を、「高齢者が子どもや若者に行う活動」「子どもや若者が高齢者に行う活動」「高齢者と子どもや若者が一緒に行う活動」に分類しているが、本講座は、三つ目の「高齢者と若者が一緒に行う活動」として設定した。

2．プログラムの概要

（1）プログラムのコンセプト

育児中の母親世代と中高年世代の居場所づくりのツールとして、日本古来より伝承される水引を選び、月1回学ぶ講座型の世代間交流プログラムとした。水引は、1,400年の歴史をもつ伝統工芸であり、和紙をよって水のりで固め周囲を絹糸で巻いたもので、贈物の包み紙を結ぶための特別なひもである。お祝のときには赤と白や金と銀、お葬式のときには黒と白のものなどを使う。現在は色や種類が増え、アクセサリーや飾りにも用いられる。水引を世代間交流プログラムのツールとして選んだ理由は、筆者の友人に水引を教えられる講師がいたことによるが、「和」のものを作ることは、若い母親にも中高年にも好む人はいると考えたこと、高齢者から子育て世代に教えるのではなく、高齢者も子育て世代と同じように学ぶことで、水引を習いながら自然にお互いに教える行動が生まれると考えたこと、子育て世代が子どもを連れていける場所で、少しの時間だけ育児から離れて自ら学べる時間を持てることが重要と思ったことにある。講座の目的は、地域の子育て世代の母親と中高年世代が集う場所で、子どもを皆で見守りながら、ともに学

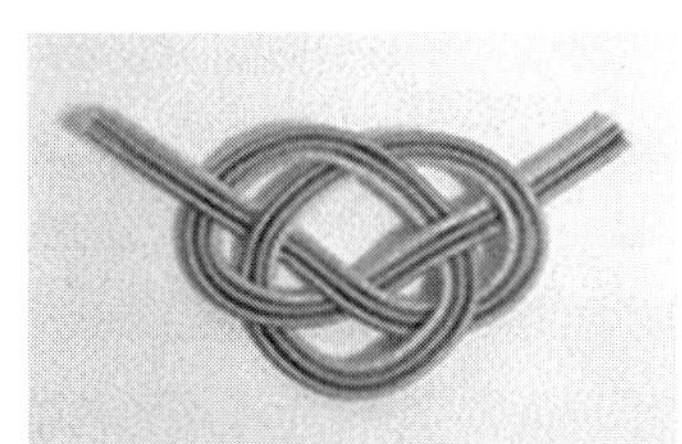
写真１　水引の基本の結び「あわじ結び」

写真２　水引のお正月飾り

び、地域の中で互いの世代への関心を醸成することであり、それを講座のゴールとして目指した。

（2）試験期間

試験的に水引講師に来学してもらい、学生や少人数の地域住民を集めて多世代交流型の水引講座を行った。「水引を結ぶのは面白い。最初は覚えるのが大変だけど、できると嬉しい。」との声があった。学生と高齢者では色の選び方も異なり、「その色合わせが綺麗ね。若い人のセンスは違うわね。」などと自然な交流が生まれ、大変好評であった。参加者として設定した子育て中の母親が子どもと一緒に安心して水引を学べるようにするため、保育ボランティアを募ることとした。看護学科の学生や保育経験のあるアルバイトさんにお願いした。後に地元の社会福祉協議会のボランティアセンターにプログラム登録を行い、定期的に来てもらえることとなった。参加者を集めるための広報活動としてチラシを作成し、近隣町内会や地域包括支援センター、保健センターに配布した。子育て世代３組、中高年世代６名の参加者を得て、講座開始となった。

写真３　クリスマス飾りを皆で作成

写真４　学生による保育ボランティア

（3）プログラム構成

プログラムの運営場所は、大学の和室（36 畳）を利用した。子育て中の母親が子どもを連れて訪れ、同じ空間で子どもが遊んだり、這い這いしたりできるスペースと、多世代が水引を習うスペース、授乳やおむつ交換スペースを設置し、自由に行き来できるようにした。運営スタッフは、水引講師１～２名、保育ボランティア２～９名、看護学科の教員１名である。ボランティアは、子育て経験のある一般人ボランティアと、子どもの発達を学んだ看護学科の学生であった。参加者の推移を表１に示す。プログラムは、月１回、午後に２時間半開催した。受付後、自由に着席し、全体の挨拶、自己紹介、子どもの紹介に続き、水引の作品づくり

表１　参加者の推移

年度	子育て世代	中高年世代	計
2017 年	3	6	
年度途中～		2	11 人
2018 年	1（継続）	8（継続）	
年度途中～		1	10 人
2019 年	5	9（継続）	
年度途中～	2		16 人

注）下線部にて初回データを測定した。

表２　参加者の属性

項目		子育て世代 n=10		中高年世代 n=9	
年齢		35.2	(3.5)	63.2	(10.7)
子どもの月例（初回）		10.7	(4.6)		
世帯	夫婦と子ども	9	(90)	2	(22.2)
	夫婦と子どもとひとり親	1	(10)	0	(0)
	夫婦	0	(0)	2	(22.2)
	単独	0	(0)	5	(55.6)
何人目の子ども	１人目	9	(90)		
	２人目	1	(10)		

注）単位：年齢、子どもの月例は mean（SD）、
　世帯と子どもの人数は人（%）

となる。作品ができて一息ついたころに、お茶とお菓子を配り、お茶の時間を持った。

水引講座は、全体へのインストラクション後、不明点については個別に教えながら１回で１つの作品が仕上がるようにした。まず基本の「あわじ結び」（写真１）を修得し、少しずつステップアップし、季節の行事の準備ができる内容とした（例：４月こいのぼり、５月紫陽花、９月ハロウィン、12 月お正月しめ縄飾り）。水引は人によって習得するスピードが異なり、個別のフォローが必要なため、水引講師と相談し、全体の参加人数は 10 名程度が良いと設定したが、徐々にそれをオーバーする参加者数となり、講師を常時２名体制とし、教員も講師の補助をした。子どもは保育ボランティアが迎え入れ、遊ぶスペースに誘導した。子どもが母親から離れないときには、母親が抱っこ紐等で抱きながら、そのまま講座に参加した。子どもの人数に応じて、保育ボランティアの増員が必要となり、区の社会福祉協議会ボランティアセンターに依頼した。

写真５　多世代交流水引講座の様子

（４）参加者の行動と世代間交流の深化

①子育て世代の行動

講座において子育て世代に見られた行動では、初回は、子どもが場所に慣れず、また母親が自分に関係ないことに集中しようとしていることを察知し、泣き、母親はそれをあやしていることが多かった。保育ボランティアが促しても子どもは遊ぶスペースにいかず、同スペースで母親が子どもを抱っこ紐で抱いたまま、水引を習う姿が見られた。６ヵ月後には、子どもが慣れてきた様子で、おもちゃの音のする方に行き、遊び、しばらくして母親のもとに帰ってきて膝に座るなどの行動があった。これは子どもの成長による。12 ヵ月後には、子どもが会場に来ると自分で靴下を脱ぎ、おもちゃの方にいく姿が見られた。子ども同士でおもちゃを取り合う姿も見られた。12ヵ月後には、母親が水引作成に集中できるようになり、隣に座った高齢者に水引の分からないところを聞く、子どもが成長したことを高齢者にほめられ、笑顔で応じる姿が見られた。また、6ヵ月後以降、子どもの成長について心配している母親が、看護教員や保育ボランティアに相談する姿も見られた。

②中高年世代の行動

中高年世代に見られた行動では、友人と参加し、講座に参加した母子を笑顔で見ていた。初回は必死に水引の基本を習得しようとする姿が見られた。6ヵ月後には、高齢者が「子どもさんにお菓子をあげてほしい」と、お菓子を持参する、

カテゴリ	多世代との接点をもつ、 異世代への関心を示す行動	初回	6カ 月後	12カ 月後
知り合いや身内の会話	友人と参加する	○	○	○
	水引の方法を聞く	○	○	○
	水引の方法を隣に教える	○	○	○
	子どもが泣くのであやす	○	○	
	近況を話す		○	○
世代を超えた会話	高齢者が子育て中のお母さんに話しかける		○	○
	高齢者が子育て中のお母さんにお菓子をあげる		○	○
	母親が高齢者にお礼をいう		○	○
	母親が高齢者に話しかける			○
	多世代でも水引を教えあう		○	○
	母親が子育てについて教員やボランティアに相談する		○	○
子どもの存在や成長を喜ぶ	参加の母子を笑顔でみる	○	○	○
	母親が高齢者と子どもの話をする			○
	子どもが歩けるようになったことを喜ぶ			○
	子どもが場所に慣れてきたことを喜ぶ			○

図1　世代間交流の度合いの変化

多世代で水引を教えあう、終了後の会場の片づけを手伝うなどの行動や近況を話すなどが見られた。12 ヵ月後には、家で作った水引の作品を持参して披露していた。また参加者の子どもが歩けるようになったことや場に慣れて泣かなくなったことを皆で喜ぶ様子が見られた。

③世代間交流の深化

子育て世代と中高年世代を観察したデータから、多世代との接点や異世代への働きかけに焦点化して分析し、接点の多寡や異世代への関心を軸として分類したところ、【知り合いや身内の会話】【世代を超えた会話】【子どもの存在や成長を喜ぶ】となった。それぞれの行動の出現した時期について図示した（図１）。

３．講座の意義

母親の感想のなかには、「子育てと家事以外にこうやって外出し多世代の方と交流したり、水引を習ったりして生活に張りが出てきた」などがあり、太田[1)]が述べた「育児に追われ、日中は子どもと二人きりという閉塞感のある生活」から一息つける場所であったと考えられる。母親は子どもが他の子どもや保育ボランティアと遊ぶ様子から、子どもが他者と触れ合えることは子ども自身にも良い経験になるととらえていた。子育てについて看護教員や保育ボランティアに相談をしており、異世代から育児の情報を得る機会となっていたと考えられる。本講座のなかで子どもが歩けるようになったことを高齢者に褒められたことは、子育て中の母親にとって、子どもの成長に地域の人から関心を寄せられたことにほかならず、心理的援助を受けた経験であったと推察される。

中高年世代参加者はすべて初年度あるいは２年目からの継続であり、今後も継続を希望していた。本講座の中高年世代の感想には「同世代の方たちとの交流は日頃ありますが、若い方たちとの交流がとてもエネルギーをもらえます」など若い世代との交流に癒される様子があり、世代間交流の機会を貴重なものとして受け止めていた。つまり、中高年世代参加者にとって重要な居場所となっていたと考えられる、多世代交流水引講座は両世代の居場所を提供し、互いの世代への関心を育んだ可能性がある。

4．継続における課題

参加者の推移では、中高年は全員が継続していたが、子育て世代は継続する人と１年で終了する人に分かれた。仕事復帰や子どもの保育園入園による終了がほとんどであるが、「親だけでも参加を継続したいが、保育園のお迎えの時間と重なってしまうので来られない」という意見もあった。子どもの成長に伴う生活時間の変更に対応できるとよいだろう。プログラム運営では、子どもの人数に応じて、特に３年目に保育ボランティアの増員が必要となったが、学生ボランティアの継続において、平日は授業があることや高学年となると国家試験勉強に専念したく、学生のみではまかなえないという課題があった。そのため区の社会福祉協議会ボランティアセンターに依頼した経緯があった。ボランティアごとに、参加動機を把握し支援することが必要であろう。現在、新型コロナウイルスの感染拡大防止のため、大学では入校制限があり、地域住民への講座は休止している。再開を望む声が多く、講座を再開した後も、感染予防と交流を両立することが課題である。

おわりに、本講座の立ち上げと運営を通し、地域の中で意図的に世代間交流を持つために必要と考えたことを述べたい。目的を定めた後は、まずは実施者の出来る範囲で多世代を組み合わせたプログラムをイベント的にでも試行してみること、地域の多機関の人々と協力体制を作ること、参加者の安全を確保し、ボランティアも楽しめる循環的な仕組みにすることである。

引用・参考文献

1）太田睦　2002　育児不安は生活不安－父親のフルタイム育児体験，大日向雅美（編）こころの科学 103 号、特別企画　育児不安　日本評論社　67-71.

2）文部科学省　2012　超高齢社会における生涯学習の在り方に関する検討会：長寿社会における生涯学習の在り方について～人生 100 年いくつになっても学ぶ幸せ「幸齢社会」～，　16-17. https://

www.mext.go.jp/component/a_menu/education/detail/__icsFiles/afieldfile/2012/03/28/1319112_1.pdf (2021 年 7 月閲覧)

3）糸井和佳　2021　多世代交流型水引講座における地域の子育て世代と中高年世代の体験に関する記述研究 , 日本世代間交流学会誌 10 (1・2) 15-24.

4）内田勇人, 藤原佳典, 西垣利男, 香川雅春, 作田はるみ, 下村尚美, 木宮高代, 濱口郁枝, 東根裕子, 矢野真理　2012　高齢者による育児支援行動が高齢者の心身の健康と母親の育児ストレスへ及ぼす影響 , 日本世代間交流学会誌 2 (1) 33-39.

5）McCrea, J.M., Smith, T.B.　1997 Types and Models of Intergenerational Programs, Newman, S. et al., Intergenerational Programs: Past, Present, and Future, Taylor& Francis 83-91.

要約

古来伝承される「水引」を学ぶ多世代交流型水引講座を大学で創設した。対象は地域の子育て世代と中高年世代であり、講座の目指すところは、子どもを連れて訪れることのできる居場所づくりと、地域の中で互いの世代への関心を醸成することである。大学の和室で水引を習ったり、子どもが遊んだり、授乳などができるスペースを準備し、水引講師と保育ボランティアを配置した。はじめは母親が子どもを抱きながら参加していたが、6 か月後には子どもが保育ボランティアとともに遊び、母親も水引を集中して学べるようになっていた。中高年は、講座に参加した母子を笑顔で見ており、6 か月後には子どもにお菓子をあげたり、隣の席の母親に水引を教えたり、12 か月後には子どもが歩けるようになったことを喜んでいた。参加観察による世代間交流の様相を時系列でみると【知り合いや身内の会話】が多かったのが【世代を超えた会話】が増え【子どもの存在や成長を喜ぶ】という世代性関心を示す交流に深化していた。参加者の感想から、子育て世代は、外出しリフレッシュできる機会であり、中高年世代は、若い方たちとの交流によりエネルギーをもらえる場所と感じており、地域における多世代交流の一形態として両世代の居場所となっていたと考えられた。

糸井　和佳

帝京科学大学医療科学部看護学科教授　博士 (看護学)

専門は地域看護学。高齢者と子どもの世代間交流観察スケールを作成し、地域の子育て中の母親と中高年が交流する多世代交流型水引講座を創設した。

Summary

Community Intergenerational MIZUHIKI Lecture Program for Parenting, Middle Aged and Older Persons

We created the intergenerational lecture program to learn traditional Japanese crafts MIZUHIKI at University. The purpose of this program was to make a place to visit with their child for mother and middle-aged and older persons, and to foster their generative concern. Qualitative observation showed developed interactions such as "multi-generational conversations" and "being pleased with the growth of children". The intergenerational MIZUHIKI lecture program might be a comfortable place.

Waka Itoi

Professor, Faculty of Medical Sciences, Department of Nursing, of Teikyo University of Science, Ph.D., R.N. Her major is Community Nursing.

Dr. Waka ITOI created community intergenerational observational Scales (CIOS-E, CIOS-C), and the intergenerational MIZUHIKI lecture program for parents and middle and older persons in the community.

第13章　行事食伝承事業における高齢者と高校生の世代間交流

矢野　真理・作田　はるみ
坂本　薫・内田　勇人

1．はじめに

日本人の生活のなかには、日常生活とは別に特別なハレの日がある。ハレの日には毎年同じ時期にめぐってくる年中行事と誕生から成人、結婚、還暦といった人生の節目にあたる人生儀礼の２種類がある。年中行事や人生儀礼時における食、すなわち行事食は、伝統的な祝いや祭り時に地域特有の食べ物として作られ、日常生活の節目を彩り、生活に喜びを与えてきた。そこにはその地域に根ざした生活にあう形での家族の幸せや健康を願う意味がこめられている[1)]。しかし、近年における農業人口の減少、輸入食品の増加、食の外部化や核家族化の進行により、郷土料理や行事食を家庭で作る機会は減少し、伝統的な地域の料理が親から子へ伝承されない傾向にあることが指摘されている[1)]。

地域の食は、我が国の文化の発展に寄与するだけでなく、人々の精神的な豊かさや生き生きとした暮らしと密接に関係しており[2)]、先人によって培われてきた地域の食文化を次世代に伝えることは、その地域に暮らす人々の生活の質の向上や健康増進を図るうえで今後益々重要になるといえる。

本稿では、高齢者がこれまで地域で親しんできた食に関わる知恵や技術を次世代である高校生に伝える行事食伝承事業の実践事例と交流の効果について報告する。

2．プログラムの概要

2015年３月、著者らは兵庫県Ａ市高齢者大学と体育館スポーツ教室に在籍する高齢者、A 市内 B 高等学校に在籍する生徒を対象に行事食に対するアンケート調査を実施した。その結果から行事食の認知度や経験度、高齢者が伝承したい行事食と高校生が学びたい行事食が明らかになった（表 1）[3]。

表 1　高齢者と高校生の行事食に対するアンケート結果

認知度	多くの行事食において、高齢者より高校生の方が認知度が低かった。 正月、節分、七夕、お月見、大みそかの行事食の認知度は、高齢者と高校生は同程度であった。
経験度	多くの行事食において、高校生より高齢者の方が食べた経験がある人の割合が高かった。 盂蘭盆のそうめん（七夕も含む）、だんご、七夕の赤飯、大みそかの巻きずし（秋の祭りも含む）、秋の祭りのちらしずしは、高校生の方が食べた経験がある人の割合は高かった。
高齢者が伝承したい行事食と高校生が学びたい行事食	高齢者は、伝えたい行事食として正月の行事食を挙げる人が多かったが、高校生の関心は低かった。高齢者と高校生の双方が伝承したい、学びたいと思っている行事食はきんとん（正月）、七草粥、おはぎ（春分）であった。

2015 年 7 月、行事食伝承調理実習（以下、調理実習と略す）への参加希望調査を実施し、参加者は兵庫県 A 市高齢者大学と体育館スポーツ教室に在籍する高齢者 19 名（女性、平均年齢 70.8 ± 4.0 歳）、A 市内の 4 つの高等学校に在籍する 24 名（男子 3 名、女子 21 名、平均年齢 16.5 ± 0.9 歳）となった。

（1）実習の内容

事前学習会

2015 年 8 月、著者らがコーディネーターとなり高齢者参加者グループを対象とした約 2 時間の事前学習会を実施した。

最初に調理実習の趣旨、高校生の学校生活の状況を説明し、行事食に関する知識、調理実習の手順を確認してグループにより調理法に差異がないように配慮した。後半は、グループに分かれて自己紹介や調理実習の進め方等を話し合う時間とした。

表2　調理実習の詳細

	第1グループ	第2グループ
日時	2015年8月　夏休み　2日間 10:00 ～ 12:00	2015年10月　授業終了後　2日間 15:30 ～ 17:30
場所	兵庫県A大学調理室	兵庫県B高等学校調理室
参加人数	高齢者15名 高校生9名(男子2名、女子7名)	高齢者4名 高校生15名(男子1名、女子14名)

調理実習

参加者は、開催場所の定員数や学校行事の日程により2グループに分かれそれぞれ2回、同じメンバーで調理実習を行った(表2)。

両グループともに1グループ5～6名(高校生2～4名、高齢者1～4名)の4グループに分かれ、表1のアンケート結果[3]を参考にして、1回目はおはぎ、

調理実習1回目　おはぎ

調理実習2回目　巻きずし

２回目は巻きずしを調理した。

調理実習は、グループ内での自己紹介から始まり、もち米とうるち米の違いを確認したり、コーディネーターから出題された「海苔の表はどちらでしょう。」等のクイズをグループ内で考えてそれぞれ発表した。高校生は行事食（おはぎや巻きずし）の調理経験がなかったため、全体で実習内容を確認した後、高齢者が高校生に調理手順や技術を指導し、見本を見せながら高校生の調理を補助する形で一緒に調理した。その後、感想や行事の思い出を話しながら試食、片づけのプログラムを行い、約２時間交流した。

３．世代間交流の効果

調理実習初回の開始前と調理実習２回目の終了後、心身の健康度や高齢者に抱くイメージ、行事食に対する関心度についてアンケート調査を実施した。

その結果､高齢者による高校生への行事食伝承事業に参加して交流することで、高齢者の地域共生意識における「自分の近所に１人暮らしの老人がいたら、その老人のために日常生活の世話をしてあげたい」、世代継承の意識における「若者の良き助言者となりたい」、高校生が抱く高齢者イメージの「温かい」、「正しい」、「話しやすい」、「はやい」、「大きい」、「親切である」、「やさしい」、「頼りがいがある」の各得点が高くなった。また、行事食に対する関心度において、高齢者、高校生の参加者全員が実習後も行事食を伝承すべきだと思うと回答した。

地域共生意識は、信頼感や連帯感に基づく人間関係を基本として地域の問題に取り組み、その地域の自治を築こうとする意識や態度であり[4]、世代継承の意識は、世代の育成と継承の双方を意味している[5]。高齢者イメージは、先行研究に従い[6]「温かい－冷たい」等の相反する形容詞を対語にして、いずれが高齢者イメージとしてあてはまるかを評価した。

先行研究を見ると、高齢者の若者への利他的行動（外的な報酬を期待せず、他者のために自発的に行う行為自体が目的の行動）に対する若者のポジティブな反応が世代性の向上に影響する[7]、高齢者は子どもとのふれ合いを通してポジティブな感情を抱きやすく、それが高齢者の子どもとふれ合いたいという欲求や行動、心身の健康に影響する可能性が指摘されている[8)]。村山[9)]は、高齢者と子どもの心的な親密感を高めることが有意義な関係性の構築に重要であり、そのためには、両世代が交流する場所と十分な時間が確保され、その中でコミュニケーションを通じた交流が必要であると報告している。調理実習に参加した高校生は、行事食（おはぎや巻きずし）の調理経験がなく、調理実習では、高齢者が高校生に実習の手順や技術を指導しながら一緒に調理し、お互いに行事の思い出を話しながら試食や片付けといった活動の中で自然にコミュニケーションを深め、親密感を高めたと考えられる。短期間だったが、行事食伝承事業に参加して交流することで、高齢者の地域共生意識および世代継承の意識、高校生が抱く高齢者イメージが向上した要因であると考える。

4．まとめ

高齢者による高校生への行事食伝承事業に参加して交流することで、行事食の伝承に関心をもつだけでなく、高齢者の地域共生意識および世代継承の意識、高校生が抱く高齢者イメージが向上する効果が期待できることがわかった。

感想をたずねてみたところ、高齢者からは、「実習前から高校生と接する機会はないので楽しみだった。」、「高校生は自分たちの説明や行事にまつわる話を熱心に聞いてくれた。」、「一緒に調理実習ができてとてもうれしかったし、楽しい時間だった。」と話していた。高校生からは、「高齢者の人は優しかった。」という声が多く聞かれた。

少子高齢化、核家族化が急速に進行し、地域における人との交流やふれあいの機会も減少している中、地域性に着目した高齢者による若者への行事食伝承事業の取り組みは非常に有意義だと考える。参加者は、調理実習後も全員が行事食や地域の郷土料理などを次世代に伝えていくべきだと思うと回答し、行事食伝承に関心を持ち続けていることがわかった。

今後は、行事食伝承事業が継続できるシステムを構築し、内容について検討を重ね、世代間交流のもたらす効果をさらに評価、検証していきたいと考えている。

引用・参考文献

1） 渕上倫子，桑田寛子，石井香代子，他．2011 特別研究「調理文化の地域性と調理科学：行事食・儀礼食」－全国の報告－行事食・儀礼食の認知・経験・喫食状況，日本調理科学会誌 44，436-441.

2） 冨岡典子，江原絢子 2009 日本の食文化－その伝承と食の教育 15 章行事と地域の食文化，アイケイコーポレーション 141-150.

3） 矢野真理，作田はるみ，内田勇人，他． 2018 高齢者による高校生への行事食伝承事業に関する調査研究－行事食に対する意識調査結果－，日本食生活学会誌 29 (1) 53-63.

4） 田中国夫，藤本忠明，直村勝彦 1978 地域社会への態度の類型化について－その尺度と背景要因－，心理学研究 49，36-43.

5） 大場宏美，藤原佳典，村山陽，他．2013 世代間交流プログラムの評価に向けた日本語版 generativity 尺度作成の試み，日本世代間交流学会誌 3，59-65.

6） 藤原佳典，西真理子，渡辺直紀，他．2007 児童の高齢者イメージに影響をおよぼす要因－"REPRINTS" 高齢者ボランティアとの交流頻度の多寡による推移分析から－，日本公衆衛生雑誌 54，615-625.

7） 田淵恵，三浦麻子 2014 高齢者の利他的行動場面における世代間相互作用の実験的検討，心理学研究 84，632-638.

8） 村山陽，高橋知也，村山幸子，他．2014 高齢者における「世代間のふれ合いにともなう感情尺度」作成の試み - 高齢者の心身の健康との関連 -，厚生の指標 61，1-8.

9） 村山陽 2009 高齢者との交流が子どもに及ぼす影響，社会心理学研究 25，1-10.

要約

近年における農業人口の減少、核家族化の進行、食品加工技術の進展等により、行事食や伝統的な地域の料理を家庭で作る機会が減少し、それらが親から子へ伝承されていない傾向が見られる。先人によって培われてきた地域の食文化を次世代に伝えることは、その地域に暮らす人々の生活の質の向上や健康増進を図るうえで今後益々重要になるといえる。本稿では、高齢者がこれまで地域で親しんできた食に関わる知恵や技術を次世代である高校生に伝える行事食伝承事業の実践事例と交流の効果について報告する。

行事食伝承調理実習（以下、調理実習と略す）の参加者は、兵庫県 A 市高齢者大学と体育館スポーツ教室に在籍する高齢女性 19 名、A 市内の 4 つの高等学校に在籍する生徒24名（男子3名、女子21名）であった。

最初に高齢者参加者グループを対象とした約2時間の事前学習会を実施した。その後、調理実習は、2グループに分かれそれぞれ2回行った。全体で実習内容を確認した後、高齢者が高校生に調理手順や技術を指導し、高校生の調理を補助する形で一緒に調理した。その後、感想や行事の思い出を話しながら試食、片づけのプログラムを行い、約2時間交流した。

高齢者による高校生への行事食伝承事業に参加して交流することで、高齢者の地域共生意識、世代継承の意識、高校生が抱く高齢者イメージの各得点が有意に高くなった。また、行事食に対する関心度において、高齢者、高校生の実習参加者全員が実習後も行事食を伝承すべきだと思うと回答した。

高齢者による高校生への行事食伝承事業に参加して交流することで、高齢者の地域共生意識および世代継承の意識、高校生が抱く高齢者イメージが向上する効果が期待できることがわかった。また行事食伝承事業の参加者全員が実習後も行事食の伝承に関心を持ち続けていることが明らかになった。地域における人との交流やふれあいの機会も減少している中、地域性に着目した高齢者による若者への行事食伝承事業の取り組みは非常に有意義だと考える。

矢野　真理

神戸女子短期大学幼児教育学科

〒650-0046　兵庫県神戸市中央区港島中町4-7-2

神戸女子短期大学講師。博士（環境人間学）（兵庫県立大学）。専門は、健康教育学。現在は、親子の身体活動について調査研究を行っている。

坂本　薫

兵庫県立大学環境人間学部

〒670-0092　兵庫県姫路市新在家本町1-1-12

兵庫県立大学環境人間学部・大学院環境人間学研究科教授。博士（学術）（神戸大学）。専門は食物学。食物のおいしさに関わる実験を行いながら、行事食や郷土料理についての調査研究を行っている。「次世代に伝え継ぐ日本の家庭料理」（農山漁村文化協会，2017-2021）などの著作がある。

作田　はるみ（編著者紹介欄 p.277 参照）

内田　勇人（編著者紹介欄 p.276 参照）

Summary

Intergenerational Exchange between the Elderly and High School Students in the "Project of Passing on the Food" Events

In recent years, due to the decrease in the agricultural population, the trend toward nuclear families, and the development of food processing technology, the opportunities to prepare traditional local foods and events at home have decreased, and there is a tendency that these foods are not being passed on from parents to children. It will become more and more important in the future to pass on to the next generation the local food culture nurtured by our ancestors in order to improve the quality of life and health of the people living in the region. In this paper, we report on a practical example of a project to pass on the wisdom and skills related to food that elderly people have been familiar with in their communities to the next generation of high school students, and the effects of this exchange.

The participants in the event of cooking practice for the purpose of passing on the traditional foods (hereinafter referred to as the cooking practice) were 19 elderly women enrolled in the University for the Aged and the Gymnasium Sports Class in A City, Hyogo Prefecture, and 24 students (3 boys and 21 girls) enrolled in four high schools in A City.

First, a two-hour pre-study session was held for the group of elderly participants. Then, the cooking practice was divided into two groups and each group was given two sessions. After confirming the contents of the training with the whole group, the elderly instructed the high school students on the cooking procedures and techniques, and assisted the high school students in cooking together with them. Afterwards, the students shared their impressions and memories of the event, tasted the food, cleaned up, and interacted with the elderly participants for about two hours.

By participating in the project to pass on traditional foods to high school students, the scores of the elderly in terms of their awareness of coexistence with the local community, awareness of generational succession, and the image of the elderly held by high school students were significantly higher. In addition, all of the participants, both elderly and high school students, answered that they thought that the traditional foods should be handed down even after the training.

By participating in and interacting with the project in which elderly people handed down traditional foods to high school students, it was found that the elderly people's awareness of coexisting with the local community and of passing on food from one generation to the next, as well as the image of elderly people held by high school students, was improved. In addition, it was found that all participants in the project continued to be interested in the transmission of information on traditional foods even after the training. As opportunities for interaction and contact with people in the community are decreasing, it is meaningful to work on the project to pass on traditional foods by the elderly to young people, focusing on the local characteristics of the community.

Mari Yano

Department of Education, Kobe Women's Junior College
4-7-2, Minatojima-nakamachi, Chuo-ku, Kobe, Hyogo, 650-0046, JAPAN
Tel:+81-78-303-4700　E-mail：myano@kwjc.kobe-wu.ac.jp

Mari Yano is a lecturer of the Department of Education, Kobe Women's Junior College of Hyogo, Japan. She received her PhD in Human Science and Environment in 2020 from Graduate School of Human Science and Environment at University of Hyogo, Japan. Her major is Health Education. She is promoting research on physical activity of the parent and child.

Kaoru Sakamoto

School of Human Science and Environment, University of Hyogo
1-1-12, Shinzaike-honcho
Himeji, Hyogo, 670-0092, JAPAN
Tel: +81-79-292-9323 E-mail: sakamoto@shse.u-hyogo.ac.jp

Dr. Kaoru Sakamoto is a professor of School of Human Science and Environment at University of Hyogo, Graduate School of Human Science and Environment at University of Hyogo, Japan. She received her Doctor's degree in Philosophy from Kobe University, Japan. Her specialty is food science. She is promoting research on event foods and local cuisine while conducting experiments on the deliciousness of food. She has written books such as "Japanese Home Cooking Passed on to the Next Generation" (Rural Culture Association Japan, 2017-2021).

Harumi Sakuda (See p.277)

Hayato Uchida (See p.276)

第14章　地域ボランティアとの世代間交流を通じた高校生のキャリア発達に及ぼす影響：３年間の縦断調査から

村山　陽

1．はじめに

近年、進路意識や目的意識が希薄なままにとりあえず大学へと進学する若者が増加している。こうした傾向は、フリーター志向の広がりや就職後の早期離職などの問題へとつながることが懸念されている[1)]。「キャリア教育・進路指導に関する総合実態調査(平成25年)」によれば、「将来の生き方や進路について考えるため、指導してほしかったこと」について、「自分の個性や適性を考える学習」が29.9%と最も高く、次いで「社会人・職業人としての常識やマナー」が26.5%となっており、進路選択に限らず社会人として望まれる行動や社会とのかかわりなどの将来を展望した期待が強くなっている。こうした中で、学校が地域と協働したキャリア教育のあり方が注目されており、その実践例が報告されている[2)]。

青年の職業観の形成には、キャリアのモデルとなる人物の存在が重要であるとされている[3)]。キャリアモデルを活用したキャリア教育の実践例として、自分の希望する職業に就いている人へのインタビューや、キャリアモデルに関するレポート作成が行われ、その有効性が検証されている[4) 5)]。古野[6)]は、「憧れの先輩モデル」を提唱し、伝記に載るような偉人から父親、母親、親戚、あるいはOB・OG、会社の先輩等から働き方や職業観を学ぶことで自身のキャリアデザインが確立していくと指摘している。本稿では、地域ボランティアがキャリアモデルとして青年のキャリア発達を促す試みとして、都立A高校における世代間交流型プログラムの取り組みに着目する。

2．プログラムの概要

都立A高校では、2007年度より「奉仕」（以下、奉仕）の体験学習として高校1年生と地域ボランティアとの世代間交流活動を取り入れており、地域のボランティア団体を講師として招いて複数のプログラムを実施している。奉仕は、「社会の一員であること及び社会に役立つ喜びを体験的に学ぶことを通して、将来、社会に貢献できる資質を育成する」ことを目的として、2007年度から東京都全都立高校に設置された必修教科である。本教科は、在学中に35単位時間（1単位時間は50分）以上学習することとされており、校内の授業（事前学習、事後学習）と校外の体験学習から構成されている[7]。2016年4月からは奉仕を発展させた教科「人間と社会」が導入されている。

A高校の体験学習は10のプログラムから構成されており、生徒はその中から2つのプログラムを選択する仕組みになっている。体験学習開始前に、各種団体が来校して各プログラムに関する発表を生徒にする機会（オリエンテーション）が設けられており、それを聞いたうえで生徒は自分の興味や関心にあったプログラムを選択する。「事前学習」では、各プログラムの担当教員により、授業に参加する目的や意識を明確にするための授業を行っている。また、体験学習中には、授業終了後に感想や課題等を用紙に記入する時間を設けており、それを各プログラムの担当教員が確認をしてコメントをつけて返却をしている。さらに、「事後学習」として生徒が授業で学んだことを整理して発表する機会を設けている。授業は、生徒20～25人に対して1つの地域のボランティア団体に所属している地域ボランティア4～6人程が講師として入り、グループワーク形式で進められる（全8回:12時間）。本プログラムの進行については、同校の奉仕担当教員が地域ボランティアと調整しながら進めている。各プログラムにはそれぞれ1～2名の担当教員がおり、授業に参加して資料配布や点呼、引率および地域ボランティアとの連絡調整等を行っている。ただし、生徒への指導は地域ボランティアに任されており担当教員は直接的な指導は行わない。2012年度のプログラム概要は表1に示す。

表１　プログラムの概要[8)]

講座名	団体	内容
絵本の読み聞かせ	地域の NPO 法人	地域の高齢者ボランティアが実技指導を行い、その成果として生徒が近所の保育園を訪問して園児に絵本の読み聞かせを実演する。
紙芝居	地域の紙芝居ボランティア団体	地域の紙芝居ボランティアの指導を下に紙芝居を創作し、その読み方や表現方法を学習する。紙芝居が仕上がったら、近くの保育園を訪問して園児の前で実演をする。
手話	地域の手話サークル	地域の聴覚障碍者との交流を通して聴覚障害の理解を深めるとともに、手話サークルのボランティアから手話コーラスを習って発表する。
リサイクル	地域の NPO 法人	地域で活動している環境ボランティアからリサイクルについて学び、ゴミをリサイクルして工芸品を作成する。出来上がった作品を近所の高齢者施設に持っていき高齢者と交流をする。
イベントのごみを減らす	地域の NPO 法人	地域で活動している環境ボランティアからディッシュリユースの方法を学び、廃油から石鹸づくりなどを体験する。講座中には、リサイクル施設の現場見学を行う。
落ち葉の腐葉土づくり	地域の NPO 法人	地域で活動している環境ボランティアから環境について学習し、新聞紙でエコバッグを作成したり、近くの公園の管理人と協力して落ち葉の腐葉土づくりを行う。
林道に木道を作る	地域の環境ボランティア団体	地域の環境ボランティアから、環境問題やエネルギー問題について学び、林道の木道（ボード）づくりを行う。完成品は、実際に木道として使用される。
開発途上国支援	地域の NPO 法人	地域の海外ボランティアから開発途上国の実態について学び、バングラディッシュの子どもたちの教材（アルファベットカード等）を作成する。作成したものは現地に届けられる。
高齢者との共生	校区の社会福祉会	地域の高齢者ボランティアから認知症についての学習や車いす体験や高齢者疑似体験を行い高齢者の理解を深める。その後、近くの高齢者施設を訪問して高齢者と交流をする。
仲間との共生	校区の社会福祉会	地域で活動しているボランティアから「心の病気」について学び、精神障害者の方と一緒にとうふ作りを経験する。その他に、ゲームを通して自分自身についての理解も深める。

3. 生徒の職業選択に及ぼす影響

１年時にプログラムに参加した生徒における３年時の職業選択に及ぼした影響を検討するため、2014年12月（プログラム終了から約２年後）にアンケート調査を実施した。その結果、「１年生の時の奉仕授業は、現在のあなたの職業に対する意識に影響を及ぼしていると思いますか。」の質問に、４割程の生徒が「とてもそう思う」あるいは「少しそう思う」と回答していた。また、その影響の内容について自由記述からは、「将来の進路への関心が高まった」、「自己の役割を理解した」、「積極的な姿勢を学んだ」、「思いやりの気持ちを学んだ」、「多様な生き方や価値観に気づいた」が挙げられた（表２）。

表２　自由記述回答のカテゴリー化

カテゴリー	自由記載の回答欄
将来の進路への関心	福祉施設の見学や勉強はその両方への進みたいという思いを強めた。 子どもとふれあったことで保育士になりたいと思った。 職業について関心が持てるようになった。
自己の役割の理解	人のために何ができるか考えるようになった。 人のためになることをする大切さや楽しさが分かった。 ボランティアに参加したいと思った。
積極的な姿勢	自ら進んでやることは、苦ではなく、楽しく笑顔になるとわかった。 自分の仕事は最後まで果たす責任感を感じることができた。 どのような姿勢で物事に取り組むべきかを考えて行動するようになった。
思いやりの気持ち	耳が聞こえない人がどれだけ大変かを、少しわかったような気がした。 相手の気持ちなどを見る視線が変わった。 高齢者のことを考えられるようになった。
多様な生き方や価値観への気づき	いろんな人の話が聞けたことで、いろんなことを知ることができた。 知らなかった世界の状況を少し知れた。 様々な職業があることがわかった。

4．まとめ

本稿では高校１年生を対象に、キャリアモデルとなる地域ボランティアとの世代間交流型プログラムを実践している都立A高校の取り組みに着目した。４割強の生徒は、このプログラムに参加したことが高校３年時の職業選択に影響したと回答していた。そして、地域ボランティアとの交流を通して将来の進路への関心を高めるだけでなく、思いやりの気持ちや多様な生き方や価値観への気づきを得ていることが認められた。

A高校における地域ボランティアとの世代間交流が生徒のキャリア発達にポジティブな影響を及ぼしていた理由として次のことが挙げられる。一つ目に、A高校の体験学習には多種多様なプログラムが用意されていることである。A高校の体験学習は10のプログラムから構成されており、生徒はその中から２つのプログラムを選択するシステムになっている。また、体験学習開始前には、各種団体が来校して各プログラムに関する発表をする機会（オリエンテーション）が設けられており、それを聞いたうえで生徒は自身の興味や関心にあったプログラムを選択する時間が設けられている。こうした自由意志による選択の機会が、生徒の能動的かつ主体的な授業参加を促すとともに、内発的な動機づけによる学びにつながったと考えられる。

二つ目に、体験学習の事前学習および事後学習の実施である。藤田[9]は、事前学習において体験活動の目標を達成するうえで必要な知識の獲得が促され、さらに事後学習を行うことでその力は確実なものとなると指摘している。A高校では、事前学習として、各プログラムの担当教員により、授業に参加する目的や意識を明確にするための授業を行っている。また、体験学習中には、授業終了後に感想や課題等を用紙に記入する時間を設けており、それを各プログラムの担当教員が確認をしてコメントをつけて返却をしている。事後学習には生徒が授業で学んだことを整理して発表する機会を設けている。すなわち、生徒はただ漠然と体験学習に参加するのではなく常に目的意識をもちながら授業に臨み、そこで学んだことや気づいたこと、課題等を記録する作業を繰り返し行っている。こうした一連のプロセスが、生徒の発見学習を促していると考えられる。

三つ目に、学校と地域の各種団体とのつながりである。A高校における体験学習のプログラムは、地域ボランティアと奉仕担当教員との協働により長い時間をかけ信頼関係を構築することで少しずつ作り上げられたものである。A高校では、奉仕が必修化された当時の奉仕担当教員が、地域のボランティアセンターや社会福祉協議会に問い合わせをするなどして一つひとつ地域ボランティアとの関係性を築いていった。そして、学校側では体験学習以外にも地域ボランティアとの関わりを維持するための様々な試みをしている。例えば、体験学習の学内発表会には、体験学習に参加した地域ボランティアが招待されており、そこで生徒が発表する姿を微笑ましく見守る姿が見受けられる。A校における体験学習のプログラムは、地域ボランティアと奉仕担当教員との協働により長い時間をかけ信頼関係を構築することで少しずつ作り上げられたものであり、奉仕担当教員の異動後もその関係は引き継がれている。こうしたことからも、地域の事業所や公的機関やキャリア教育コーディネーターと協働しながら、学校と地域ボランティアとの信頼関係の上にプログラムを作っていくことが重要であると思われる。

引用・参考文献

1）文部科学省　2006　高等学校におけるキャリア教育の推進に関する調査研究協力者会議報告書－普通科におけるキャリア教育の推進－、平成18年11月.〈http://www.mext.go.jp/b_menu/shingi/chousa/shotou/023/toushin/06122007/all.pdf〉（2013年11月15日）

2）文部科学省国立教育政策研究所生徒指導･進路指導研究センター　編　2016　変わる！キャリア教育、ミネルヴァ書房.

3）Bandura、A.　1971　Psychological Modeling:Conflicting Theories、Aldine De Gruyter（バンデューラ、A. 原野広太郎･福島修美訳 1975 モデリングの心理学－観察学習の理論と方法－金子書房.）

4）佐藤浩章　2006　キャリアモデルを活用した教育の可能性、ベネッセ教育センター若者の仕事生活実態調査報告書 121-125.

5）室雅子　2012　ライフコース選択へのキャリアモデルインタビューの有効性、椙山女学園大学教育学部紀要 5 125-136.

6）古野庸一　1999　キャリアデザインの「必要性」と「難しさ」、リクルートワークス研究所

「Works」35 4-7.

7）東京都教育委員会　2007　平成19年度奉仕体験活動の必修化に向けて、東京都教育委員会〈http://www.kyoiku.metro.tokyo.jp/buka/shidou/houshi.htm〉（2014年2月26日）

8）Murayama、Y et al. 2021　Effects of Participating in Intergenerational Programs on the Development of High School Students' Self-Efficacy、Journal of Intergenerational Relationships、(in press).

9）藤田晃之　2014　キャリア教育基礎論－正しい理解と実践のために－、実業之日本社.

要約

近年、学校が地域と協働したキャリア教育のあり方が注目されており、その実践例として世代間交流型のプログラムが報告されている。本稿では教科「奉仕」における体験学習として、高校1年生を対象に地域ボランティアとの世代間交流を通したプログラムを実践している都立A高校（総合学科高校）の取り組みに着目する。A高校では、2007年度より奉仕の体験学習として高校1年生と地域ボランティアとの交流活動を取り入れ、地域のボランティア団体を講師として招いて複数のプログラム（①絵本の読み聞かせ、②紙芝居を学ぼう、③手話を学ぼう、④環境ボランティア、⑤イベントのごみを減らそう、⑥リメイク手工芸、⑦林道に木道を作ろう、⑧開発途上国支援、⑨高齢者との共生、⑩仲間との共生）を実施している。本プログラムは、校内の授業（「事前学習」「事後学習」）と校外の体験学習（「体験学習」）から構成されている。生徒は希望するプログラムに振り分けられ、前期と後期に2つのプログラムを受講した。授業は、生徒20～25人に対して1つの地域のボランティア団体に所属しているボランティア4～6人程が講師として入り、グループワーク形式で進められる。プログラム終了後2年間にわたりその効果を検証したところ、体験学習を通して参加生徒のキャリア発達の基礎スキルの一部が向上した。また、4割強の生徒が体験学習の職業選択への影響があったと回答しており、自由記述から「思いやりの気持ち」や「多様な生き方や価値観への気づき」とともに「自己の役割の理解」等の影響が示された。こうしたことから、体験学習における子どもや高齢者、そして障害者など様々な人との関わりが、多様な価値観や考え方を理解することにつながるとともに生徒自身の役割や生き方を考えるきっかけになったと思われる。

村山　陽（編著者紹介欄 p.277参照）

Summary

The Effects of an Intergenerational Exchange with Community Volunteers on Career Development of High School Students : A Three-year Longitudinal Study

In adolescents, career exploration has been considered an essential developmental task. Nevertheless, in recent years, the number of adolescents with difficulties with career decision-making has grown in Japan and other countries. Given these circumstances, many local governments in Japan have introduced intergenerational programs as part of career education. Therefore, we focused on intergenerational programs at High School A to clarify their effects on students' career developments. High School A is a Tokyo metropolitan high school with integrated courses that combine regular and specialized courses. Starting in 2007, Tokyo Metropolitan High Schools introduced "service-learning" as a compulsory subject for all high-school students. It consists of in-school lectures (pre-learning, post-learning) and hands-on learning outside the school. As part of the service-learning subject, High School A invites local volunteer group members to be instructors for the multiple hands-on learning programs that it conducts for all first-year students, twice a year, once in the first semester and once in the second semester. The hands-on learning comprises 10 programs (Reading picture books aloud, Picture card story-telling, Sign language, Recycling, Reducing waste produced at events, Making humus from fallen leaves, Building a board walk on a woodland road, Supporting developing countries, Coexistence with the elderly, Coexistence with others).These volunteers comprise many generations and are members of a single local volunteer group that takes 20 to 25 students. Questionnaires were administered to students after the program. The results indicated that students evaluated the program highly and about 40% of them felt an influence in their job selection. According to the free-response answers on the impact on career decision-making, some students considered or created a concrete vision of their future through the programs. Furthermore, it was shown that students seem to learn diverse values, ways of living, and prosocial behavior from volunteers. Hence, creating intergenerational programs in local communities can be an effective method of resolving difficulties surrounding career decision-making or career indecision among adolescents.

Yoh Murayama (See p.277)

第 15 章　園児来校型ふれ合い体験を通して生徒に生じた感情と学び

叶内　茜・筧　敏子

1. はじめに

中学校の家庭科では、平成 20 年告示の学習指導要領より、保育学習の一環として生徒と乳幼児が直接交流をする体験型の学習「ふれ合い体験」が全面実施されている。ふれ合い体験は生徒と乳幼児の双方にとって、日常の中でかかわる機会の少ない相手との貴重な異年齢交流の場となっている。

ふれ合い体験を通して生徒が乳幼児に対して肯定的なイメージを持つようになる (藤原・猪野 2002) ことや、生徒の自尊感情が向上する (叶内・倉持 2014)、生徒の親性準備性が育まれる (伊藤 2007) 等の効果があることが先行研究により明らかになっており、「育てられている時代に育てることを学ぶ」(金田 2003) ことができるふれ合い体験の意義は大きいといえる。

また、乳幼児にとってはふれ合い体験でかかわる生徒が、先生や園児仲間とは違ったかかわり方をしてくれる人、日常とは違う雰囲気をもたらしてくれる存在 (天野 2015) であり、大人ばかりの環境で育つことの多い乳幼児の状況から社会性の育ちを認めるという指摘もある (矢萩 2007)。このように、ふれ合い体験は生徒と乳幼児の双方にとって互恵的な体験となっている。

一方で、少子化や核家族化などの影響によって、生徒の中にはふれ合い体験を行う以前に、全く乳幼児とかかわった経験のない生徒もみられる。そのような中で、すべての生徒がふれ合い体験を通して乳幼児と直接かかわる機会を得ることは、生徒が将来の子育てイメージを持つことにつながるだけではなく、将来のライフスタイルにかかわらず地域社会の中で皆が子育ての担い手となり、ともに子どもの育ちを支え合っていくという考え方を持てるようになるためにも必要なことである。

2．さまざまなふれ合い体験

ふれ合い体験は、活動場所や交流相手によって、大きく４つに分けられる（叶内・倉持 2019）。１つ目は、生徒が保育所や幼稚園、認定こども園を訪問して園児と交流を行う「乳幼児施設訪問型（就学前施設訪問型）」のふれ合い体験である。この形のふれ合い体験は、最も多くの中学校で実施されている。２つ目は、保育所や幼稚園、認定こども園に通う園児が中学校に来校し、学校内で交流を行う「園児来校型」である。３つ目は、生徒と園児または乳幼児親子が地域の子育て支援センターや児童館などの施設に集まって交流を行う「地域交流拠点訪問型」である。４つ目は、０～２歳頃を中心とした乳幼児親子が中学校に来校し、学校内で交流を行う「親子来校型」である。いずれのふれ合い体験も生徒にとって多くの学びがあり、有意義な活動となっている。各学校でどの型のふれ合い体験を扱うのかについては、地域の実態や、家庭科教員がめざす授業の目的に応じて選択されている。

3．園児来校型ふれ合い体験の事例

ここでは、先に述べた４つの型のふれ合い体験のうち、「園児来校型」のふれ合い体験を取り上げる。東京都内にある公立中学校に近隣の公立保育所の園児を招いて交流を行った実践である。

（1）活動の目的

ふれ合い体験は、中学校第３学年の技術・家庭（家庭分野）の「幼児の生活と家族」に関する学習の一環として実施された。授業実践者である筧氏は、「実際に園児とふれ合うことにより、園児の心身の発達や遊びについての理解を深める。園児とのふれ合い体験を通して、年長者としてのかかわり方について考える。」という目的のもと、全 10 時間の保育学習の中に、１時間（50 分）のふれ合い体験を計画した。ふれ合い体験のような生徒と園児との交流は、職場体験などの家庭科以外の時間でも行われている場合があるが、家庭科のふれ合い体験では、事前に子どもの発達や特徴について丁寧に学び、ふれ合い体験後も体験から得たことをさらに深める事後学習の時間が設定されていることが特徴である。

（2）活動内容と工夫

ふれ合い体験時の活動内容を図１に示す。交流を始める前の全体のあいさつの中で、園の先生から安全上の注意事項を説明していただいた。生徒にとっては、保育の専門家から話を聞くことのできる貴重な機会となっていた。

交流の時間には、生徒４～５名と園児２～３名を１グループとして、８つのグループに分かれ、グループ毎に生徒が準備した遊びを一緒に楽しんだ。１時間という限られた時間ではあったが、絵本の読み聞かせや２種類の遊びの活動を取り入れたことで、短時間であっても園児のさまざまな姿を知ることができた。帰り際には、生徒と園児の互いに離れがたい様子もみられ、双方にとって充実した交流の時間となったことがうかがえた。

（3）ふれ合い体験後の事後学習

ふれ合い体験後の事後学習では、活動中の記録やふり返りをもとに生徒の経験をワークシートにまとめ、クラス全体で共有化した。ワークシートの内容は、一緒に過ごした際の園児の様子や特徴的だと感じた点、園児と楽しくかかかわるために生徒が行った工夫の中で、うまくいった点・うまくいかなかった点、保育者の話や保育者の園児へのかかわりの様子を観察して気がついた点等についてまとめた。生徒たちは、自分の経験を言語化することで自らの経験をふり返るとともに、クラスで共有化をすることを通して、自分とは異なるアプローチのしかたで園児とかかわっていた他の生徒の経験を知る機会となっていた。また、保育者のさまざまな園児への働きかけの様子を観察することを通して、保育の専門家から園児とのかかわり方のコツを学び、幼児とのかかわり方の工夫についてさらに学習を深めていた。

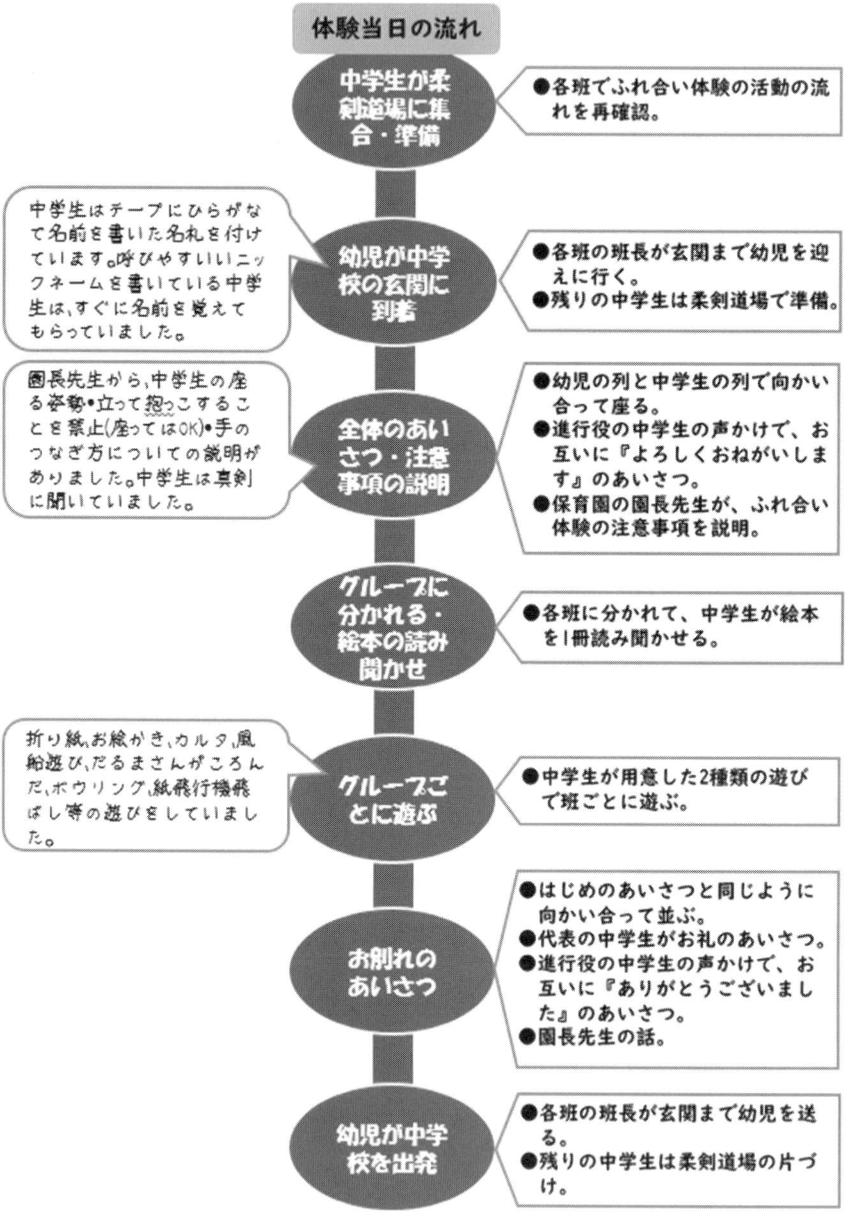

体験当日の流れ

中学生が柔剣道場に集合・準備
- 各班でふれ合い体験の活動の流れを再確認。

幼児が中学校の玄関に到着
- 各班の班長が玄関まで幼児を迎えに行く。
- 残りの中学生は柔剣道場で準備。

中学生はテープにひらがなで名前を書いた名札を付けています。呼びやすいいニックネームを書いている中学生は、すぐに名前を覚えてもらっていました。

全体のあいさつ・注意事項の説明
- 幼児の列と中学生の列で向かい合って座る。
- 進行役の中学生の声かけで、お互いに『よろしくおねがいします』のあいさつ。
- 保育園の園長先生が、ふれ合い体験の注意事項を説明。

園長先生から、中学生の座る姿勢・立って抱っこすることを禁止(座ってはOK)・手のつなぎ方についての説明がありました。中学生は真剣に聞いていました。

グループに分かれる・絵本の読み聞かせ
- 各班に分かれて、中学生が絵本を1冊読み聞かせる。

グループごとに遊ぶ
- 中学生が用意した2種類の遊びで班ごとに遊ぶ。

折り紙、お絵かき、カルタ、風船遊び、だるまさんがころんだ、ボウリング、紙飛行機飛ばし等の遊びをしていました。

お別れのあいさつ
- はじめのあいさつと同じように向かい合って並ぶ。
- 代表の中学生がお礼のあいさつ。
- 進行役の中学生の声かけで、お互いに『ありがとうございました』のあいさつ。
- 園長先生の話。

幼児が中学校を出発
- 各班の班長が玄関まで幼児を送る。
- 残りの中学生は柔剣道場の片づけ。

図１　ふれ合い体験時の活動の流れ（叶内・倉持 2019）

4．ふれ合い体験を通して生徒に生じた感情と学び

生徒のワークシートを授業後に回収し、記述をさらに詳細に分析した結果からは、次のことが読み取れた（叶内・筧 2020）。

ふれ合い体験時に生徒が感じていた不安としては、園児のケガや、園児が生徒の準備した活動を楽しめているのか、ということへの不安に関する記述が目立った。こうした不安からは、生徒が自分たちよりもケガにつながるような行動を起こしやすいという園児の特徴を理解していることや、園児が楽しめるようにふれ合い体験に真剣に向き合い、準備をしてきたことが読み取れる。

また、生徒が楽しいと感じた経験については、園児と一緒に過ごしたこと自体が生徒にとって楽しい経験であり、さらに園児が生徒の準備した活動に積極的に参加し、園児が楽しむ姿を見ることができたこと、園児が生徒に興味を持ってくれたことが挙げられた。先に述べた、園児が活動を楽しめるかという生徒の不安に対して、実際に園児の楽しむ姿を見て自分自身も楽しい気持ちを持つことができたことは、今後も生徒が幼い子どもとかかわるうえでの自信につながるのではないだろうか。

一方で、生徒は楽しい場面だけではなく、園児が自己中心的な態度をとったり、自分が興味のない活動には露骨につまらなそうな態度をとったりするといった、幼児らしさを目の当たりにする場面もあったようだ。こうした園児の一面に触れられたことは、生徒が幼児理解を深めていくうえでとても意味のある経験といえるだろう。生徒の中には今回のふれ合い体験が幼児とかかわるはじめての機会であった者もいる。また、幼児とかかわることに難しさを感じ、困った状態のままで体験が終わってしまうケースも想定される。こうした経験によって生徒が幼児とかかわることへの自信を失わないように、今回の授業実践では、事後学習の中で家庭科教諭が丁寧に生徒の発言を拾い、生徒がふれ合い体験中に起こった事象を前向きに捉えられるように補足をしながら進めていた。このように、事後学習時に同じような状況を経験した生徒同士で対処法を共有する活動や、家庭科教員・保育者から生徒へのフォローの場を作り、今後の幼児とのかかわりにつなげてい

くことが必要であるといえる。

効果的なかかわり方の工夫としては、園児と目線を合わせることや、園児が理解できるように簡単な言葉を使って話すなどの声かけの工夫を、かかわりの中で生徒が体験的に学習していたことが読み取れた。

5．おわりに

本章では、園児来校型のふれ合い体験の一実践を取り上げ、ふれ合い体験を通して生徒に生じた感情と学びの内容をまとめた。ふれ合い体験中の生徒たちは、元気いっぱいの園児に圧倒されている様子や、園児と一緒に遊びを楽しむ様子、園児の反応に戸惑う様子、そして背中を丸めて園児と目線を合わせ、優しく見守る温かなまなざしが印象的であった。園児たちもまた、交流を思いっきり楽しみ、充実した表情をしていた。こうした直接的な交流体験は、子どもたちの心を豊かにしてくれる。しかし、新型コロナウィルスの流行以降は、ふれ合い体験の実施が難しくなってしまい、直接かかわり合うことのできる機会が失われてしまった。こうした状況でも可能な相互交流の方法を模索するとともに、一日も早く、また交流ができるようになる日が来ることを願うばかりである。

引用・参考文献

天野美和子 2015「園児と生徒との“ふれ合い体験活動”における園児の経験」保育学研究 53(2) 138-150.

藤原由美子・猪野郁子 2002「生徒の園児ふれ合い体験学習に関する研究」島根大学教育学部紀要（教育科学）36 27-35.

伊藤葉子 2007「中・高校生の家庭科の保育体験学習の教育的課題に関する検討」日本家政学会誌 58(6) 315-326.

金田利子編著 2003『育てられている時代に育てることを学ぶ』新読書社.

叶内茜・筧敏子 2020「園児来校型ふれ合い体験を通して中学生に生じた感情と学び；ワークシートの記述分析から」日本世代間交流学会第 11 回全国大会（オンライン）.

叶内茜・倉持清美 2014「中学校家庭科のふれ合い体験プログラムによる効果の比較；園児への

肯定的意識・育児への積極性と自尊感情尺度から」日本家政学会誌 65(2) 58-63.
叶内茜編著・倉持清美監修 2019『家庭科保育学習生徒と乳幼児のふれ合い体験事例集』.
矢萩恭子 2007「次世代育成としての乳幼児とのふれあい体験；生徒・高校生の「保育体験学習」に関する実践の検討」田園調布学園大学紀要 2 125-153.

要約

本稿では都内の中学校に近隣の保育所の園児を招いて交流を行った「園児来校型」のふれ合い体験の実践を取り上げ、ふれ合い体験を通して生徒に生じた感情と学びについてまとめた。体験時に生徒が感じた不安としては、園児のケガや、園児が生徒の準備した活動を楽しめているのか等の不安が挙げられた。生徒が楽しいと感じた経験については、園児と一緒に過ごしたこと自体が生徒にとって楽しい経験であり、さらに園児が生徒の準備した活動に積極的に参加し園児が楽しむ姿を見ることができたこと、園児が生徒に興味を持ってくれたこと等が挙げられた。一方で、生徒は園児が自己中心的な態度をとったり、自分が興味のない活動には露骨につまらなそうな態度をとったりするといった幼児らしさに触れる場面もあった。こうした園児の一面を知ることは、生徒が幼児理解を深めていくうえで意味のある経験である。効果的なかかわり方の工夫としては、園児と目線を合わせることや、園児が理解できるように簡単な言葉を使って話すなどの声かけの工夫を、かかわりの中で生徒が体験的に学習していた。

叶内　茜

川村学園女子大学 生活創造学部 生活文化学科

〒 270-1138　千葉県我孫子市下ヶ戸 1133

川村学園女子大学 生活創造学部 生活文化学科 専任講師。博士（教育学）（東京学芸大学）。専門は家庭科教育学、保育学。現在の研究テーマは、生徒と乳幼児の世代間交流、子どもの食育。

筧　敏子

国分寺市立第二中学校。

都内公立中学校で 40 年近く家庭科教員をしている。

Summary

Emotions and Learning of Students through Interaction with Preschool Children

This paper focuses on the practice of a "school visit type" interaction experience, in which children from a nearby nursery school were invited to a junior high school in Tokyo for an exchange program. The students' concerns during the experience included whether the children were injured and whether they enjoyed the activities that the students had prepared. As for the experiences that the students found enjoyable, they said that spending time with the children was an enjoyable experience for them, and that they could see the children actively participating in the activities that the students prepared and enjoying themselves, and that the children took an interest in the students. On the other hand, the students were sometimes exposed to the infantile nature of the children, such as their self-centered attitudes and their blatantly boring attitudes toward activities they were not interested in. Learning about these aspects of preschoolers is a meaningful experience for students to deepen their understanding of young children. In order to interact effectively with the children, the students learned through experience how to make eye contact with them and how to talk to them using simple words so that they can understand.

Akane Kanouchi

Department of Life and Culture, Faculty of Creative Life, Kawamura Gakuen Woman's University

1133 Sageto, Abiko-shi, Chiba Pref. 270-1138, JAPAN

Tel: +81-4-7183-6831 E-mail: a.kanouchi@kgwu.ac.jp

Dr. Akane Kanouchi is a Senior Lecturer of the Kawamura Gakuen Woman's University, Japan. Her Major are Home Economics education and Childcare. Her research themes are intergenerational interaction between students and young children, and Food and Nutrition Education for children.

Toshiko Kakehi

Kokubunji Municipal Second Junior High School.

She has been a home economics teacher for nearly 40 years at several public junior high schools in Tokyo.

第 16 章　世代間交流が生まれる学校システム

溝邊　和成

1．はじめに

およそ 10 年前、文科省 (2012) は、超高齢社会における生涯学習政策のあり方として、多様な学習機会の提供とともに、ライフステージに応じた縦のつながりも重視する世代間交流の促進を掲げている。個人や社会の多様性を尊重し、それぞれの強みを活かしてともに助け合い、社会に参加することが可能なシステムが求められており、学校システムの一つの取り組みとして「聴講生制度」や「シニアスクール」が考えられる。

本稿では、筆者が過去数年間で調査成果として発表・報告した論文等をレヴューする形で、「聴講生制度」と「シニアスクール」を取り上げ、生涯学習社会における世代間交流が生起する学校システムとしてその概要を紹介する。

2．聴講生制度

「学び直し」に着目した溝邊 (2017a) では、溝邊 (2015) の報告をもとにして、異世代となる地域住民と児童・生徒がともに授業を受ける異年齢同居型の学校システムとなる「聴講生制度」(初等・中等教育段階) を紹介してきた。紹介例として、愛知県丹羽郡扶桑町、福岡県糟屋郡須恵町に加え、福岡県筑紫郡那珂川町 (現 那珂川市) の聴講生制度であった。

2002 年に全国に先駆けて始まった扶桑町の聴講生制度 (小中学校) では、「1 学級２名まで」「受講生の孫、子の在籍する教室は避ける」等の高齢者の受け入れルールが一定程度示されているものの、「地域の学校理解」や「地域の安全強化」「授業の質向上」につながっていくとともに高齢者が中学生の「よき相談者」となったり、その教室が「ふれあい・生きがいの場」となったりしていた。開校（2002年）されて以降10年間の調査では、小学校よりも中学校の人数が７倍ほどであり、中学校での人気が高いことがわかる。

全国で２番目にスタートした那珂川町の聴講生制度も、基本的には、前者の扶桑町と大差はない。開校（2005年）後の10年ほどの受け入れ状況は、小学校、高等学校は、20名前後であったが、中学校はその倍近くになる。中学校で選択された教科については、のべ人数50名中20名近くが英語であった。数学、社会、音楽、美術などは、６、７名程度であったことがわかった。

須恵町の聴講生制度（全国３番目に開始）も、いわゆる「生涯学習・リカレント教育の場の一つ」として、また「地域に開かれた学校」として取り組まれていた。溝邊ら（2015）の調査結果から、聴講生を受け入れている中学校の生徒のほとんどが聴講生に対して肯定的な意見を述べていたことがわかった。また、聴講生を受け入れたクラス担当となった教員も聴講生は「学ぶ喜び」を感じ、生徒との「ふれあい」を楽しんでいると回答し、授業を乱される心配もなく、むしろ聴講生から学ぶことが多いと受け止めていることがわかった。

扶桑町高齢者等実態調査報告書（2014）では、趣味を持つ人の割合が多く、友人・知人との交流や、旅行・娯楽、趣味のサークル活動などが希望する項目の上位を占めていることがわかった。今後は、同好の者が集える活動や教養講座の開設、児童生徒に関わるボランティア活動等を含むプログラムの運営が期待される。

上記事例とは、若干異なる聴講生制度も見られる。高知県土佐郡土佐町では、聴講生制度として、「生涯楽習学校」が開かれている（溝邊ら 2017）。この町では、「できるときに　できる人が　できることを」を合言葉に、学校教育で行われる様々な活動の支援をする学校応援団（学校支援ボランティア）が設定されており、そこに登録・参加している人たちがボランティアを行いつつ、この制度を利用し、学び直すことができる生涯学習の機会保障を行っている。１クラス２名の制限や学年・科目の自由選択などの設定は、先の扶桑町や須恵町と同じシステムである。溝邊ら（2017）の調査では、高齢者（聴講生）と関わる学びの経験ありと回答する児童・生徒は、全体の８割を占め、そのほとんどが小学校時代であった。中学校の聴講生制度では、小学校時代に高齢者との交流経験を有する生徒が関わっているのが特徴である。そのため、児童よりも生徒の方が高齢者（聴講生）と一緒に勉強する活動や勉強を教えてあげる体験を肯定的にとらえ、関わる意識も高かった。また、生徒たちが高齢者との交流で教えてもらいたいと期待する内容として、歴史（一般）をはじめ、地域の歴史、昔の遊びなどであった。それらの項目は、一緒に学びたい内容としても挙げられていた。生徒たちが高齢者に教えてあげたい内容は、現代の社会や現代的な遊びに続き、電子機器の操作等が見られた。

神奈川県中部大磯町・中学校（２校）、鳥取県伯耆郡伯耆町・中学校（２校）、佐賀県東松浦郡玄海町・小中学校（１校）を対象とした中学校聴講生制度に関する調査（溝邉ら 2016）では、次の点が明らかとなった。いずれも生涯学習確立のための再教育の場とともに地域住民と生徒との触れ合いを通して質の高い教育をめざしている。これら３地域の聴講生制度では、受講の受け入れ学年・受け入れ人数は、全学年で各クラス２名までとされ、受講期間も原則１年となっている。受講料無料（教材費など実費）、給食可（実費）であり、学校行事等への参加もすべて可とされている。

自分の現在の仕事に関係した「公民」を受講している受講生は、「今更ながら、なるほどそうだったのだと再認識する場面も度々、（略）非常に有意義なものになっている」と記している（鳥取県：男性）。また佐賀県の受講生（女性）は、外国経験もあり、英語に関心を示し、英語を中心に数科目を受講している。「今どきの中学生の考えを知ることができたり、活気にあふれる姿にふれることができたりして、楽しむことができている」との感想があった。こうした学び合う場を求め、その目的に合う選択ができる点、自己充実を図っていることがわかる。今後、聴講生のニーズに応える点として、参加しやすい聴講スタイルを用意することや通学方法等の課題も挙げている（神奈川県：中学校教頭へのインタビューより）。

３．シニアスクール

溝邉（2017b）の報告では、2006 年より制度化された北海道札幌市のシニアスクールを取り上げている。小学校の空き教室を利用した講座制（全 50 講座）である。５月下旬から 12 月下旬まで夏休みを含む２期制で、毎週水曜日午前中に行われる。活動内容は、スクールとして独自の内容が取り組まれる一方で、全時間の半分程度に児童との世代間交流活動が設定されている。調査の結果から、次のようにまとめられる。まず、本スクールに参加した高齢者は、その期間内で全学年の児童との交流活動に参加している。そこでは、ものづくり、楽器演奏等に加え、昔の暮らしを調べるインタビューへの協力など多彩な活動が工夫されていた。児童は「交流活動は楽しい」としながら、仲良くなる自信がそれほど強くなく、またスクールに参加する高齢者にとっては、教えることは楽しかったりするが、教えることへの自信がなかったり、不安であったりすることも見られた。しかしながら、双方とも「一緒に学ぶ」ことを期待しており、「科学実験」「料理」「ものづくり」「合奏」「昔遊び」などが希望として挙がっていた。

中学校のシニアスクールに関する報告には、京都府相楽郡精華町の事例もある（MIZOBE K.,2017）。学校と地域との協働事業を推進することを通し、学習環境を整え、学校生活の安定を図ることを目的に、平成 21 年に学校運営協議会を発足させ、その取り組みの一つとしてシニアスクールを設定している。その特徴は、次の通りになる。

・ ４月初めにシニアスクールの受講申し込み受付・開講説明があり、５月から開講。翌年３月下旬に閉校式がある。
・ ５月から翌年２月まで毎月 10 講座以上が開講される。造形（絵画、押し花等）、音楽（コーラス）、英語、社会科（町の歴史）、国語（読み聞かせ）、技術･家庭（パソコン、手芸、寄せ植え・ガーデニング）とともに、現学習指導要領に含まれていない茶道や花道、写真などの活動も見られる。
・ 受講生は、中学校が行う体育会や学習発表会、収穫祭といった行事などにも参加したり、生徒と昼食会をもったりしている。また、農作業や園芸、調理実習などのサポートも行ったりしている。

このようにシニアスクールで開講されている講座は、多くの教科に対応し、定期的に実施されていることがわかった。また、中学校の行事をはじめ、学習内容に関連させた取り組みや様々な学校への支援活動も含まれており、世代間交流も自然な形で導入されている。

上記に示されたシニアスクールは、小学校または中学校と１校限定が基本型となっている。しかし、同地区で、小学校・中学校にともにシニアスクールを開いている事例も見受けられる（溝邊 2018）。岡山県岡山市に 2003 年より開かれたシニアスクールがそれに当たる。

溝邊（2018）の報告によれば、このシニアスクールは、中学校１教室（以下、K 教室と称する）、小学校２教室（以下 S 教室、N 教室と称する）の３つの教室で成り立っている。S 教室と N 教室は異なる小学校に置かれている。シニアスクールの入学式は K 教室のある中学校において合同で行われ、翌年３月末までの１年間が通学期間となり、修了書授与式も実施する。ただし、修了後も受講の継続は可能となっている。開講は、K 教室では、３日／週、S 教室は２日／週、N 教室は、１日／週の１時間目から５時間目までとなっている。講座を担当する講師陣も、開講 10 年後の 2013 年では、９教科にわたり 30 名を超えている。実施時間数が異なるものの、どの教室においても同じような内容が受講できるように、講師陣のローテーションが組まれていたり、葉のつくりの顕微鏡観察や世界の音楽、歴史上の人物など実施する内容面にも工夫がなされていたりする。

児童・生徒との交流においては、K 教室と S 教室では、それぞれの学校の運動会・体育会や文化発表会、音楽・学習発表会などに参加している。K 教室では、クラスごとに合同給食が行われたり、ふれあい講座（中学１年）が実施されたりしている。S 教室では、各学年の児童と関わりを持つようにされている。生活科に関する昔遊びやおもちゃづくり、ミシンの使用、戦争の話といった家庭科や総合的な学習の時間・社会科に関わる取り組みが行われていた。N 教室も同様であった。また、どの教室も幼稚園・保育園との交流は行われていた。

このように本スクールでは、ユニークなコンテンツを学びつつ、コミュニティサポーター（小中学校の教育活動及び幼稚園、保育園の保育を支援する人材）として活動する機会が用意されている。しかし「学校」として展開する点では、教室ごとにクラス担任が存在し、希望科目のみの受講ではなく、給食も含め、原則全教科受講型になっている。これは、先にふれた北海道や京都で展開されているシニアスクールも同様であった。

4. おわりに

本稿では、聴講生制度とシニアスクールについて概観してきた。それぞれの詳細については、引用・参考文献等に譲るが、その特徴を総括して言えば、ここで取り上げたどちらの、どのケースにおいても、「高齢者を学校に受け入れる」ことによる「個の学びの機会保障」と「交流活動の設定」がなされていたことである。高齢者の受け入れ方法として、既存の時間割や授業内容、教科目にしたがって受講していくことを中心にする場合と受講者のみが学ぶ場を保障し、受講者ニーズを配慮した内容を実施する場合に分かれる。その中で「世代間交流」の活動をどの程度組み入れていくかによって、スタイルが分かれていく。

今後は、生涯学習社会における全世代にひらかれた学びの成立を求めるならば、聴講生制度やシニアスクールに見られる学習スタイルを今一度点検し、旧来の学習システムの感覚にとらわれないで、次世代への知識・経験の伝承を提供する機会を保障したり、若年世代のもつ最新の知識・技術等を共有できる場を提供したりする学校を模索する必要があると考える。そのアイデアの一つとして、これまでの学校教育学や子どもの成長・発達論を加味した学習プログラムの作成過程に、高齢者学習の内容編成論（ex. 堀 2012）などからの検討を加えることも考えられるだろう。また互恵性（ex. Newman, S. 1997）の効果を反映させた実践的検討も具体的なプログラム作成には欠かせない視点であろう。

引用・参考文献

扶桑町（2014）扶桑町高齢者等実態調査報告書 https://www.town.fuso.lg.jp/kaigo/documents/koureisyajittaityousa.pdf（参照日 2014.08）

堀薫夫（2012）教育老年学におけるエイジングと高齢者学習の理論、堀薫夫編著『教育老年学と高齢者学習』学文社，pp.1-53.

溝邊和成・田爪宏二・吉津晶子・矢野真(2015)小中学校の聴講生制度に見られる世代間交流, 日本世代間交流学会誌, Vol.5 No.1, pp.47-55.

溝邊和成・田爪宏二・吉津晶子・矢野真(2016)中学校聴講生制度の特徴と高齢者の参加意識　資料ならびにインタビュー調査をもとに, 日本世代間交流学会第7回全国大会要旨集, p.45.

溝邊和成(2017a)リ・ラーニングをひらく学校, 草野篤子・溝邊和成・内田勇人・安永正史編著『世代間交流の理論と実践2 世界標準としての世代間交流のこれから』三学出版、pp.234-243.

溝邊和成(2017b)小学校のシニアスクールに見られる世代間交流に関する児童・高齢者・教師の意識, 兵庫教育大学研究紀要, 第51巻, pp.91-100.

MIZOBE, K. (2017) The program for the elderly: "Senior School" in junior high school, Japan, Generations United 19th Global International Conference 2017

溝邊和成・田爪宏二・吉津晶子・矢野真(2017)学校支援活動参加者を対象とした聴講生制度における世代間交流　～土佐町学校応援団「生涯楽習学校」の分析と小・中学生の意識調査をもとに～, 日本世代間交流学会誌, Vol.6 No.1, pp.49-58.

溝邊和成(2018)小・中学校の空き教室を活用したシニアスクールの世代間交流, 日本世代間交流学会誌, Vol.7 No.1, pp.47-59.

文部科学省(2012)長寿社会における生涯学習の在り方について～人生100年　いくつになっても学ぶ幸せ「幸齢社会」～、超高齢社会における生涯学習検討会 https://www.mext.go.jp/component/a_menu/education/detail/__icsFiles/afieldfile/2012/03/28/1319112_1.pdf

NEWMAN, S. (1997) History and Education of Intergenerational Programs, NEWMAN, S. et al. Intergenerational Programs: Past, Present, and Future, Taylor & Francis, pp.18-19.

要約

本稿では、筆者が過去数年間で調査成果として発表・報告した論文等をレヴューする形で、「聴講生制度」と「シニアスクール」を取り上げ、生涯学習社会における世代間交流が生起する学校システムとしてその概要を紹介する。取り上げている対象地域と学校は次の通りである。

＜聴講生制度＞

愛知県丹羽郡扶桑町(小･中学校)、福岡県糟屋郡須恵町(中学校)･筑紫郡那珂川町(現那珂川市)(小・中・高等学校)、高知県土佐郡土佐町(小・中学校)、神奈川県中部大磯町(中学校)、鳥取県伯耆郡伯耆町(中学校)、佐賀県東松浦郡玄海町(小中学校)

＜シニアスクール＞

北海道札幌市(小学校)、京都府相楽郡精華町(中学校)、岡山県岡山市(小・中学校)

どの学校においても「高齢者を学校に受け入れる」ことによる「個の学びの機会保障」と「交流活動の設定」がなされており、聴講生制度は、既存の時間割や授業内容、教科目に対して選択型の受講となっている。また、シニアスクールは、参加者のみが学ぶ場が保障され、受講生のニーズを配慮した取り組みとなっている。今後の生涯学習社会における学校システムのあり方を検討する際の一つのアイデアになる。

溝邊　和成（編著者紹介欄 p.276 参照）

Summary

School System that Create Intergenerational Exchange

In this paper, the "auditing system" and "senior school" are introduced as school systems that generate intergenerational exchanges in a lifelong learning society, in the form of a review of articles and other papers that the author has published and reported as research results over the past several years. The target areas and schools are as follows.

<Auditing system>

- Fuso Town, Niwa County, Aichi Prefecture (elementary and junior high schools)
- Sue Town, Kasuya County (junior high school), Nakagawa Town, Chikushi County (elementary, junior high and high school), Fukuoka Prefecture
- Tosa Town, Tosa County, Kochi Prefecture (elementary and junior high schools)
- Oiso Town, Naka County, Kanagawa Prefecture (junior high school)
- Hoki Town, Hoki County, Tottori Prefecture (junior high school)
- Genkai Town, Higashimatsuura County, Saga Prefecture (elementary and junior high schools)

<Senior School>

- Sapporo City, Hokkaido Prefecture (elementary school)
- Seika Town, Souraku County, Kyoto Prefecture (junior high school)
- Okayama City, Okayama Prefecture (elementary and junior high schools)

In all schools, "guaranteeing individual learning opportunities" and "setting up exchange activities" by "accepting the elderly into the school" have been implemented, and the auditing system is an elective course for the existing time schedule, class content, and subject matter. In addition, the senior school guarantees that only participants have the opportunity to learn, an approach that takes into consideration the needs of the students. This is one idea to consider when examining the future of the school system in a lifelong learning society.

Kazushige Mizobe (See p.276)

第２部

Part 2

世代間交流：諸外国

Intergenerational Exchange in the World; Several Countries

Chapter 1

Connecting and Reflecting: Intergenerational Activities that Build a Safety Net of Community

Derenda Schubert
Lindsay Magnuson
Renee Moseley

Bridge Meadows is a nonprofit located in Portland, Oregon that develops and sustains supportive intergenerational neighborhoods for families adopting children out of foster care and adults over 55. Our goal is to create a mutually beneficial network of support with a primary focus on helping children formerly in foster care to heal from trauma. This core social purpose focuses the community around the children's' needs, creating a common unifying principle that motivates and inspires people to extend beyond their comfort zones. The relationships that result become safety nets for each individual.

In order to facilitate these community connections, Bridge Meadows helps bring children, parents and elders together with a variety of activities and therapeutic programmatic offerings. Intergenerational connection activities in an environment where children have experienced considerable trauma requires knowledge, awareness and intention. Bridge Meadows addresses this by hiring mental health specialists who serve as community facilitators, as well as providing training for elders and parents in trauma-informed care. In this way, the community has a shared language that helps create a sense of safety and belonging.

Bridge Meadows offers three types of programs.

1. <u>Community-member led programs</u>: Elders bring a wealth of talent and energy to Bridge Meadows. Some offer their gifts to the community through specific classes or group facilitation. Examples include leading a writing group, teaching Spanish to children, co-facilitating a conflict resolution group, co-leading an anti-bullying task force, and facilitating a weekly intergenerational art class. Working across generations

presents particular challenges, as well as rewards. The mental health specialist helps support community members in planning to meet those challenges.

2. Community Support Specialist-facilitated programs: The mental health specialist facilitates core psycho-educational programming, using their strengthts and interests to design programs to meet community needs. For example, a mental health specialist with a background in nutrition education might design a group for elders and kids that addresses eating a diabetic-friendly diet, while also helping kids learn to cook. Or a mental health specialist may use expressive arts in the design of a depression-support group.
3. Partnerships and community-led programs: Bridge Meadows draws on the wider community of resources to support its purpose. Some partners provide programs directly to community members at Bridge Meadows, while others provide opportunities outside of the community. Bridge Meadows communities are embedded in neighborhoods, cities, regions, and states. We draw upon local partnerships to offer valuable programming (e.g., wellness classes, parenting classes, support groups). The larger community supplements the well-being and sustenance of community members through resources, educational opportunities, and expanded opportunities for volunteerism.

The core principles of our programs within the community include:

- Empowering the community: At each step, the licensed clinical therapist asks, "Am I doing something that a community member could be doing/leading/facilitating?" Helping the community, especially vulnerable children, build its own leadership, agency, and self-determination so that the licensed clinical therapist is working with community members not for them.
- Modeling the Bridge Meadows Equity Statement: Showing others how to reflect on one's biases and disrupt discriminatory actions.
- Modeling the Bridge Meadows Community Agreements: Showing others how to live the agreements with self-reflection and a willingness to address conflict.

Intergenerational Connection and Reflection Programming

Happiness Hour©

Bridge Meadows holds several regular gatherings and groups to bring the generations together. Happiness Hour © (pre-COVID) is our weekly shared meal where kids, parents and elders celebrate school achievements, birthdays, and milestones. It is a family-like gathering that is casual and open to all. Often new connections are made over a shared meal, or resources are shared.

Support Groups

Support groups are designed to prioritize relationship-building. Bridge Meadows' Support Groups are facilitated groups that gather community members together based on the role they play within the community—elder, parent, or child. The Support Groups provide an avenue for participants to deepen their connections, find support, and enhance their acceptance of one another. Support Groups provide space for processing community issues, creating a co-learning environment and reinforcing the skills needed for community living. Each group requires a slightly different style of facilitation; however all contain an intentional opening and closing structure. If possible, it is best to host wisdom, parent, teen, and kid support groups once a month.

Examples include:

- After community members identify poor listening skills as a barrier to healthy relationships, a Support Group can be an opportunity to practice and reinforce the value of listening skills as a group.
- After learning that many elders are struggling with depression in the winter, a Circle addressed this struggle.

General implementation tips:

- Use a consistent structure that community members come to know and can depend on.
- Be as transparent as possible notifying participants of the topic and a flow of the circle in advance.
- Consider using opening check ins and ice breakers.
- Create a consistent closing that offers participants an opportunity to synthesize what they experienced, heard, or learned in the group.
- Think about the space and whether the Support Group meets everyone's abilities and learning styles.

Examples include:

- Arrange the chairs so everyone can see each other.
- Use the microphone to normalize access for people with impaired hearing.
- Provide a variety of modalities including words on paper, videos,

conversation, expressive arts, and others.
- Establish agreements in advance, to ensure that all people have a voice and may contribute to the group (i.e use of microphones, no cross talk or interruptions, ask clarifying questions).

Elder Support Group provides an elders-only space to process issues related to aging, such as loss of loved ones or age-related health changes. These Groups also focus on psycho-educational topics related to the elders' participation in the community, such as the impact of trauma on our brains, clear communication, and accepting differences. At times, Support Groups are a place for processing community issues, such as the passing of a community member or a change to a family.

Elder Support Groupe implementation tips:
- Have two microphones to ensure that the facilitator and speakers can be heard.
- Use the mic like a "talking stick"—only people with a mic may talk.

Possible Topics: Grief and loss, adapting to change, communication with adult children, legacy contributions, storytelling as a way of affirming lived experience and getting to know one another.

Parent Support Group is a parent-only space that supports sharing around issues intimately connected to the roles of parents. Parent Support Group is often centered on a meal, and it often takes an informal, conversational form. Parents report that they value having this kid-free time to talk with peers who share the same journey of raising children who have been in the foster care system—"a family that looks like ours." Parent Support Group is a space for emotional support, as well as sharing resources for raising children who have experienced the impacts of trauma.

Parent Support Group implementation tips:
- Organize childcare to make it easier for parents to attend.
- Provide a meal.
- Co-plan the day and time with parents taking into account their needs and preferences.
- Use texts to build group commitment and send reminders.

Possible Topics: Understanding ADHD and deciding whether to use medication, relating to birth families, communication with teens, general check ins to be heard and seen in a group of peers.

Teen Support Group aims to unite teens who are often the most isolated with the community model.

Teen Support Group implementation tips:

- Gather teen input on what they want to do together—have them "weigh in to buy in."
- Provide a meal.
- Use text reminders.
- Identify an adult ally—elder or parent—who can support the teens' vision within community

Possible Topics: Building connection and relationship, feeling seen and heard as youth, a topic that they are passionate about.

Kid Support Group provides a kid-focused space that is fun and enhances children's bonds to one another while focusing on important community-related themes. To accommodate a broad range of ages, kid circle usually starts with an all-group opening followed by age-appropriate break-out sessions.

Successful implementation tips:

- Recruit elders and/or parents to support kid circle by being "co-guides" to lead smaller age-appropriate break-out sessions.
- Tailor the group to the topics that the kids and their parents identify as important or interesting.
- Use a variety of modalities. For example, open with a movement-based check in, read a story with each person reading a line, integrate making art, etc.
- Create group agreements.

Possible Topics: Friendship skills, bullying psycho-education, building empathy.

Community Support Group invites both elders and parents to connect.

Successful implementation tips:

- Create group agreements.

Possible Topics: Communication across differences, dealing with communication breakdowns, unpacking our assumptions about one another, team building.

Community Gatherings

Community Forum offers a space for the entire community to gather on a quarterly basis to engage with recent issues, build community and hear organizational updates. Community Forums are typically held on a weekend to ensure that most people can participate. The format usually includes a meal and informal socializing followed by a town hall discussion facilitated by staff.

Successful implementation tips:

- Provide a meal.
- Create an agenda and share as much in advance as possible.
- Use microphones to ensure that everyone can hear and delineate who "has the floor" to speak.

The Bridge Meadows intergenerational exchange activities listed above are examples of ways to both address the needs of particular age groups, while providing opportunities for all generations to connect in community. Other specific connection activities we have found successful were based around topics like ageism. The goal was to increase awareness through activities that uncover bias and ultimately that increase mutual understanding. Many activities that connect the generations, provided they are designed intentionally and with consideration for the needs of each generation, can break down the barriers so common in society today. Bridge Meadows hopes to contribute to this societal change by demonstrating the benefits of intergenerational relationships that improve quality of life for all ages.

Summary

Bridge Meadows is a nonprofit located in Portland, Oregon that develops and sustains supportive intergenerational neighborhoods for families adopting children out of foster care and adults over 55. Our goal is to create a mutually beneficial network of support with a primary focus on helping children formerly in foster care to heal from trauma. This core social purpose focuses the community around the children's' needs, creating a common unifying principle that motivates and inspires people to extend beyond their comfort zones. The relationships that result become safety nets for each individual.

The program focuses on empowering community members to build strong, interdependent relationships so that resources and solutions can be found within the community, rather than from institutions that are often overburdened and difficult to access. We believe that when people feel comfortable asking for and receiving help, bonds form that improve well-being, reducing isolation and creating a sense of extended family and a group of people who care for one another across the age spectrum. For example, in a Bridge Meadows community, younger people check in on elders, parents offer support to other parents and elders, and elders support each other, children and parents.

In order to facilitate these community connections, Bridge Meadows connects parents and elders through a variety of activities and therapeutic programmatic offerings. Intergenerational connection activities in an environment where children have experienced considerable trauma requires knowledge, awareness and intention. Bridge Meadows addresses this by hiring mental health specialists who serve as community facilitators, as well as by training elders and parents in trauma-informed care. In this way, the community has a shared language that helps create a sense of safety and belonging. Community gatherings facilitated by mental health specialists offer both informal and structured opportunities for connection. These include weekly shared meals, support groups , and classes initiated and taught by community members. The combination of shared activities across the generations, therapeutic support, and safe, quality housing, provides the structure and stability that create resilience and healing for all.

要約

ブリッジ・メドウズはオレゴン州ポートランドにある非営利団体で、養護施設から子どもを養子として受け入れる家族や55歳を越える成人にとって支えとなる世代を超えた地域を築き維持しています。私たちの目標は、かつて養護施設にいた子どもたちが負ったトラウマの治癒を主要な焦点としながら、双方にとって有益な支援ネットワークを構築することです。中核となる社会的目的は、人々が自分たちの安全地帯を越えて前進できるように促し励ます共通の統一的原則を作ることであり、コミュニティーの焦点を子どもたちのニーズに合わせています。その結果として生じる人間関係は、各個人にとってのセーフティーネットとなります。

本プログラムは、アクセスが困難でかつ過度な負担を強いられていることが多い施設においてではなく、コミュニティー内でリソースと解決策を発見できるよう、強力で相互依存的な関係を構築する力をコミュニティーの構成員にもたらすことに重点を置いています。気軽に助けを求めたり、手を借りたりすることができるようになれば、そこから結びつきが生まれます。こうした結びつきにより、幸福感が高まり孤立感が和らぐだけでなく、大きな家族であるかのような感覚が生まれ、年齢の幅を超えお互いを思いやる集団が生まれます。例えば、ブリッジ・メドウズのコミュニティーでは、若者が高齢者の様子をたずねたり、保護者が他の保護者や高齢者を手助けしたり、高齢者がお互いだけでなく子どもたちや保護者のサポートもしています。

こうしたコミュニティーのつながりを促進するため、ブリッジ・メドウズは様々な活動や治療的プログラムなどを通じて保護者と高齢者がつながる機会を設けています。子どもたちが大きなトラウマを感じたことのある環境において異世代をつなぐ活動を行うには、知識、理解、目的意識が必要です。ブリッジ・メドウズは、セラピストやコミュニティーファシリテーターとして精神衛生の専門家を雇用するだけでなく、トラウマインフォームドケアについて高齢者と保護者を教育することでこれに対応しています。これによりコミュニティーは、安心感と帰属感を生み出す共通言語を持つことができます。精神衛生の専門家がファシリテーターを務めるコミュニティーの集会では、非公式なものから体系的なものまで、人々がつながる様々な機会が提供されています。これらには、毎週行われる会食や、サポートグループ（「サークル」とも呼ばれている）、コミュニティーの構成員が発案し指導も担うクラスなどが含まれます。多世代が参加する活動や、治療的サポート、そして安全で質の高い住居が組み合わさることで、すべての人に回復力と癒しをもたらす仕組みと安定性が生まれているのです。

Author

Derenda Schubert, PhD and Executive Director of Bridge Meadows

Dr. Derenda Schubert is a psychologist with professional experience including counseling children and families as well as creating, managing, and evaluating programs in the realms of foster care, mental health, and developmental disabilities. She has held several executive leadership roles including Chief Operating Officer and Associate Director of Training at two of Oregon's largest child and family mental health agencies. She is also a former Board Member of Bridge Meadows. Dr. Schubert is an intergenerational champion, leading the team that created Bridge Meadows, advocating nationally for intergenerational solutions to complex social challenges, spearheading strategic planning, and shaping Bridge Meadows' expansive vision for the future. Dr. Schubert speaks locally and nationally on the topics of children's mental health, community building, and intergenerational living. She is an American Leadership Forum Senior Fellow and an Encore Public Voices Fellow. Every day, she is inspired by the love of her grandmothers and her children.

Lindsay Magnuson, Communications Director at Bridge Meadows

Lindsay joined Bridge Meadows in March 2018. She earned her Bachelor of Arts degree in History from San Francisco State University and is fluent in Spanish. Lindsay has over 20 years of experience in branding, marketing, research, grant writing, and PR for clients such as Adidas, Visa, Kaiser Permanente, CLEAResult, and the California Public Utilities Commission. She has managed large-scale international projects and excels at creating strategic and creative programs that address complex challenges. She has worked as a volunteer grief counselor at The Dougy Center, a Spanish teacher, and as a liaison to the homeless population with Operation Nightwatch. Her passions include writing, flamenco dance, yoga, and travel.

Renee Moseley, LCSW and Associate Director of Bridge Meadows

Renee Moseley is a Licensed Clinical Social Worker and Associate Director of Bridge Meadows. Renee manages the organization's community services, research and evaluation, and provides oversite of property management. She is also a member of Bridge Meadows' development team. Prior to joining Bridge Meadows in 2010, Renee provided program management to county and community-based agencies in Los Angeles, California focused on child welfare and adult services.

Chapter 2

CoGenerations:
A Cross-Generational Participatory Action Research Project

Rick Lathrop
David Blake Willis

Introduction

The CoGenerations Project is a participatory action research (PAR)[1] and practice effort designed to increase cross-generational dialogue, mutual mentoring, and engagement to address shared societal concerns. This project emerged from Rick Lathrop's 28 years' experience as the Founder/Executive Director of Global Service Corps (GSC)[2], a 501(c)(3) international service-learning volunteer program. Rick founded GSC in 1993 while a student at Fielding Institute (now Fielding Graduate University)[3] with the support of faculty, fellow students, and a small Fielding startup grant. Over 80% of the GSC program volunteer participants were of the ages 18–30, with programs located in Costa Rica, Thailand, Kenya, Guatemala, Tanzania, Cambodia, and Cuba.

GSC international service programs focused on addressing community and societal needs through collaboration with local organizations and the development of community training programs. Rick learned the value of establishing meaningful cross-cultural and cross-generational relationships while developing service-learning programs in collaboration with community leaders.

In response to the forced indefinite shutdown of GSC due to the Covid Pandemic in March 2020, it seemed appropriate to find a way to build on cross-cultural and cross-generational lessons learned with GSC. After observing extensive protests in early 2020 in Portland, Oregon, and elsewhere, along with societal unrest among young adults (15–35), Rick decided that GSC could build on its 27 years of working intergenerationally to address shared concerns of younger and older people.

The concept was thus hatched for the *CoGenerations Participatory Action Research (PAR) Project: Generations collaborating for the common good through dialogue, mutual mentoring, and collaboration.* The GSC Board approved the initial use of its 501(c)(3) status, office facilities, and its website to support the more domestic-focused work of the CoGenerations Project (hereafter referred to as the Project). An initial Project website page[4] was launched along with a list of Advisors[5], with additional pages being planned.

Method

Initial Project research with young adults identified key concerns shared across generations: climate change, racial and gender issues, economic and educational inequities, and health issues. Further research was initiated to better understand key concerns of young adults and how to best communicate and collaborate intergenerationally. While generations share these concerns, there is often a lack of intergenerational communication and collaboration based on mistrust and unequal access to resources. At the same time, a nationally recognized high school student environmental activist shared how a strong working relationship with his mother was instrumental in his work, evidence of cross-generational success.

The Project continued its PAR work through the further development of the Project Advisors group and initiated a series of dialogue-oriented meetings. While the project goal was to include input from all generations, we found more interest and participation among older than younger adults. Most of the interest in this project came from the following established thought leaders along with the authors of this paper:

- Harry (Rick) Moody, PhD, Distinguished Faculty Fellow at Fielding Graduate University; co-author of Aging: Concepts and Controversies, a gerontology textbook and editor of the Human Values in Aging Newsletter.
- Peter Whitehouse, PhD, Professor of Neurology, Psychiatry, Cognitive Science, Neuroscience, and Organizational Behavior at Case Western Reserve University, co-founder of The Intergenerational Schools in Cleveland, OH, USA.
- Connie Corley, PhD, Professor at Fielding Graduate University and California State University Los Angeles, as well as Associate Director of Lifelong Learning, Applied Gerontology Institute.
- Tim Stanton, PhD, Founder and Past Director of Stanford University's Overseas Studies Program, Cape Town, SA, and co-author of Service-Learning: A Movement's Pioneers Reflect on its Origins, Practice, and Future (1999).

The initial advisor group also included three younger adults and met via Zoom on several occasions to further develop Project directions. We identified some specific goals and possible next steps:

- With the engagement of young adult research assistants, identify younger people (especially high school and college-aged young adults) and organizations run by young adults and/or addressing areas of key concerns of younger people.
  - Identify and apply best practices and lessons learned.
  - Welcome collaboration and partnership.
  - Continue research to identify organizations involved in cross-generational communication and dialogue.
  - Identify and apply best practices and lessons learned.
  - Welcome collaboration and partnership.
  - Develop training modules to prepare both younger and older individuals to dialogue, share expertise, and engage together more effectively.

Results

The advisors group continued to meet to further develop Project directions and helped sponsor various PAR dialogues and planning sessions. This included discussions on how many people, organizations, or communities are likely to be impacted by the project. A core group of Fielding Graduate University students, alumni, and professors engaged with the Project and are interested in further collaboration. Expanded Project meetings included the following Fielding gatherings of alumni, students, prospective students, presenters, and guests totaling 63 participants.

- CoGenerations: A Cross-Generational Participatory Action Research Project was presented at the 2020 Fielding Alumni Summer Session and the 2021 Fielding Winter Session. Fielding President Katrina Rogers has encouraged the Project to hold an intergenerational dialogue summit to be hosted by Fielding.
  - Summit was tentatively planned for late 2021.
  - Emphasis to be on young adult involvement.
- A training development planning session with Fielding faculty, other Project Advisors, and Fielding students took place on March 10, 2021.
- A strategic planning meeting with key advisors then took place on March 31, 2021.
  - Ongoing planning sessions were scheduled throughout 2021 to further develop leadership and skill-building training in the areas

of dialogue, mutual mentoring, storytelling, appreciative inquiry, and coaching.
  - A pilot of this training program was tentatively scheduled for late 2021, ideally to coordinate with the intergenerational dialogue summit.
  - Two training programs were planned for early 2022, building on the pilot program and the research to identify interested younger and older individuals and collaborating organizations.
  - Agreed to work with Professors Corley and Willis, and Fielding staff to develop opportunities for Fielding students, including Project research opportunities for credit as part of their studies.
  - Plan to explore with Fielding the possibility of offering Project training as a certificate program.

During 2021, the Project Advisors group expanded to 18 with a core advisors group of nine; and an initial mailing list of interested parties including potential collaborating organizations totaling 100 contacts. A Project-curated library of intergenerational subjects was established and now includes articles, videos, and papers numbering over 150 items.

Discussion

Many of the Project Advisors and interested individuals have multiple networks with thousands of contacts to draw upon. The Project looks forward to disseminating information and invitations for collaboration through these networks. One key Project connection was made with a group of additional established thought leaders gathered by Peter Whitehouse through InterHub, a group affiliated with the Presencing Institute of the Massachusetts Institute of Technology.

The mission of InterHub is described as follows:

> InterHub[6] is a convening and conversation space created under the umbrella of the GAIA (Global Activation of Intention and Action) project of the Presencing Institute. We share the overarching purpose of transforming civilization through a deep exploration of learning together and appreciating our relationships to each other and nature. InterHub explores intergenerational, intergenerative, and transdisciplinary concepts and practices in the arts and sciences.

Through the connections of InterHub and others, Project advisors participated and made presentations at the following conferences:

- May 4, 2021, R & B Innovation Expo Conference

- June 17, 2021, Generations United's 21st Biennial Global Intergenerational Conference.

Another network of individuals and organizations interested in generational issues comes from Project advisor Harry (Rick) Moody's mailing list of 10,000 people for his *Human Values in Ageing Newsletter.*

Global Service Corps (GSC) also has a mailing list of over 10,000 available for promoting the work of the Project. A particular GSC connection of note is AmeriCorps, which has provided scores of GSC service-learning volunteers. Rick Lathrop has been a presenter for over five years at the annual Life After AmeriCorps (LAA) programs and may be invited to offer CoGenerations trainings in the future. Approximately 500 Corps members participate in the LAA programs each year.

The Project has not attracted the numbers of younger adults to participate as hoped, unfortunately. Young adults live and communicate in a different world than older adults. Especially since Covid-19, most young adult communication and activity has been through social media. The Project decided to learn more about social media and use this to reach out to encourage intergenerational dialogue, mutual mentoring, and engagement. This has become a central focus for future Project work.

With the assistance of two of young adult advisors, the Project launched a Facebook page, a Facebook Group page, and an Instagram page. We have also created a CoGenerations Newsletter Draft which can be found at the CoGenerations page on the GSC website[4]. We are reaching out to younger adults to assist us in further developing our social media platforms and messages before sending out the newsletter to various mailing lists.

Two specific projects initiated and supported by CoGenerations:

- The Collaborative Online Domestic and International Service-Learning (CODIS-L) program
    - Supporting community organizations addressing critical local and global issues, starting with the climate crisis, through intergenerational dialogue and action.
    - Organization and remote team members gather online to plan and act to support organizational missions and goals.
    - Initial pilot project organizational partners: Africatown[7] and Meraki People.[8]
- The Climate Dialogue Action Group
    - Utilizing intergenerational dialogue to further explore and uncover new meaning toward addressing the climate crisis

- Series of four dialogic inquiry events sponsored by Fielding Graduate University with youth, business, government, indigenous, and religious thought leaders

Since the initiation of these projects, each has expanded with a continuing interest in developing intergenerational dialogue and action. The CODIS-L project through GSC was well-positioned to address a major global issue: the war in Ukraine. We realized that CODIS-L could be adjusted for use with Ukrainian refugees and the Ukraine Refugee Support Service-Learning Program was born. [9]

Beginning in April of 2022 we gathered an advisory group[10] including representatives of two Ukraine organizations, TESOL-Ukraine and Women's Perspective, as well as individual Ukrainians, Ukrainian Americans, and other Americans interested in supporting this work.

Women's Perspectives shared results of a survey which identified the needs and interests of refugees. Conversational English training came up regularly as an area of interest and as a means of addressing trauma and improving mental health. TESOL-Ukraine posted a survey on their Facebook page to identify refugees interested in conversational English training. They identified over 100 refugees who expressed interest and provided their contact information. TESOL-Ukraine also recruited Ukrainian professional English teachers who volunteered to work with us to provide this training. Seven of our Advisory Group members with experience teaching English and/or international experience agreed to work with these Ukrainian teachers to provide conversational English workshops to Ukrainian refugees.

On July 10, 2022, we launched an eight-week virtual conversational English practice workshop pilot project. Six teams of workshop facilitators made up of one or two US English speakers and one Ukrainian English trainer. These facilitators are working with groups of three to ten Ukrainian refugees, mostly IDPs (internally displaced persons) in Ukraine who have requested assistance with conversational English. The virtual workshops take place via Zoom on Sunday evenings Ukraine time, drawing on conversational English teaching resources and the personal experiences of the facilitators. We are greatly impressed by the resilience of our new Ukrainian friends and their willingness to share and learn with us. This includes representatives of three generations of participants.

Finally, the Climate Dialogue Action Group has continued to evolve and has hosted several dialogue sessions including Equatorial and Indigenous people with future sessions planned to include representatives of business[11] and Generation Z youth.[12]

References

1 https://www.ncbi.nlm.nih.gov/pmc/articles/PMC2566051/; https://us.sagepub.com/en-us/nam/participatory-action-research/book230910
2 https://globalservicecorps.org/
3 https://www.fielding.edu/
4 https://globalservicecorps.org/intergenerational-dialogue/
5 https://globalservicecorps.org/cogens-cogenerations-advisors/
6 https://www.presencing.org/community/hubs/interhub--intergenerational-and-transdisciplinary--futuring
7 https://en.wikipedia.org/wiki/Africatown
8 https://www.merakipeople.gr/
9 https://globalservicecorps.org/ukraine-refugee-support-service-learning-project/
10 https://globalservicecorps.org/ukraine-refugee-support-service-learning-program-advisory-group/
11 https://www.msn.com/en-us/money/smallbusiness/why-every-leader-could-benefit-from-adopting-a-gen-z-mindset/ar-AAStkhc
12 https://pubify.net/how-gen-z-is-schooling-their-elders-on-climate-action

Summary

The CoGenerations Project is a participatory action research (PAR) and practice effort designed to increase cross-generational dialogue, mutual mentoring, and engagement to address shared societal concerns.

This project emerged from Rick Lathrop's 28 years' experience as the Founder/Executive Director of Global Service Corps (GSC), an international service-learning volunteer program. Rick founded GSC in 1993 while a student at Fielding Institute (now Fielding Graduate University). GSC international service programs focused on addressing community and societal needs through collaboration with local organizations and the development of community training programs. In response to the forced shutdown of GSC due to the Covid Pandemic in March 2020, it seemed appropriate to locate a new way to build on cross-cultural and cross-generational lessons learned with GSC.

Initial Project research with young adults identified key concerns shared across generations: climate change, racial and gender issues, economic and educational inequities, and health issues. Further research was initiated to better understand key concerns of young adults and how to best communicate and collaborate intergenerationally. While concerns are shared, there is often a lack of intergenerational communication/collaboration based on mistrust and unequal access to resources.

The Project continued its PAR work through the further development of the Project Advisors group and initiated a series of dialogue-oriented meetings. While the project goal was to include input from all generations, we found more interest and participation among older than younger adults.

The advisors group continued to meet to further develop Project directions and helped sponsor various PAR dialogues and planning sessions. This included discussions on how many people, organizations, or communities are likely to be impacted by the project. Many of the Project advisors and interested individuals have multiple networks with thousands of contacts to draw upon. The Project looks forward to disseminating information and invitations for collaboration through these networks. The Project has not attracted the numbers of younger adults to participate as hoped. Especially since Covid-19, most young adult communication and activity has been through social media. The Project decided to learn more about social media and use this to reach out to encourage intergenerational dialogue, mutual mentoring, and engagement. The Collaborative Online Domestic and International Service-Learning (CODIS-L) program and the Climate Dialogue Action Group have emerged from our work. CODIS-L has been adjusted for use with Ukrainian refugees and the Ukraine Refugee Support Service-Learning Program was born. The Climate Dialogue Action Group has continued to evolve and has hosted several dialogue sessions including Equatorial and Indigenous people with future sessions planned.

要約

CoGenerations プロジェクトは、世代を超えた対話、相互の助言、そして共通の社会的問題に取り組むための関与を高めることを目的とした、参加型アクションリサーチ（PAR）と実践的な取り組みです。

このプロジェクトは、国際的なサービス・ラーニングのボランティアプログラムである Global Service Corps（GSC）の創設者で、エグゼクティブ・ディレクターである Rick Lathrop 氏の 28 年間の経験から生まれました。Rick は、フィールディング・インスティテュート（現フィールディング大学院大学）在学中の 1993 年に GSC を設立しました。GSC の国際奉仕プログラムは、地域の組織と協力し、地域のトレーニングプログラムを開発することで、地域や社会のニーズに応えることことに重点を置いていました。

2020 年 3 月にコロナウイルスの世界的流行のため、GSC の活動停止が強制されたことを受け、GSC の活動から得られた異文化と世代を超えた教訓を基に、新たな方法を模索することが適切と思われました。

若年層を対象にしたプロジェクトの最初の調査で、世代を超えて共有されるべき主要な懸念事項が明らかにされました。それらは気候変動、人種やジェンダーの問題、経済や教育の不公平、健康問題です。さらに若年層の主な関心事をより深く理解し、世代を超えたコミュニケーションと協力のあり方について調査を開始しました。懸念は共有されているものの、不信感や、資源への不平等なアクセスが基になった、世代間のコミュニケーションや協力の欠如がしばしばあります。

プロジェクトは、プロジェクト・アドバイザーズ・グループのさらなる発展を通してその PAR 活動を継続し、そして、一連の対話重視のミーティングを開始しています。プロジェクトの目標は、すべての世代から意見を取り入れることでしたが、若年層よりも高齢者の関心と参加が高いことがわかりました。

アドバイザーズ・グループは、プロジェクトの方向性をさらに深めるために会合を重ね、さまざまな PAR ダイアログや集まりの企画の後援を支援しました。これには、プロジェクトによって影響を受ける可能性のある人、組織、コミュニティがどれくらいあるのか、という議論も含まれました。プロジェクトのアドバイザーや関心を持つ人々の多くは、利用可能な何千もの人とのつながりがある、多くのネットワークを持っています。プロジェクトは、これらのネットワークを通じて、協力のための情報や呼びかけを広めることを期待しています。プロジェクトは、期待されているほどには多くの若年層の参加を得られていません。特に Covid-19 以降、若年層のコミュニケーションや活動の大半はソーシャルメディアを通じて行われてきています。プロジェクトは、ソーシャルメディアについてもっと学び、これを利用して、世代を超えた対話、相互の助言、参加を促すことを決めました。これは、今後のプロジェクトの中心的な取り組みになっています。私たちの活動から、CODIS-L (Collaborative Online Domestic and International Service-Learning) プログラムと Climate Dialogue アクション・グループが生まれました。CODIS-L はウクライナ難民のために調整され、ウクライナ難民支援サービス・ラーニング・プログラムが生まれました。Climate Dialogue アクショングループは進化を続け、赤道直下の人々や先住民を含むいくつかの対話セッションを開催し、今後もセッションを予定しています。

Author

Richard K. Lathrop

Founder and Executive Director, Global Service Corps, and President, GSC International, prior to forming Global Service Corps (GSC), Rick had experience as a high school teacher, a Navy Officer, a print advertising account representative, a nonprofit administrator, and an adult holistic educator and leadership trainer. Rick's graduate studies were part of the Human and Organization Development PhD program at The Fielding Graduate University in Santa Barbara, California. At Fielding, Rick became interested in global studies, particularly in the area of sustainable development, and discovered that there were few educational programs available for adults to gain firsthand experience in the field of international development. With the assistance of a small startup grant from Fielding, he began the development of a program of short-term, "mini–Peace Corps" types of experiences to provide Fielding students and others international grass roots exposure to global issues. The concept soon expanded to include participation of adults from all walks of life interested in this kind of experience. Rick continued developing the GSC program part time while completing his studies and finished his master's degree in Organization Development in August of 1994. With the indefinite shutdown of GSC due to Covid in March 2020, Rick has been applying GSC lessons learned to the new CoGenerations Project.

David Blake Willis

Professor of Anthropology and Education at Fielding Graduate University (2008-Present) and Soai Buddhist University (Japan, 1986-2009), taught and did research at Oxford, Grinnell, Kyoto University, Kobe University, and the University of Washington. His interests in anthropology, sustainability, social justice, immigration, leadership, and the communitas of organizations, cultures, and systems, particularly on a global scale, come from 38+ years living in traditional cultural systems in Japan and South India. David's work has included transformational leadership, transformative education, human development in transnational contexts, the Creolization of cultures, comparative education, citizenship, transcultural communities, transnational diaspora, and Dalit/Gandhian liberation in India. Volunteer work has been important, too, for David, including responses to the Kobe Earthquake (1995), the Indian Ocean Earthquake and Tsunami (2004), the 3/11 Earthquake and Tsunami in Northern Japan (2011), and more recently work as a trainer for Friendly Water for the World in India and the United States. David's collaborative publications with colleagues include Leadership in Sustainability (2015, 2021); World Cultures: The Language Villages (2016); Reimagining Japanese Education: Borders, Transfers, Circulations, and the Comparative (2011); and Transcultural Japan: At the Borders of Race, Gender, and Identity (2007).

Chapter 3

Teaching Caring: Successful Intergenerational Service-Learning Projects

A. Patricia Aguilera-Hermida

I am a professor in the United States. I was in the last class with my students and we were talking about their learning experience. They worked with older adults in a retirement community in a service-learning project. One student was thanking me for the class. She mentioned that she did not have grandparents and before this class, she did not have any type of interaction with older adults. She expressed that she was scared of them. But now, she was considering working with this population for the rest of her career. She loved working with older adults. A service-learning intergenerational experience can be transformative for students and have a long-lasting effect.

Teaching caring refers not only to teaching about aging or implementing an intergenerational program but also caring about the older population. This chapter will describe ageism and some of its consequences, and the relevance of intergenerational service-learning projects in higher education. Finally, I will explain some projects that I do with my students.

The world is aging, but are our societies prepared for it? Economically? Do we have enough services? Are we mentally prepared? Currently, there is a growing population of older adults around the world (Kumagai, 2016; United Nations, 2019), there is a shortage of professionals to work with them (Lester et al., 2020; Mori & Shima, 2020), the image of elders is not always positive (Butler, 1969), and there is an intergenerational divide.

Furthermore, many of our societies around the world face ageism, discrimination based on age. Ageism refers to negative attitudes against older adults based on stereotypes and prejudices (Aguilera-Hermida, 2020; Burnes, et al., 2019; Butler, 1969). Ageism, like many other forms of discrimination, starts with stereotypes that become prejudice (Rosell, et al. 2020). People assign negative or positive attributes to a group of individuals. Those attributes are internalized as a reality and based on prejudices, individuals think of, feel, and treat people accordingly. For example, there is the misconception that older adults are vulnerable or fragile. However, a person who is 68 will not have the same level of frailty that a person who is 95. Once we assign the attribute to the group of people, we start thinking that all older adults share the same characteristics (Rahman & Jahan, 2021).

Why do we have to talk about ageism if this chapter is about intergenerational programs? The answer is because ageism is ingrained in many cultures and has negative consequences for people, whether they are older adults or not. Ageism is internalized throughout the entire lifespan, and can operate unconsciously (Aguilera-Hermida, 2020; Rosell et al., 2020).

Due to ageism, older adults face other problems such as fewer job opportunities, lower quality in health care services (diagnosis and treatment), fewer resources allocated for the aging population, among others. There is a devaluation of the knowledge and experience of older adults. Society is alienating them (Nair, 2014; Powell, 2014). Ageist attitudes negatively affect the image and relationship between young and older adults (fear, distaste, mistreatment, avoidance, etc.) (Macdonald & Levy, 2020). But most importantly, ageism has negative consequences in the way people age and in the way they see themselves.

How can we face this new reality? Intergenerational programs provide a set of countermeasures for challenging such negative, deficit-oriented conceptions of old age. They not only are a pathway for a more sustainable and integrated society (Kaplan et al., 2017; Kuraoka, 2020) but also for stopping or reducing ageism. Many programs around the world prove that intergenerational programs between older adults and younger people have positive benefits for both generations (Giraudeau & Bailly, 2019; Gualano et al., 2018; Kaplan et al., 2017). Generations United (2021) reported that young adults and college students showed higher rates of civic engagement, increased entrepreneurial capabilities and occupational skills, and expressed higher levels of self-confidence and efficacy. Older adults decreased social isolation, improved quality of life, purpose in life, self-worth, self-esteem, and cognitive health. They also reduced falls and frailty. All ages showed a greater sense of belonging and connection with others of different ages after they participated in intergenerational programs.

During service-learning projects, students learn while they are doing service in the community. Innovative educational models, such as service-learning projects, open up channels to stimulate academic, social, and personal learning (June, 2020; Martínez-Usarralde & Chiva-Bartoll, 2020; Gresh et al., 2021; Ruiz-Montero et al., 2019). Service-learning projects allow students to acquire technical (useful), practical (ethical and directed to people), and critical knowledge (guided by justice, inclusion, and equality) (Martínez-Usarralde & Chiva-Bartoll, 2020). Intergenerational projects can be delivered as service-learning projects in high schools and universities.

Intergenerational service-learning projects promote a commitment to social justice and change through awareness-raising activities. Burnes et al., (2019) found that interventions based on education, intergenerational programs, and a combination of both were effective to reduce ageism. Students are in contact with older adults, and they have the opportunity to question and reduce their ageist beliefs (Ruiz-Montero et al., 2019; Ruiz-Montero et al., 2020; Yoelin, 2021).

It is imperative to question and transform young adults' unquestioned ageist attitudes so they can become professionals who want to work with older adults. As Söllner (2014) suggested, educational institutions should generate materials, processes, and environments that promote ethical principles such as inclusion, honesty, integrity, cooperation, respect, justice, and sustainability. Effective learning experiences offer foundations for responsible and transformational leadership among young adults. Students need not only to learn about aging but also about caring about older adults. The goal is to create an inclusive and respectful society for all stages of development.

The following section mentions different intergenerational service-learning projects that I have implemented in Behavioral Sciences and Education courses at Pennsylvania State University. I hope it is helpful for other professionals.

Experiential Learning

Objective: Participants will learn about adult development and aging while volunteering within a retirement community or other service-provider for older adults.

Suggested population: High school and/or higher education. Any semester. Students from general education or interdomain classes and from different majors.

Delivery Method: Face-to-face

Procedure: The professor contacts a provider who is willing to accept student volunteers (senior centers, schools for older adults, retirement communities, etc.). Both professionals establish schedules and activities that students can do. They also plan a facility tour for students where they can see the facility, understand the rules, and be aware of training/requirements they have to complete. After that, students sign up for activities and volunteer for a minimum of 5 hours per semester. Students have to complete a journal where they reflect on their learning experiences. By the end of the course, they have to investigate a topic related to the aging population and integrate their experiential activities. They present the project to their classmates.

Results: Students enjoy choosing a topic and informing their classmates about it. Student quote: "I had a great experience working with [name] and seeing the older population in a different light. I feel happy I took this class".

Recommendations: Students must participate in enjoyable activities such as group music sessions, happy hours, craft time, chorus, bonfire, festivals, photography trips, etc., so they have opportunities for positive interactions. If the activities are only transporting seniors, helping them to eat, or something similar, the experience may reinforce negative stereotypes that students might have about older adults. In cases where some personnel are not fully cooperative, it is particularly important to have at least one or two true allies who are committed to the program and can promote it among the older adults. Furthermore, older adults should be willing to participate in the activities with students.

Guided Autobiography and Scrapbook

Objective: Students will learn through applied service and fieldwork in the community with older adults.

Suggested population: Higher education. Students from behavioral and social sciences (psychology, gerontology, human development, education, health sciences, etc.).

Delivery method: Face-to-face.

Procedure: Students will participate in a two-month intervention based on Positive Psychology and Narrative Therapy. The format is a workshop (8 two-hour sessions) where college students and older adults develop a guided autobiography and a scrapbook. As emerging professionals, students will use strategies to promote a positive group experience and sensitize older adult participants to develop a heightened sense of self-awareness, social acceptance, and self-esteem. There is a specific list of questions/prompts that students will use every session (Birren & Deutchman, 1991). They are related to health, body image, successes and challenges, the meaning of life, family, etc. For example, students would ask about family (What was best about your family? Family heroes? Family favorites?) or love (Who in your life made you feel loved and why? How have your ideas of love changed over time?) In return, students will learn about the aging population by listening to the older adults' experiences. During the sessions, both generations will portray the older adult experiences in a scrapbook. At the end of the workshop, all the participants will showcase their final products.

Results: Students and older adults usually develop an emotional bond that creates a positive view of the other generation. Older adult quote: "I am grateful. Your students are different, they are not like other students". Student quote: "The scrapbook project was one of the most life-changing moments I've had".

Recommendations: The student's questions/prompts are crucial for an enjoyable conversation and process. Furthermore, students need time to talk about their experiences/questions/challenges with the professor. The professor and/or the authority from the facility has to be present during the time that students and older adults are working, so they can respond to any emergencies/problems. I recommend the professor pair two students per older adult so they can help each other.

Educational Lectures

Objective: Students will conduct a literature review and present the latest research findings on specific topics that increase and/or maintain older adults' health and well-being.

Suggested population: Higher education. Students from advanced classes and/or interested in older adults.

Delivery method: It is preferred a face-to-face modality, but it can be delivered online.

Procedure: The professor develops a partnership with a school for older adults, senior center, or retirement community and establishes the dates and times to deliver the information. Students are organized in teams (2-3) and present each week (6-8 weeks depending on the number of students). They will review and synthesize empirical research and present it to older adults in understandable language. Students choose their topic and should include an interactive/experiential component (e.g. if they are talking about the benefits of meditation, they may include a meditation practice).

Results: Both groups highly value the interaction and the knowledge.

Recommendations: Give the students at least 4 or 5 weeks to develop the literature review. Work in the classroom with them so they know how to work in groups. Invite them to choose a topic that they are personally interested in, so they get engaged with the literature. After that, they will look for what has been done with older adults. The professor should authorize all the presentations and activities before they are carried out (make sure they are appropriate and accurate).

Intervention to Promote Wellbeing

Objective: Students will develop and implement an intervention to promote wellbeing.

Suggested population: High school and/or higher education. Students from behavioral and social sciences (psychology, gerontology, human development, education, health sciences, etc.).

Delivery method: Face-to-face or online. This was successful online during COVID-19 pandemic. It helped young and older adults overcome loneliness and/or isolation.

Procedure: The professor explains the theoretical framework (Positive psychology) and provides the structure of the intervention so students can create a safe and friendly space. The whole intervention will be organized by the students (teams of 4). They develop the recruitment methods and promote the intervention (students' grandparents, local library, retirement community, a school for older adults, etc.).

Each week one team will be the leader, but all the sessions will have the same structure: Activities to promote a positive narrative (people think and/or talk positively about themselves), a positive mood (body-learning strategies or art-evoking strategies that make people feel good), and activities where participants have fun (jokes, games, riddles, funny stories, etc.). Furthermore, all the activities have to be for people from 8 years old to 95 years old (if there are a lot of participants, the leading team can do subgroups/breakout rooms). The leading team will choose and prepare the specific activities for their session. The activities should promote interaction and participation in a safe and friendly space. Students have to complete a final paper including the objective, justification, theoretical background, procedure (including supporting materials for the activities), and results, so it is documented and they can repeat it in the future.

Results: Here are two comments from participating students:

> "One of the most influential aspects of this intervention was our older participants who presented advice for the younger students.

> This really made the younger students open up with their personal experiences. When we can be vulnerable around each other then we can grow closer to other people and form healthy social bonds. ... The more we can adapt to, look forward to, and embrace change, the more successful we will become at maintaining happiness, growth, balance, and inner peace."
>
> "Overall, the intervention was a great success. It provided everyone with a good experience and resources to use in the future. Each group did a fantastic job providing fun and interesting activities that everyone could enjoy. This intervention was a great way to reach out to our community and provided a space for social interaction with older adults without the risk of COVID-19 pandemic."

Recommendations: The professor should be clear that the intervention is for everybody, not only for older adults, so students engage all the participants (classmates and older adults). Avoid the thought that students are "helping" older adults. It reinforces frailty. Older and young adults must see each other as capable to bring something positive to the interaction. The knowledge of both generations should be equally valued.

Conclusion

Most of the students reported a positive experience during the intergenerational service-learning projects and they were no longer afraid or reluctant to work with other adults in the future. Professors should be aware that students will see the world through their young lenses and their developmental perspective. For example, a young adult's perspective may be that everyone wants new and different experiences like they do. Because of this, they may judge the lifestyle of an older adult who does not share their views. They may say something like "poor senior, they must feel very lonely and depressed", when in reality the older adult is happy and very social in the community. Professors should talk with students about these misconceptions, so students are clear that what is important for life satisfaction at one age does not necessarily have to be important for life satisfaction at another age.

A more sustainable, connected, and inclusive society cannot be created in one day or with one program. But service-learning intergenerational projects represent a step in the right direction, whereby young adults tend to gain a more balanced and positive attitude towards older adults and an openness toward building relationships with them.

References

Aguilera-Hermida, A. P. (2020). Fighting Ageism through Intergenerational Activities, a Transformative Experience. Journal of Transformative Learning, 7(2), 6-18.

Birren, J. & Deutchman, D. E. (1991). Guiding autobiography groups for older adults. Baltimore: The Johns Hopkins University Press

Burnes, D., Sheppard, C., Henderson Jr, C. R., Wassel, M., Cope, R., Barber, C., & Pillemer, K. (2019). Interventions to reduce ageism against older adults: A systematic review and meta-analysis. American Journal of Public Health, 109(8), e1-e9.

Butler, Robert N. "Age-ism: Another Form of Bigotry." Gerontologist 9.4 (1969): 243–46.

Germán Bes, C., Hueso Navarro, F., & Huércanos Esparza, I. (2011). El cuidado en peligro en la sociedad global. Enfermería Global, 10(23), 221-232.

Giraudeau, C., & Bailly, N. (2019). Intergenerational programs: What can school-age children and older people expect from them? A systematic review. European journal of ageing, 1-14.

Generations United (2021). Fact Sheet: Intergenerational Programs benefit everyone. Gonzales E., Kruchten, & Whetung, C. Retrieved from: https://www.gu.org/app/uploads/2021/03/2021-MakingTheCase-FactSheet-WEB.pdf

Gresh, A., LaFave, S., Thamilselvan, V., Batchelder, A., Mermer, J., Jacques, K., Greensfelder, A., Buckley, M., Cohen, Z., Coy, A., & Warren, N. (2021). Service learning in public health nursing education: How COVID-19 accelerated community-academic partnership. Public Health Nursing (Boston, Mass.), 38(2), 248-257. https://doi.org/10.1111/phn.12796

Gualano, M. R., Voglino, G., Bert, F., Thomas, R., Camussi, E., & Siliquini, R. (2018). The impact of intergenerational programs on children and older adults: A review. International Psychogeriatrics, 30(4), 451-468. https://doi.org/10.1017/S104161021700182X

June, A. (2020). Participation in intergenerational Service-Learning benefits older adults: A brief report. Gerontology & Geriatrics Education, 41(2), 169-74. http://doi.org/10.108/02701960.2018.1457529

Kaplan, M., Sanchez, M., & Hoffman, J. (2017). Intergenerational pathways to a sustainable society. Springer International Publishing.

Kumagai, F. (2016). Family issues on marriage, divorce, and older adults in Japan. Springer Verlag, Singapor.

Kuraoka, M. (2020). Multigenerational Cyclical Support System: Programs in Japan for "Designing a Sustainable Society through Intergenerational

Co-creation". In Kaplan, M., L.L. Thang, M. Sanchez, & J. Hoffman (Eds.), Intergenerational Contact Zones: Place-based strategies for promoting social inclusion and belonging (pp. 217-227). New York: Routledge.

Lester, P. E., Dharmarajan, T. S., & Weinstein, E. (2020). The looming geriatrician shortage: Ramifications and solutions. Journal of Aging and Health, 32(9), 1052-1062. https://doi.org/10.1177/0898264319879325

Macdonald J. & Levy S.R. (2020). Addressing stereotypes of aging and interest in careers working with older adults through education, Gerontology & Geriatrics Education, 42(3), 363-379, DOI: 10.1080/02701960.2020.1854246

Martínez-Usarralde, M. J., & Chiva-Bartoll, Ó. (2020). Inclusivity and social justice through service-learning in the era of biopolitics. Humanistic Futures of Learning, UNESCO. 116-120.

Mori, J., & Shima, C. (2020). Text, talk, and body in shift handover interaction: Language and multimodal repertoires for geriatric care work. Journal of Sociolinguistics, 24(5), 593-612. https://doi.org/10.1111/josl.12434

Nair, L. V. (2014). Ageing in India- A conceptual clarification in the background of globalization. European Scientific Journal. 10(2) 379-392.

Powell, J. (2014). Towards a globalization of aging. Canadian Journal of Sociology/Cahiers Canadiens De Sociologie, 39(2), 255-267.

Rosell, J., Vergés, A., Irribarra, D. T., Flores, K., & Gómez, M. (2020). Adaptation and psychometric characteristics of a scale to evaluate ageist stereotypes. Archives of Gerontology and Geriatrics, 90, 104179.

Ruiz-Montero, P., Chiva-Bartoll, O., Salvador-García, C., & Martín-Moya, R. (2019). Service-learning with college students toward health-care of older adults: A systematic review. International Journal of Environmental Research and Public Health, 16(22), 4497. https://doi.org/10.3390/ijerph16224497

Ruiz-Montero, P. J., Chiva-Bartoll, O., Salvador-García, C., & González-García, C. (2020). Learning with older adults through intergenerational service learning in physical education teacher education. Sustainability (Basel, Switzerland), 12(3), 1127. https://doi.org/10.3390/su12031127

Söllner, A. (2014). Globalization, greed, and exploitation. How to break the baleful path? Journal of Business Economics, 84(9), 1211-1235.

United Nations (2019). Department of Economic and Social Affairs, Population Division (2019). World Population Prospects, Volume II: Demographic Profiles (ST/ESA/SER.A/427)

Yoelin, A. B. (2021). Intergenerational service-learning within an aging course and its impact on undergraduate students' attitudes about aging. Journal of Intergenerational Relationships, 1-16. https://doi.org/10.1080/15350770.2021.1881019

Summary

This chapter presents a detailed explanation of how to implement intergenerational service-learning projects that have been successful at Penn State Harrisburg, a university in the United States of America. Intergenerational service-learning projects are designed to help students to acquire technical, practical, and critical knowledge while impacting positively the community where they live. Furthermore, intergenerational programs between older and young adults are a positive alternative to fight against ageism (discrimination based on age) and promote social justice.

Each intervention describes the objective, suggested population, delivery method, procedure, results, and recommendations. Professors should avoid the narrative are "helping" older adults. It reinforces frailty (and ageism). Older and young adults must see each other as capable to bring something positive to the interaction. The knowledge of both generations should be equally valued. The four projects are:

1. Experiential learning. Students volunteer for a minimum of 5 hours doing enjoyable activities with seniors in retirement communities and investigate a topic related to the aging population where they integrate their experiential activities.
2. Guided autobiography and scrapbook. Students will participate in a workshop (8 two-hour sessions) where college students and older adults develop a guided autobiography and a scrapbook about the older adults' life and experiences. By working together, students and older adults create a positive bond that allows them to see each other's generation in a positive way.
3. Educational lectures. Students will conduct a literature review and present the latest research findings on specific topics that increase and/or maintain older adults' health and well-being. It can be delivered online or face-to-face and it should include activities that the audience can do on a daily basis (for example, the topic is balance and students will include some balance exercises). Therefore, the research should have practical implications.
4. Online intervention to promote wellbeing. Teams of 3 or 4 students will deliver an intervention. It includes activities to promote a positive narrative (people think and/or talk positively about themselves), a positive mood (body-learning strategies or art-evoking strategies that make people feel good), and activities where participants have fun

(jokes, games, riddles, funny stories, etc.).

In all the interventions, students and older adults reported a positive experience. Also, students had transformative and positive outcome, and were prone to work with older adults in the future. Intergenerational service-learning programs are a pathway to a more inclusive, integrated, and sustainable society.

要約

本章では、アメリカ合衆国にある大学、ペンシルベニア州立大学ハリスバーグ校で成功を収めた世代間サービス・ラーニングプロジェクトの実施方法について詳しく説明します。

世代間サービス・ラーニングプロジェクトは、学生たちが生活するコミュニティーにポジティブな影響を与え、学生が技術的知識、実用的知識、不可欠な知識を身に付けられるよう設計されています。さらに、高齢者と若者による世代間プログラムはエイジイズム（年齢に基づいた差別）と闘い、社会的正義を推進するためのポジティブな選択肢でもあります。

各介入時には、目標や、推奨される対象者、伝達方法、手段、結果、そして推奨事項が説明されます。教授は、学生が高齢者を「助けている」というナラティブを避けなければなりません。これは高齢者の虚弱さ（そしてエイジイズム）を助長します。高齢者も若者も、お互いをこの場にポジティブなものをもたらすことができる存在だと思わなければなりません。両世代の知識は、同等に評価されるべきである。４つのプロジェクトは以下のとおりです。

1. 体験学習。学生は、退職者向け居住施設の高齢者と楽しい活動に取り組みながら最低５時間のボランティア活動をし、高齢化に関するトピックを調査して、体験活動に組み込みます。
2. 指導による自伝とスクラップブック。ワークショップ（２時間のセッション×８回）に参加し、大学生は高齢者と共に、高齢者の人生と経験についての自伝とスクラップブックを指導の下に作成します。共同作業を通じて、学生と高齢者につながりが生まれ、お互いの世代をポジティブに考えられるようになります。
3. 教育的講義。学生は、高齢者の健康と幸福感の向上・維持に資する特定のテーマについて、文献レビューを行い、最新の研究結果をプレゼンします。発表はオンライン上または対面で行い、発表内容には聞き手が日常的に実践可能な活動を含めるべきです（テーマがバランスの場合は、バランス感覚を養う運動を紹介するなど）。このため、実用的意義をもつ研究である必要があります。
4. 幸福感を増進するオンライン上の介入。３人または４人の学生から成るチームが介入を行います。ポジティブなナラティブ（自分自身についてポジティブに考えたり語ったりする）、ポジティブな雰囲気（楽しい気分にさせるボディラーニングの手法やアートを呼び醒ますような手法の活用）、そして参加者が楽しめる活動（ジョーク、ゲーム、なぞなぞ、面白い話等）などが含まれます。

どの介入も、学生と高齢者に好評でした。また、学生は変化をもたらす影響やポジティブな影響を受け、将来的には高齢者に関わる仕事につきたいと考えるようになりました。世代間サービス・ラーニングプログラムは、より共生的で、誰もが受け入れられる持続可能な社会への道を拓くものです。

Author

Ana Patricia Aguilera-Hermida

Dr. Patricia Aguilera-Hermida is a professor in undergraduate and graduate levels in Human Development and Family Studies and Psychology. She has a master's degree in family therapy and a doctorate in Lifelong Learning and Adult Education. Her research focuses on intergenerational studies, education for older adults, use and acceptance of technology, and her passion: neuroplasticity and cognitive reserve. She promotes healthy aging and is a fighter against ageism.

Dr. Aguilera has participated in different projects with high social impact; for example, she was the creator of a school for older adults in Mexico City that has more than 1200 adults. Recently, she created a training program to maintain cognitive functions. In this chapter, Dr. Aguilera shares detailed steps on how to successfully implement intergenerational projects within universities. Intergenerational programs are a powerful tool to create more inclusive societies for all ages. Therefore, Dr. Aguilera shares specific tips that can help any professional interested in intergenerational projects.

Chapter 4

Conserving and restoring social systems: Lessons learned from "naturalizing" intergenerational relations in three diverse programs in Canada

Theresa Southam

Abstract

In 2018, two facilitators from Nelson, British Columbia, Pat Gibson and Theresa Southam, trained at the Intergenerational Leadership Institute at Penn State University. Over 2500 miles away from their home town, they joined facilitators from across North America with the common cause of increasing intergenerational relations in their communities. Upon their return, the two Nelson facilitators worked with Learning in Retirement (LIR), a group of over four hundred adults age 50+ who join LIR to explore old and new interests in a relaxed and stimulating learning environment. In early 2019, the facilitators offered an eight-week training on building intergenerational relationships through LIR for 12 registrants. Three of the training participants were subsequently interviewed in 2021. They were representatives of (1) a local chapter of Citizens Climate Lobby (CCL), (2)

Nelson Izu-shi Friendship Society (a group which promotes friendship between Canada and Japan), and (3) the Columbia Basin Alliance for Literacy (CBAL) Tech Tutoring program. The researcher wanted to discover whether the nature of intergenerational relations in the participants' programs had changed since their training.

In this chapter, the three case studies of intergenerational programming are also informed by two major research efforts. Simard's 2018 research on exchanges of communication and resources between trees of many ages in old growth forests allows us to better understand ideal "naturalized" intergenerational systems. Lowenhaupt-Tsing's (2015) ethnography of communities set-up to forage for mushrooms as well as efforts to restore the Satoyama Woodlands in Japan, is offered to the reader as a metaphor for "naturalizing" not only our relations amongst generations but with the environments in which we live.

Background

The ultimate goal of intergenerational programming may be to restore the intergenerational nature of social systems so that they are more resilient and sustainable (Kaplan, Sanchez, & Hoffman, 2018; Mitrofanenko, Muhar, & Penker, 2015; Tchernina & Tchernin, 2002). Although multigenerational relations are not necessarily intergenerational, i.e. we can live side by side but not cooperate for the greater good (Villar, 2007) the return to multigenerational households is a case in point. For example, in the US, the number of multigenerational households has returned to its 1950s state of about 20% of the population having fallen to only 12% in 1980 (Cohn & Passel, 2018). 64 million Americans living multigenerationally, such as adults living with their parents, may be a coping strategy for surviving racial inequities, economic strife, and disastrous events related to the climate crisis.

However, increased multigenerational living may not, alone, be enough to rebuild intergenerational intelligence (Biggs, Haapala, & Lowenstein, 2011) and solidarity (Hodgkin, 2014)- both potential benefits of intergenerational relations. Intergenerational programming can be a tool introduced outside the home and later practiced inside one's home, to reintroduce and nurture intergenerational relations. Intergenerational relations can counteract a trend towards individualistic problem-solving that has been reinforced by capitalist doctrines (Leath, 2017; North & Fiske, 2012). The effectiveness of intergenerational programming to "naturalize" may rely on the degree, continuity, and depth of engagement (Kaplan, 2004).

Depth of Engagement

The Intergenerational Depths of Engagement Model (IDEM) recognizes that demographic and social changes over the past century have weakened intergenerational ties in families and communities (Kaplan, 2002). The IDEM describes the growing variety and numbers of artificial means that are used to help "people of different generations get to know one another and share in the richness of each other's lives" (Kaplan, 2002). This researcher was trained in the activities that constitute the beginning steps of this model and then trained older adults in her own community in instigating these activities (Penn State College of Agricultural Sciences, 2018). This resulted in what could be called the "intergenerationalization" of three organizations: Citizens Climate Lobby, Izu-Shi Society, and Columbia Basis Alliance for Literacy. Three years later, I returned to the project leads and asked them to reflect on naturalizing intergenerational relations, in other words, ways to move up the depth of intergenerational engagement continuum as illustrated in Figure 1, below.

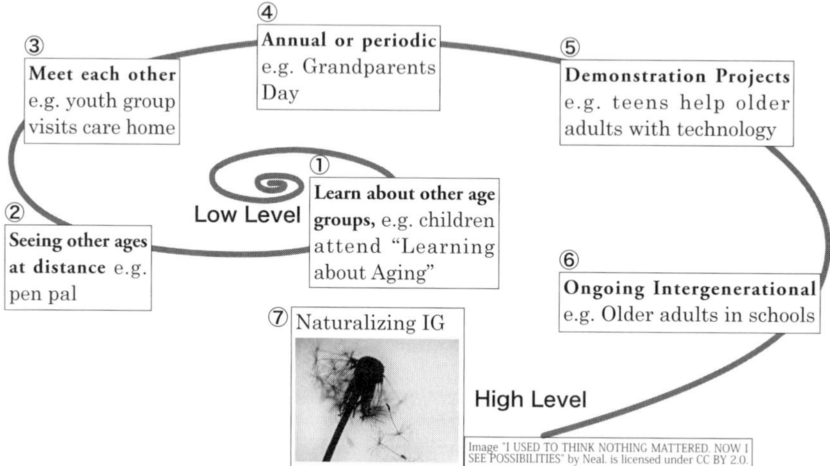

Figure 1: IDEM as a Spiral (adapted fromKaplan, 2002)

Naturalizing Intergenerational Relations: Three Cases

Nelson Izu-shi Friendship Society – A Way of Being Intergenerational

Photo: 2019 intergenerational exchange participants, Brent Irving and Celeste Moola, in Izu-shi, Japan, in March 2019. They are taking part in a Japanese calligraphy lesson given by a teacher as part of an exchange activity organized by Izu-shi hosts.

When Grace Devaux and John Armstrong joined the Nelson Izu-shi Friendship Society, a group which aims to deepen friendship and mutual understanding between communities from Canada and Japan, they tried from the beginning to shift the organization's focus to becoming intergenerational in its programming by including local people of all ages. After attending the intergenerational training offered through Learning in Retirement, Grace reflected "It's easy to plan an event and not include all ages, so John and I started to intentionally make children feel welcome. For example, we brought toys to the kite building and gardening events" (personal correspondence, 2021). "At each of our seasonal cultural events in Nelson, we made sure that we had Japanese things that kids would like," Armstrong noted.

By 2017, Nelson Izu-shi's exchange had transformed from involving grade eight children only to being a mixed group of kids and adults. In 2019, a second exchange to Izu-shi included five kids and teenagers and eleven adults. Bi-weekly orientations to Japanese culture leading up to the exchange strengthened involvement and relations amongst the Canadian participants of all ages. To increase the intergenerational nature of the exchanges, Friendship Society representatives had actively recruited families for travel and learning in Japan through the exchange, but when the exchange group got to Japan, outings were planned and homestay placements arranged not necessarily in their own family groups. Armstrong and Devaux explained that they wanted to encourage participants to interact with each other intergenerationally even outside of their family groups. In all cases, the participants of different ages acted as equal members of the group exploring this new culture and its mysteries. Armstrong mentions situations in Japan where younger exchange participants were able to use technology to orient themselves whereas older participants were relying on more traditional methods of finding their way around.

During the pandemic, the Nelson Izu-shi Friendship Society continued with their cherry blossom viewing Hanami and Canada Day events. Instead of being in-person, in Nelson, social media was used to organize the event and share photos. Zoom was used to celebrate virtually together. Kids and adults from both Nelson and Izu-shi participated enthusiastically, happy to see their friends again. Armstrong says "I remember trying to organize it and the family said their child in Nelson had already heard from another child in Izu-shi on social media that this was happening".

Armstrong says the Nelson Izu-shi Friendship Society has been in existence for 30 years and until 2017 spent all of its energy on exchanges for junior high students. "Grace and I wanted to broaden the relationship to become a true sister city and not just something for junior high school students" says Armstrong. He goes on to say "it is so easy to be separated into our own lanes. We try to be inclusive". Intergenerational has become a way of being for the Friendship Society.

Columbia Basin Alliance for Literacy (CBAL) – Intergenerational a Goal and a Value

When the pandemic hit, CBAL's Tech Tutoring program, premised on in-person sessions where teens help older adults with technology, was postponed. CBAL turned its attention to a program whereby older adults and Grade 8 students in the school's indigenous education program met on Zoom to learn to listen deeply and tackle difficult conversations. Truth and Reconciliation Commission of Canada (2015) has brought increased awareness of the need for conversations about the attempted eradication of Indigenous cultures through residential schools (Austen, 2021) and other means.

Joan Exley says CBAL has programs at all points on IDEM. "One of our directions is naturalizing intergenerational in our society. There is room for all of these levels of engagement. You don't move away from the lower levels." Exley believes there is a tipping point where intergenerational becomes a value of an organization not a goal. For example, the deep listening group has continued to meet on Zoom and wants to create an intergenerational space for sharing stories. They are looking at installations of displays at a skate park that is adjacent to a long-term care home. The displays are meant to act as conversation provocations for impromtu in-person intergenerational meetings.

"It's OK there were new opportunities that I didn't foresee" says Exley, "sometimes intergenerational programming is done as a task, but it's really important that intergenerational relations are held as a foundational value for everything we do. You want both."

Local Chapter of Citizens Climate Lobby (CCL) – Lifelong Learning Intergenerationally

In 2017, after the intergenerational training sponsored by LIR, Mike Geisler and Ron Robinson, liaised with Laura Nessman, the sustainability coordinator at Selkirk College to organize a letter writing campaign with students. Although Geisler was happy to increase engagement of youth in addressing the climate crisis, he felt his efforts were more at the lower levels of IDEM. He wanted CCL to do more to naturalize intergenerational relations in their group.

Fortunately, another CCL organizer, Laura Sacks, was also making efforts to have the group become more deeply intergenerational. At the time she was feeling very sad about all she had learned about the climate crisis. "This is our children's future," Sacks says.

In 2016, Alyssa Taburiaux contacted Sacks after Sacks gave a presentation at her school. Taburiaux was 16 when she attended her first CCL meeting at Sacks encouragement. Sacks says,

> I was so worried that Taburiaux was wondering why she sacrificed her Saturday morning. I was the next youngest person at the group and I was in my early 50s. But Taburiaux was so excited to bring the information to her school. She was a catalyst for a lot of the information sharing.

Later Taburiaux and another youth, Linn Murray, travelled across the country to the capital with Sacks. Sacks remembers,

We got assigned meetings with politicians. I was to meet with Elizabeth May, the then leader of the Green Party. Murray said his dream was to meet May. We were able to squeak both youth in to the meeting. Then the Trans Mountain pipeline was approved. Taburiaux and Murray got poster board and pens together, made signs, and we all went to demonstrate at parliament hill.

Photo: Alyssa Taburiaux and Linn Murrary in Ottawa, as part of CCL trip speaking for the planet. Photo credit: Keith McNeill

Taburiaux says that without Sacks many doors would not have opened for her. "I'd have an idea", Taburiaux said, "Laura would help me form it. We'd arrive at the idea of a petition and Laura would show me how to make a parlimentary petition and then she'd go out and get signatures. I got a job with a non-profit right out of high school. My interviewer knew the work of CCL and especially Laura". Taburiaux says that her friends will say that old people, the boomers especially, have caused all the problems we find ourselves in today. But since her collaborations with CCL that kind of mass stereotyping has never felt true. "There are so many giving elders," Taburiaux says. Some older people have resources that younger people don't and they are willing to help. For example, Sacks drove Taburiaux to CCL meetings on weekends and evenings when transit wasn't an option and she acted as mentor on the Ottawa trip.

Taburiaux and Murray have gone on to work for the planet as: lake stewards, park naturalists, deep canvasers for a not-for-profit, post-secondary students, joining the youth climate core and volunteers for the radio program Ecocentric. Sacks believes these long-term intergenerational relationships create learning on both sides that yield many benefits including addressing the climate crisis as a lifelong pursuit.

Discussion

From the cases above we can see that intergenerational programming can lead to a way of being, adopting intergenerational relationships as a value, and long-term systemic change for a more sustainable world. In forest ecologist Susanne Simard's research (Simard, 2018) we find a metaphor for Sack's intergenerational efforts at CCL. Simard has documented intergenerational relations amongst trees in old growth forests. Mycorrhizal fungal networks link the roots of trees in forests thereby facilitating inter-tree communication and sharing of resources. Older trees, titled "mother trees", help younger trees survive. The trees recognize kin and influence the behavior of neighbor through signaling. Thanks in part to Simard and other forest ecologists, forests are valued not as individual trees but as systems. This intergenerational point of view on forests underlies, for some, the necessity of conserving old growth forests. Simard said in a recent interview (Canadian Broadcasting Corporation Radio One, 2021) what "I was discovering with these Western scientific tools had long been known for thousands of years by the First Nations of Canada and the north and in the U.S" (para. 23). In my experience indigenous communities also value intergenerational relations as part of a healthy human community.

In the CCL case study Sacks collaborated with youth in acting for the planet, sharing resources, approaches, and knowledge. Sacks acted as an elder would in indigenous communities (Doman, 2011; Paul, McKenzie, Raibmon, & Johnson, 2019). Sacks was like one of the "mother trees" in Simard's work.

If Simard teaches us about the importance of intact intergenerational systems, then ethnographer Anna Lowenhaupt-Tsing teaches us about how these systems, if lost, can be restored. To harvest wild mushrooms, for personal use or for augmenting income, immigrants establish camps. In these camps the mushroom foragers are able to maintain cultural values like intergenerational living. Food preparation, camp layout, storytelling, and other types of problem-solving helps maintain the cultural practices of immigrants and supports their survival in the US economic landscape (Lowenhaupt-Tsing, 2015). In the camps, immigrants can maintain their way of being rather than relenting to constant calls for assimilation. Lowenhaupt-Tsing's mushroom harvester communities are reintroducing intergenerational relationships as Izu-Shi does in their sister city work.

The final metaphor from Lowenhaupt-Tsing relates to Satoyama—landscapes in Japan, where "more than human social relations" occur (p. 259). Satoyama allows us to reflect on, as Joan Exley of CBAL said, what it means to adopt values versus goals. Today one goal of restoring community forests in Japan is to encourage the growth of the matsutake mushroom for selling and eating. But to restore woodlands for matsutake encourages a suite of other living things: pines and oaks, understory herbs, insects, birds. Restoration enhances diversity and the healthy functioning of ecosystems. Some kinds of ecosystems, advocates argue, flourish with human activities. In this case, extending social systems to include other living things is good for everybody. The value becomes the health of everything! Activist farmer Kokki Goto explains Satoyama like this: "When people say 'Things were better in the old days,' what they have in mind, I believe, is the joy of doing things together with many people. We have lost that joy" (p. 261). Focusing on the goal, in this case, flourishing matsutake, can also lead to a valuing of things we didn't even realize we'd lost. Adopting a restorative approach can also be a way of recognizing and appreciating the interdependence between all things.

In the Future

These three cases and the associated stories of mother trees and Satoyama landscapes further elucidate our understanding of why naturalizing intergenerational relations is important. Where do these organizations travel on IDEM? In the future, it would be interesting to map the journeys of organizations on IDEM in more detail and for longer periods of time including their connections with and inspiration of other organizations. What do networks of places and organizations where intergenerational relations flourish look like in a community? How do intergenerational relations grow in a community? Are they like mycorrhizal networks and 'kin friendly'? Are disturbances like those in Satoyama landscapes helpful? What role can the natural environment play in intergenerational relations? These cases indicate that many organizations are reaching 'naturalization', at least in their groups, and that the journey and the result are fulfilling.

References

Austen, I. (2021). 'Horrible history': Mass grave of indigenous children reported in Canada. Retrieved from https://www.nytimes.com/2021/05/28/world/canada/kamloops-mass-grave- residential-schools.html

Biggs, S., Haapala, I., & Lowenstein, A. (2011). Exploring generational intelligence as a model for examining the process of intergenerational relationships. *Ageing and Society, 31*(7), 1107-1124.

Canadian Broadcasting Corporation Radio One. (2021). A pioneering forest researcher's memoir describes 'Finding the Mother Tree'. Retrieved from https://www.cbc.ca/radio/quirks/may-1-lightning-cleans-the-atmosphere-a-142-year-and-counting-experiment-and-more-1.6007496/a-pioneering-forest-researcher-s-memoir-describes-finding-the-mother-tree-1.6007500

Cohn, D. V., & Passel, J. S. (2018). A record 64 million Americans live in multigenerational households. Retrieved from https://www.pewresearch.org/fact-tank/2018/04/05/a-record-64-million-americans-live-in-multigenerational-households/

Doman, C. (2011). A peek into the journey to become an Aboriginal Elder. Retrieved from http://www.canberra.edu.au/monitor/2011/march/31_aboriginal-eldership

Hodgkin, S. (2014). Intergenerational solidarity: An investigation of attitudes towards the responsibility for formal and informal elder care in Australia. *Health Sociology Review, 23*(1), 53-64.

Kaplan, M., Sanchez, M., & Hoffman, J. (2018). *Intergenerational pathways to a sustainable society.* Cham, Switzerland: Springer International.

Kaplan, M. S. (2002). Intergenerational Programs in Schools: Considerations of Form and Function. *International Review of Education / Internationale Zeitschrift für Erziehungswissenschaft, 48*(5), 305-334.

Kaplan, M. S. (2004). Toward an intergenerational way of life. *Journal of Family and Consumer Sciences, 96*(2), 5.

Leath, S. (2017). Being better than my dad. SAGE Open, 7(1), 2158244017697163.

Lowenhaupt-Tsing, A. (2015). *The mushroom at the end of the world: On the possibility of life in capitalist ruins.* Princeton, New Jersey: Princeton University Press.

Mitrofanenko, T., Muhar, A., & Penker, M. (2015). Potential for applying intergenerational practice to protected area management in mountainous regions. *Mountain Research and Development (Online), 35*(1), 27-38.

North, M. S., & Fiske, S. T. (2012). An inconvenienced youth? Ageism and its potential intergenerational roots. *Psychological Bulletin, 138*(5), 982-997.

Paul, E., McKenzie, D., Raibmon, P., & Johnson, H. (2019). As I Remember It: Teachings (ʔəms taʔaw) from the Life of a Sliammon Elder. Retrieved from http://publications.ravenspacepublishing.org/as-i-remember-it/index

Penn State College of Agricultural Sciences. (2018). The ILI - Nelson, B.C. Chapter. Retrieved from https://aese.psu.edu/extension/intergenerational/program-areas/intergenerational- leadership-institute/the-ili-nelson-b-c-chapter

Simard, S. W. (2018). Mycorrhizal networks facilitate tree communication, learning, and memory. In Baluska, F., M. Gagliano, & G. Witzany (Eds.), *Memory and learning in plants* (pp. 191-213). Cham, Switzerland: Springer.

Tchernina, N. V., & Tchernin, E. A. (2002). Older people in Russia's transitional society: Multiple deprivation and coping responses. *Ageing and Society, 22*, 543-562.

Truth and Reconciliation Commission of Canada. (2015). *Truth and reconciliation commission of Canada: Calls to action*: Truth and Reconciliation Commission of Canada.

Villar, F. (2007). Intergenerational or multigenerational? A question of nuance. *Journal of Intergenerational Relationships, 5*(1), 115-117.

Summary

This chapter utilizes three case studies of intergenerational programming in the small town of Nelson, British Columbia, Canada:

(1) a local chapter of Citizens Climate Lobby (CCL),

(2) the Izu-Shi friendship society (a group which promotes friendship between Canada and Japan),

and (3) the Columbia Basin Alliance for Literacy (CBAL) Tech Tutoring program (where young people tutor older adults in technology) as well as two major research projects — one on exchanges between trees of many ages in old growth forests in North America and another on the restoration of the Satoyama Woodlands in Japan—in order to better understand ideal "naturalized" intergenerational systems.

The case studies and the forestry research projects can teach us about maintaining and restoring systems, both natural and human, that have become 'broken'. Communities become less resilient and sustainable when people are segregated by age and disconnected from their local environment. Healthy communities include relations, not only intergenerationally between humans, but amongst humans and all living and non-living things. In these weak systems intergenerational relations are the exception not the norm and residents are relatively unaware of their natural surroundings. When relations are weak there are fewer opportunities to exchange resources amongst generations and species.

The action research discussed in this chapter set about increasing sustainability in a community through naturalizing intergenerational relations in organizations. Initiated at the Intergenerational Leadership Institute at Penn State University, the research included an eight-week training on building intergenerational relationships with 12 older adult community leaders in Canada and then, three years later, follow-up interviews with leaders of projects that emerged from the training. The research findings build on the Intergenerational Depths of Engagement Model (IDEM) and combined with the research from the fields of forestry lead to questions which may be investigated in the future such as: How do intergenerational relations grow in a community?

Are intergenerational relations in humans like mycorrhizal networks and 'kin friendly'?

Are disturbances like those in Satoyama landscapes of Japan helpful for human intergenerational relations as well?

What role does the natural environment play in intergenerational relations?

The case studies indicate that organizations are reaching 'naturalization' of intergenerational relations, the culminating stage in the IDEM, at least within their groups. However, communities may be more sustainable if intergenerational relations are naturalized not only in select organizations but that these organizations inspire other organizations to emulate their efforts so that eventually whole communities experience naturalized intergenerational relations.

要約

本章では、カナダのブリティッシュ・コロンビア州の小さな町ネルソンで行われた

(1) 市民気候ロビー（CCL）支部

(2) 伊豆市友好協会（カナダと日本の友好を深める会）

(3) コロンビア流域リテラシー連盟（CBAL）の技術指導プログラム（若者が高齢者に技術の指導をする）

といった世代間交流プログラムの3つの事例を紹介します。そして2つの大きな研究プロジェクト（北米の原生林における多樹齢層の交わり、日本の里山再生）の事例をもとに、「自然化」に関する理想的な世代間システムの理解を深めることを目的とします。

このようなケーススタディと森林研究プロジェクトは、自然界と人間界の両方において「壊れてしまった」システムの維持と復元について教えてくれます。人々が年齢によって分断され、地域環境から切り離されると、地域社会は弾力性と持続可能性を失います。健康的なコミュニティには、人間同士の世代間の関係だけでなく、人間とあらゆる生物・非生物の間の関係も含まれます。このような脆弱なシステムにおいて、世代間の関係は標準的なものではなく例外であり、住民は自然環境に対して無関心になりがちです。関係性が弱いと世代間や種間においての資源交換の機会も少なくなります。本章で取り上げるアクション・リサーチは、組織における世代間の関係を自然化することで、コミュニティの持続可能性を高めることを目的としています。

ペンシルベニア州立大学の世代間リーダーシップ研究所で始まったこの研究では、カナダ在住の12人の高齢コミュニティリーダーを対象に、世代間の関係構築に関する8週間のトレーニングを行いました。3年後に、トレーニングにより養成されたプロジェクトのリーダーに対してフォローアップインタビューを行いました。分析の結果、世代

間関与の深さモデル（IDEM）に基づき、森林分野での研究と組み合わせることによって、以下のような将来的に調査すべき質問を導き出しました。

コミュニティにおいて世代間関係はどのように育まれるのでしょうか？

人間における世代間関係は、菌根のネットワークや「親類縁者」のようなものなのでしょうか？

日本の里山景観のような攪乱は、人間の世代間関係にも有用なのでしょうか？

自然環境は世代間関係においてどのような役割を担っているのでしょうか？

これらのケーススタディは、組織の人数が少なくても、そのグループ内でIDEMの頂点にある世代間関係の「自然化」に到達していることを示しています。しかし、世代間関係が一部の組織で自然化されるだけではなく、そういった組織から刺激を受けた他の組織が、その努力を模倣し、最終的にはコミュニティ全体が世代間関係の自然化を経験するようになれば、コミュニティはより持続可能なものになると思われます。

Author

Theresa Southam

Theresa Southam is a 2020 PhD in Human and Organizational Development and continues her research as a Fielding ISI Fellow and as a CMMI Fellow. She is coediting a book and writing a chapter for Fielding University Press on unexpected leadership including in older women. This chapter on “naturalizing” intergenerational relations for Sangaku Press in 2022 adds to her publishing on the continuous development of older adults including two articles in the Journal of Certified Senior Advisors: Positive Aging Perspectives and a New Paradigm: Foray (4A) into Aging and Living from Inside Out: The Value of Conscious Aging and the Foray (4a+) Beyond Self Paradigm. Theresa has contributed blog posts, book reviews, and recently published a portfolio piece for the Journal of Anthropology and Aging Academics as Allies and Accomplices: Practices for decolonized solidarity. Her dissertation 27,000 Sunrises: Everyday Contributions of Grateful and Giving Age 70+ Adults can be found here. As the mother of three amazing adults you’ll find her with them, in her garden, on her bike, skiing in the winter wonderland where she lives or surfing the waves of the west coast of Canada.

Southam, T. (2021a). Crone Development: Influences on Older Women Leading Major Projects. Paper presented at the Aging & Social Change: Eleventh Interdisciplinary Conference, Online. https://cgscholar.com/cg_event/events/J21/about

Southam, T. (2021b). PORTFOLIO: Academics as Allies and Accomplices: Practices for Decolonized Solidarity. Anthropology & Aging, 42(2), 150-165.

Chapter 5

The Role of Self-directed Leadership in the Development of Intergenerational Activities and Programs: A Personal Journey

Grace Hampton

Five years ago, when I told friends and family that I was signing up for a Pennsylvania State University program designed for older adults interested in taking on leadership roles in the field of intergenerational programming, they expressed extreme surprise. To be honest, I could not blame them because I have always avoided any program designed for older adults. This isn't because I didn't make the age cut-off for programs designed for the elderly, but rather because I had no interest in being a part of any program or experience designed to "serve" older adults. I mistakenly assumed that all such programs dwell primarily on addressing older adults' so-called deficits and challenges while overlooking potential new applications of their talents and other assets.

In this chapter, I will describe my experience with a leadership training program– which is identified as the "ILI" (Intergenerational Leadership Institute). In the process, I will highlight several compelling features of the ILI model that intrigued me to the point of concluding, "This program is definitely for me." The decision to sign up for the program led me to some of the most stimulating and meaningful experiences of my adult life.

Before delving into my experiences with the ILI program, here are a few words about the model itself. It is publicized as a certificate training program "for older adults 55 years of age and older who are seeking new lifelong learning experiences, skills, and volunteer opportunities to contribute to innovation and change in their communities." The program begins with an eight week (16-hour) mini-course in intergenerational studies which concludes with ILI participants who have complementary skills and interests forming intergenerational project groups. This is followed by monthly "intergenerational seminars" in which ILI participants further discuss and provide feedback and support for their respective intergenerational programs and plans [1].

1 For more information about the ILI model and related replication efforts, see: https://aese.psu.edu/outreach/intergenerational/program-areas/intergenerational-leadership-institute

The ILI was set up to embrace people with diverse life experiences such as myself. I've worn many hats, lived many lives, and experienced many careers – including as an artist, arts educator, and senior level administrator at Pennsylvania State University. Yet, somehow, I felt a yearning for new, unscripted opportunities for further self-development, self-fulfillment and service to others. Fortunately, the ILI was there to open new horizons for learning, growth and contributions to the lives of others.

What I learned and how I learned:

Building competence: A major emphasis of the ILI is the training function – of helping participants gain the competencies needed to design well-organized and creative programs for community residents of all ages. These competencies include working with individuals at many points along the age spectrum, designing appropriate activities, coordinating the program with other community agencies, designing effective, sustainable intergenerational programs, and promoting contacts, social relationships, interactions, and bonds between people from different generations.

Much of what we learned was generated through interaction among ILI participants as we shared our pre-ILI life experiences and lessons learned from our ILI-related program planning and implementation efforts. The commitment to this process of convivial learning was underscored by the growing sense of camaraderie and mutual support among ILI participants.

Expanding my social world:

A big part of my ILI program experience was the sense of connection and mutual appreciation established among my teammates.

From the first day of the program, I realized that I had much in common with the 9 other ILI participants in my program cohort. We were all: drawn to the goals of "leadership," interested in making a difference in the world around us, creative in how we embraced our professional and private lives, excited by new challenges, vehemently critical of negative portrayals of older adults, and appreciative of the "self-directed leadership" orientation of the ILI program model.

This sense of connection and shared mission was particularly strong with my project group – which consisted of Sandy Lopez, Fran Scalise, and later Dorothy Christensen.

After many hours of discussion and deliberation, the focus, title, and parameters of our group project took form.

How ILI projects are formed – The evolution of "Weaving Wisdom":

Our project team members – all with diverse histories, interests, etc. – eventually worked out a program model that reflected the intersection between our skills, interests, and experiences. The compromise took the form of naming the project "Weaving Wisdom".

Weaving Wisdom uses the art of fabric makings in Africa and America to provide a framework for planning activities, school curricula, and interactive exhibits that promote intergenerational and intercultural understanding in diverse cultural contexts, including West African and Gullah/Geechee culture of the Lowcountry (South Carolina) and cultural arts of Ghana.

During one of the early ILI training sessions, Sandy Lopez, Fran Scalise, and I began a conversation about the Gullah people from the low country of South Carolina. The Gullah people are descendants of Africans who were enslaved on the rice, indigo, and Sea Island cotton plantations of the lower Atlantic coast. Many came from the rice-growing region of West Africa. The nature of their enslavement on isolated island and coastal plantations created a unique culture with deep African retentions that are clearly visible in the Gullah Geechee people's distinctive arts, crafts, foodways, music, and language. Sandy and Fran had lived for many years in South Carolina and were familiar with the people and the arts and crafts of the Gullah people. I had recently retired from Penn State and had researched, taught and lectured on the arts and crafts of the African Diaspora. We began to discuss how we might collaborate on a project that used the traditional arts, crafts, quilting, Kente Cloth from Ghana, to bring about in-depth conversations between generations about the use of these objects. We envisioned the richness of the discussions and stories shared between generations about the history, culture, and events surrounding the making of quilts, baskets, and weavings made by the Gullah and Akan people from Ghana. It is from these conversations that Weaving Wisdom was born.

In the summer of 2017, the group organized a Weaving Wisdom workshop at our local public library in downtown State College, Pennsylvania. The workshop was composed of two sessions. The morning session introduced adult participants to sweetgrass baskets, Kente and Adinkra cloth, followed by sharing personal experiences with quilt and basket making and drawing similar experiences between quilting and adinkra and Kente cloth. Children, ages 5 through 12, accompanied by at least one parent, joined the adults for the afternoon session. In this session, the children learned how baskets are woven and used to separate the grains from the chaff years ago. They also learned that the Colors and patterns of Kente cloth represent life events and qualities and characteristics of Akan people and their culture. With the assistance of the adults, the children learned to make straw woven bracelets using colors that had special meanings to the child.

Dorothy Christenson joined the Weaving Wisdom project in 2019, bringing years of teaching in the elementary classroom. She added a solid curricular structure to the project. Between 2017 and 2021, Weaving Wisdom conducted workshops for public school art teachers regarding the incorporation of quilting and Kente cloth into the curriculum, engaged in a summer camp program, and participated in a collaborative intergenerational Fair. In addition, Sandy taught two courses for Penn State's Osher Lifelong Learning Institute on Charleston and the South Carolina Low country, during which aspects of Weaving Wisdom were discussed. Future plans for the project include developing a comparative cultural component for the project, expanding the project to include Amish quilting, and developing a replicable model that could be made available to groups and individuals interested in developing similar projects.

In retrospect, these and other activities and accomplishments of Weaving Wisdom were made possible because we coalesced as a group and took ILI's intergenerational leadership training and application journey together.

Through intensive dialogue with other ILI participants, we found our direction, based on the intersection of our interests, talents, and skills.

- Sandy, a retired university history and sociology professor, had a longstanding interest in the Gullah people and their relationship with traditional African crafts.
- Francis, also with a deep knowledge about the Gullah people and a history of supporting the arts, has a son teaching in a high school in the low country region of South Carolina.
- Dorothy, a recently retired elementary school teacher, contributed her exceptional organizational skills and experience in developing structured curricula and educational workshops on a wide variety of topics.
- On my end, I was able to contribute what I have learned from my experiences and interests in teaching about the influence of traditional African arts and culture – on contemporary American art.

Other ILI inspired projects

--**SAVOR** (Sharing and Valuing Our Relationships): State College Meals on Wheels and Penn State students come together for regularly planned meals, fellowship and recreational interests.

--**Intergenerational Pen Pal Program enhancement**: Program assessment and strategic planning for this program run by RSVP-Centre County.

--**Food that's Real for the Family Meal**: A series of family gatherings aimed at enjoying healthy foods together.

--**Intergenerational Program Development in China**: A resource review of intergenerational strategies for addressing aging-related challenges in China.

--**Doing Good With Wood**: A project that brings people together to learn design, woodworking entrepreneurship and philanthropy.

Two additional ILI projects that engaged a large number of members of the Centre County community include an Intergenerational Fair and full-day retreat designed to jump start a county-wide planning process that would generate ideas for additional intergenerational programs that improve the local quality of life.

The ILI's "self-directed volunteer leadership" development approach:

A key element of the ILI model is its "self-directed volunteer leadership development" orientation. "ILI participants have latitude in determining the nature and depth of their involvement in local intergenerational practice" (Kaplan, Greenwood-Junkermeier, & Bradley, 2019, p. 1).

In developing our Weaving Wisdom project, our project team members felt good about taking on the responsibility for creating the basic structure, focus, and ways of operating for our project. We realized this was different from the "management" orientation of many senior volunteer programs, whereby program parameters related to how participants' roles are created and maintained tend to be set at the onset of program involvement.

We all appreciated this distinction. The ILI model allowed us to be proactive in creating new intergenerational programs and in negotiating our roles as part of the process of going from "learner," to "participant," to "leader."

One point of clarification is in order. The concept of "self-directed leadership" in the ILI context is not just having the participants do what they want to do. It is about facilitating and welcoming participants' efforts to find the intersection between (1) what each participant "brings to the table" (i.e., their life experiences and their intergenerational program interests, histories of program involvement, and planning and implementation skills) and (2) the needs, conditions, and assets of the communities in which they live and work. So, in other words, as ILI participants frame their choice of volunteer activities to be meaningful to themselves, they are also considering how their efforts are meaningful to others such as in terms of community service or improving quality of life for others.

In conclusion, my involvement with ILI has become a "never ending Journey." One that is filled with opportunities for personal growth, improvement and fulfillment. I plan to continue my involvement with ILI and see where the road leads me.

References

Kaplan, M., Greenwood-Junkermeier, H. & Bradley, L. (2019). Unlocking the potential of older adult volunteers: The Intergenerational Leadership Institute model as a resource for bolstering Extension. Journal of Extension, 57(5), Oct., Article 5FEA3. Available at: https://tigerprints.clemson.edu/joe/vol57/iss5/5/

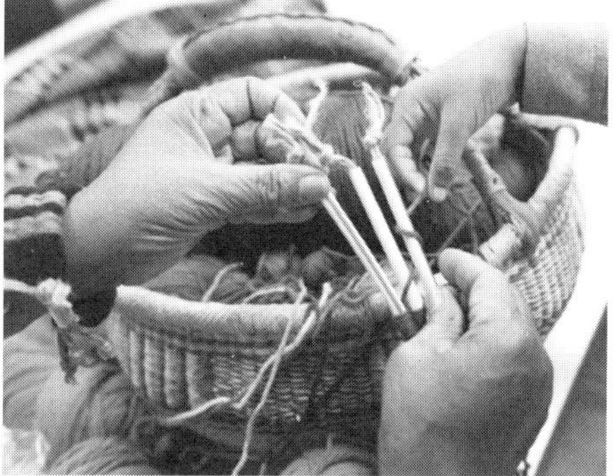

Summary

Taking on new challenges at any age is a rewarding experience; however, it is incredibly fulfilling when the challenges and rewards come later in life.

This chapter tells the story of how I gained new insights about aging, leadership, and intergenerational communication through "the retooling" I received through my participation in a program designed for older adults wishing to find fresh approaches to leadership and community engagement.

This chapter describes the journey, and development of programs designed to increase communication between generations.

In particular, I describe my work with the "Weaving Wisdom" program, which uses the art of fabric makings in Africa and America to provide a framework for planning activities, school curricula, and interactive exhibits that promote intergenerational and intercultural understanding in diverse cultural contexts, including West African and Gullah/Geechee culture of the Lowcountry (South Carolina) and cultural arts of Ghana.

The Weaving Wisdom project team coalesced through shared experiences with the Intergenerational Leadership Institute, a certificate self-directed leadership training program offered through Pennsylvania State University.

要約

いくつになっても新しいことにチャレンジするのは楽しいことですが、それが人生の後半になると、より一層充実したものになります。

この章では、リーダーシップやコミュニティ活動への新たなアプローチを模索する高齢者のためのプログラムに参加し、「再調整」することで、加齢、リーダーシップ、世代間コミュニケーションについて、どのように私が新たな洞察を得たかということについて述べます。

この章では、世代間のコミュニケーションを促進するためのプログラムの開発と、その過程について説明します。

特に「布つくりの知恵」プログラムでの私の仕事について説明します。それは、アフリカとアメリカの布作りの技術を応用して、西アフリカ、サウスカロライナ州ローカントリーのガラ／ジーチー文化、そしてガーナの文化的芸術などを含む、多様な文化背景の中で、世代間そして文化間の理解を深めるための活動、学校カリキュラム、対話型の展示を計画するための枠組みを提供するものです。

布つくりプロジェクトチームは、ペンシルバニア州立大学が提供する自己管理型リーダーシップ研修プログラム、世代間リーダーシップ研究所での経験を共有することで結成されました。

Author

Grace Hampton

Dr. Grace Hampton is Professor Emerita of Art, Art Education and Integrative Arts, and former Vice Provost and Senior Faculty Mentor at The Pennsylvania State University. In addition, she has held professorships at Northern Illinois State University, California State University at Sacramento, Jackson state University, and the University of Oregon at Eugene and also served at the National Endowment for the Arts in Washington D.C. Dr. Hampton has received two Fulbright Specialist Awards and currently serves as a Generation to Generation Fellow at the Encore Foundation. She conducts research and publishes in the areas of African and African American arts and culture, community development through the arts, and intergenerational communication.

Chapter 6

The Macrosad Chair and Intergenerational Reference Center: A case of engaged evidence-informed knowing in Spain

Mariano Sánchez
Andrés Rodríguez
Carolina Campos

Introduction

Intergenerational interactions are a core feature of human life. In any society that we may consider, intergenerational relationships are always in place at some degree because all human beings are not only engendered by a previous generation but with no exception, once we are born we need to be raised by someone from an older generation. Thus, an intergenerational flow gets started, generations in place take care of new generations that will welcome future new generations.

Therefore, the real issue in intergenerational studies and practices is not mainly about the potential extinction of connections between generations – something that will not happen – but about what type of intergenerational processes, in which extent, where, and when we would need to have in place so that our ever-changing and aging communities and societies are livable and can actually flourish. In this regard, we still have a huge window for innovation to leverage. This paper tries to contribute to rethink how intergenerational interactions may be facilitated effectively, especially among nonkin.

A few years ago the Government of Japan coined "Society 5.0" as an ideal type and a model to represent a new society mainly guided by scientific and technological innovation while still human-centered. Deguchi et al. (2020) have explained that in this model we should acknowledge the importance of getting involved with others through "engaged knowing" able to enhance "human co-becoming", i.e., knowing that really makes other persons become part of our own lives. In this paper we would like to add another important insight to this claim, namely that we should pay attention as well to specific situations where these "other persons" whom we engage belong to different generations.

It is with this perspective in mind that we intend to share the principles and initial outputs of a unique intergenerational experience being carried out in our country somehow in line with the trailblazing industry-academia collaboration model put forward by H-UTokyo Lab (Hitachi-UTokyo Laboratory, 2020). What follows is an account of two symbiotic and unprecedented initiatives in our country, the Macrosad Chair in Intergenerational Studies at the University of Granada (henceforth the Chair) and the Macrosad Intergenerational Reference Center in Albolote (henceforth CINTER). Through showcasing this intergenerational *joint venture*, we argue that the combination of the Chair and CINTER in the way presented below it is an example of intergenerational engaged evidence-informed knowing that allows for both organizational and human co-becoming.

Rationale

In September 2018 the CINTER was launched as a private initiative by Macrosad – a social cooperative with more than 25 years of experience in the care and educational sectors in Andalusia, the most southern region in Spain. CINTER is an intergenerational shared site combining day services for older adults – already in place – and a new nursery school for 0-3 year olds. There are many of these centers in the world but just a few in Spain. The innovative nature of CINTER was enhanced by the parallel inauguration of the Chair on the same year thanks to a collaborative agreement between Macrosad and the University of Granada (henceforth UGR). The Chair's ultimate purpose is serving as a platform for permanent (re)creation and transfer of knowledge between the intergenerational studies field and the practice of intergenerationality, especially in the communitarian and social services spheres. In the end, this Macrosad-UGR agreement aimed to contribute to the strengthening of relations between people from different generations as a means for promoting the happiness, well-being and socioeconomic progress of individuals and communities, with special attention to the generational groups that need more support.

Which was the originality in this context? Firstly, there was Macrosad, to our knowledge the only social cooperative in Spain that embraces intergenerationality as one of its key identifying and strategic values across areas and services – Macrosad hires some 4,500 employees who run several nursing homes, adult day care centers, early childhood schools, early care and home care services in Andalusia. Secondly, we had UGR as partner, a leading institution in the Spanish intergenerational field with a long tradition in intergenerational research and training. Thirdly, the new CINTER constituted the right living lab to prove that this symbiotic initiative between a social cooperative and a university around intergenerational practices had to work differently because of the particular relational and time-bound nature associated to these practices (Sánchez & Díaz, 2020).

For this triangular setting – Macrosad, CINTER and the UGR Chair – to function properly a good and flexible connecting rationale was required so that an ad hoc successful collaboration with a strong intergenerational stance was really feasible. The following three elements constitute the basis of the collaborative system put in place: (i) an evidence-informed approach (Smart, 2019); (ii) integration of the Chair's team as part of CINTER's community (i.e., center's users, their relatives and caregivers, and CINTER's staff and directors); (iii) the implementation of dialogic co-working by means of a mixed Macrosad-UGR executive board responsible for the Chair's day-to-day strategic decision-making in terms of intergenerational developments both at CINTER and beyond – at all Macrosad's centers.

Implementing an evidence-informed approach has driven us to count on lived experience, practice expertise and research evidence when planning and carrying out intergenerational programs and activities. We use the best available validated knowledge from research that it is combined intentionally with the experience and professional knowledge of people (e.g., educators, psychologists) and organizations (e.g., Macrosad, UGR) involved. Furthermore, we adapt our actions specifically to both each particular context of application and the people to whom these actions are addressed – i.e., older people, children, staff and families involved at CINTER daily. At the heart of this approach remains a strong interest in fostering person-centered happiness and well-being, caregiving, humanization of services, and the strengthening of relationships – we deem relationships to be the ultimate vehicle that makes everything intergenerational to work well and be interconnected.

The integration of the Chair's team as CINTER members involves fluid horizontal communication and trust building. Researchers at the Chair develop a scholarship of application and engagement (Boyer, 1990) in the sense that they are continuously asking themselves, within a framework of co-responsibility and human co-becoming, what they might do that it is helpful to the CINTER community.

Regarding the decision-making process, it is in the executive board – integrated by staff from Macrosad and UGR – where organizational co-becoming is more evident. Dialogic co-working in this board is intergenerational because board members are at different stages of their careers in the intergenerational field. Moreover, this co-working embraces engaged knowing as far as both organizations are willing to interweave and mutually influence each other as they build together – without prejudices and through active listening and co-learning – a shared intergenerational agenda.

For one illustrative example of how such three-fold model is working it makes sense to share a story on how the intergenerational coordinator at CINTER has recently approached her capstone undergraduate mini-thesis. She has carried out applied research to identify key features of intergenerational practices which have a real capacity to promote relationship building. This piece of research has been supervised by the head of the Chair – this supervision has been an intergenerational mentoring practice by itself –, it has involved staff from different services in Macrosad – a mix of experienced and unexperienced intergenerational practitioners – and its findings have been used to provide staff at CINTER and other Macrosad centers with new evidence-informed implementation principles for their intergenerational work. This output has been possible only through a combination of her expertise as intergenerational coordinator, the support of the Chair's board, the intergenerational work experience shared by her colleagues at CINTER and Macrosad, and the tutoring by a researcher from the Chair, everything in an atmosphere of trust, co-creation and intergenerational sharing of evidenced knowledge, lived experience and professional expertise. We believe that this example goes much further and deeper than traditional translational knowledge. Actually, we posit that it should be considered an example of intergenerational engaged evidence-informed knowing since different organizations and generations of intergenerational practitioners and researchers have collaborated and made each other part of their own personal lives and professional/organizational endeavors.

Some of our projects

In a similar vein, and in permanent connection with Macrosad and CINTER, the Chair carries out various projects pursuing research, training, knowledge dissemination and other services enabling the development of intergenerational relationships in Andalusia, Spain and the wider international context. The Chair also offers consultancy services addressed to organizations, public bodies, foundations and individuals wishing to adopt an intergenerational perspective in their work and willing to participate in the kind of engaged evidence-informed knowing just described.

Research carried out by the Chair revolves mainly around intergenerationality and happiness. For instance, we are involved in a project evaluating the impact that intergenerational engagement may have on the health and well-being of CINTER's users. Furthermore, through continuing observation, analysis and study of intergenerational practices as they happen at CINTER, and in close collaboration with intergenerational practitioners at the center, we have been able to introduce, evaluate and make improvements as CINTER moves on. For instance, during the current COVID-19 pandemic we have been involved in the planning of intergenerational activities of reference in conditions of physical distance and in full compliance with the new safety health-related measures introduced. From the Chair we are also involved, again with an engaged evidence-informed knowing mindset, in producing specific job descriptions for each staff position at CINTER, a scarce resource in the intergenerational field.

In addition, we are continuously seeking for new developments in intergenerational practices. Results from this research are used, among other purposes, for the continuous training of professionals involved at CINTER and other Macrosad services. In this sense, and conscious as we are that we live in a network society where information needs to be spread, we also publish a series of documents that can be consulted and downloaded for free by people interested in expanding their knowledge about intergenerational relationships and practices. To date we have published two documents whose short descriptions follows.

The first one, published in 2020, is a *Guide to intergenerational work in the first cycle of Early Childhood Education*. It is especially addressed to people involved in the field of early childhood education. It focuses on questions such as the concept of intergenerational work, how this work may fit in the early childhood stage, possible changes to be expected both in children and in people from other generations interacting with them, and the awareness and involvement in intergenerational practices of school teachers and families.

The second document in the series, a *Guide to intergenerational centers. Concept and keys to start up*, has been released in 2021. This is the first guidebook published in our country dedicated to explaining what's an intergenerational center, its typology and the main ideas to take into account when planning one of these spaces aimed at fostering interactions between generations. In line with the evidence-informed approach aforementioned, all the information gathered for the preparation of the guidebook came from a mix of professional and lived experiences along with robust scientific evidence.

Conclusion

In the end, this unique intergenerational collaboration across sectors between Macrosad and UGR through the Chair and CINTER expects to help providing better care for people from different generations in a humanized and fully engaged way. Likewise, we intend to learn from these people and with them at every step we take, co-creating new applied and engaged knowledge as we keep investigating, ensuring that all we do is always informed by evidence, and facilitating to our utmost knowledge co-creation and transferring in a transparent and public way.

References

Boyer, E. L. (1990). *Scholarship reconsidered. Priorities of the professoriate*. Jossey-Bass.

Deguchi, A., Kajitani, S., Nakajima, T., Ohashi, H., & Watanabe, T. (2020). From monetary to nonmonetary society. In Hitachi-UTokyo Laboratory (Ed.), *Society 5.0. A people-centric super-smart society* (pp. 117-143). Springer Open.

Hitachi-UTokyo Laboratory. (Ed.). (2020). *Society 5.0. A people-centric super-smart society*. Springer Open.

Sánchez, M., Díaz, P. (2020). Intergenerational Relationships. In D. Gu, & M. E. Dupre (Eds.), *Encyclopedia of Gerontology and Population Aging* (pp. 274-286). Spring Nature.

Smart, J. (2019). *Needs assessment. Families and children expert panel practice resource*. Australian Institute of Family Studies.

Summary

A few years ago the Government of Japan coined “Society 5.0” as an ideal type and a model to represent a new society mainly guided by scientific and technological innovation while still human-centered. This model should acknowledge the importance of getting involved with others through knowledge that really makes other persons become part of our own lives.

This chapter presents an unprecedented and unique experience in Spain of such engaged knowledge at an organizational level from an intergenerational perspective.

The Macrosad Intergenerational Reference Center in Albolote (CINTER) is an intergenerational shared site combining day services for older adults and a nursery school for 0-3 year olds. CINTER's innovative spirit was reinforced by the concurrent launch of the Macrosad Chair in Intergenerational Studies at the University of Granada (the Chair) on the same year thanks to a collaborative agreement between Macrosad – a social cooperative — and the University of Granada (UGR). The Chair’s ultimate aim is to promote the transfer of knowledge within the intergenerational studies field to strengthen intergenerational practices in the socio-educational sector.

The originality and innovation in this regard was the partnership’s threefold articulation around Macrosad, the UGR Chair and CINTER. Macrosad is the only social cooperative in Spain that has adopted intergenerationality as a core identity feature and strategic value across all services and areas. UGR is a reference higher education institution in the Spanish intergenerational sector with a large tradition in intergenerational research and training. In addition, CINTER has provided the appropriate living laboratory to demonstrate that this symbiotic initiative between a social cooperative and a university around intergenerational practices had to operate differently because of the relational and time-bound nature of these practices. The core of this system of engaged knowing consists of three elements: (1) an evidence-informed approach (valuing lived experience, practice expertise and research evidence); (2) integration of the Chair’s research team as part of CINTER’s community; and (3) dialogical collaborative work through a combined Macrosad-UGR executive board responsible for the Chair’s daily strategic decision-making.

The Chair carries out various projects pursuing research, training, knowledge dissemination and other services enabling the development of intergenerational relationships. It also offers consultancy services addressed to organizations, public bodies and individuals wishing to adopt an intergenerational perspective.

In the end, this intergenerational scheme aims to provide better care and more happiness to people from different generations within the context of a society focused on scientific and technological innovation.

要約

数年前、日本政府は「Society 5.0」という言葉を、人間中心でありながら、「科学技術の革新によって導かれる、新しい社会の理想型モデル」として提唱しました。このモデルでは、他者を自分の生活の一部とするような知見を通して、他者と関わることの重要性が認識されなければなりません。

本章では、世代間の視点からの組織レベルでの、非常に興味深い知見について、スペインでの前例のないユニークな経験を紹介します。

アルボロテのマクロサド世代間レファレンス・センター（CINTER）は、高齢者向けのデイサービスと０～３歳児向けの保育園を組み合わせた、世代間で共有する場所です。CINTERの革新的な精神は、社会的協同組合であるMacrosadとグラナダ大学（UGR）の協力協定により、同じ年に、グラナダ大学の世代間研究のMacrosad講座が同時に発足したことにより強化されました。講座の最終的な目的は、社会教育部門における世代間研究の分野と世代間実践分野との間での知見の移転を促進することです。

この点での独創性と革新性は、Macrosad、UGRのMacrosad講座、CINTERの３つを軸とした３重の結合にあります。Macrosadは、スペインで唯一、世代間交流をアイデンティティの中核とし、それをすべてのサービスや分野にわたり戦略的価値観として採用している社会的協同組合です。UGRは、世代間研究およびトレーニングにおいて長い伝統を持つ、スペインの世代間部門におけるリファレンス高等教育機関です。さらに、CINTERは、世代間実践をめぐる社会的協同組合と大学との間の、この共生的な新たな取り組みが、これらの実践の関係性と時間的制約のためにそれぞれが異なる運営をしなければならなかったことを示すのに適したリビングラボラトリーを提供してきました。この知のシステムの中核は、３つの要素から構成されています。(1) エビデンスに基づくアプローチ（実体験、実践の専門知識、研究のエビデンスを重視）、(2) CINTERのコミュニティの一部としての講座の研究チームの統合、(3) 講座の日々の戦略的意思決定を担うMacrosad-URR合同の執行委員会による対話的共同作業です。

Macrosad講座は、研究、研修、知識の普及、および世代間関係の発展を可能にするその他のサービスを追求する様々なプロジェクトを実施しています。また、世代間交流の視点を取り入れたいと考えている組織、公共団体、個人を対象としたコンサルティングサービスも提供しています。

最後に、この世代間計画は、科学技術のイノベーションを重視する社会の中で、異なる世代の人々により良いケアと幸福を提供することを目的としています。

Author

Mariano Sánchez
Head, Macrosad Chair in Intergenerational Studies, University of Granada.

His trajectory in the intergenerational field started in 1999. He had been member of the founding group of the International Consortium for Intergenerational Programmes and after initial training as Intergenerational Specialist at the University of Pittsburgh (USA) he decided to support the development of the intergenerational field in Spain. He was invited to chair the INTERGENERATIONAL NETWORK, a national initiative supported by the Spanish National Institute for Older People and Social Services.

Dr. Sánchez got involved as founding member in the Journal of Intergenerational Relationships, of which he was co-editor for a seven years. He has also been a member of the Advisory Committee of the Centre for Intergenerational Practice, Beth Johnson Foundation (UK) and a founding member of the European Map of Intergenerational Learning network.

His research includes the direction of several national and European projects, and he has participated as a speaker in numerous national and international conferences dedicated to intergenerational issues.

Since May 2018 he is the inaugural Head of the Macrosad Chair in Intergenerational Studies at the University of Granada, the only of its kind in the country. This Chair is responsible for supporting the development of the Macrosad evidence-informed Intergenerational Reference Center.

Andrés Rodríguez
CEO of Macrosad SCA.

Andrés Rodríguez-González holds a degree in Executive Master in Management from the Loyola University of Andalusia and ESADE. For more than 25 years he has been the promoter and CEO of Macrosad, an Andalusian leading social cooperative that provides education and care services for children and the elderly.

Mr. Rodríguez-González is as well the promoter and president of the Business Circle of Care for People (CECUA), an employer association reaching more than 8,000 professionals, 159 centers and ultimately providing services to more than 21,000 users. He is also a member of the Board of Directors of CEAPs (Business Circle of Assistance to People), the leading organization in the country within the sector of attention to dependence.

He currently combines his degree in International Marketing and Commercialization at UNIR with the vice-presidency of the Ageing Lab Foundation and the Social Council of the University of Jaén. He has also been director of public and private institutions such as the Economic and Social Council of the province of Jaén, CEPES-Andalusia, CITOLIVA Foundation or FAECTA, holding various responsibilities, and has participated in the design and development of more than 10 strategic business sectorial and territorial plans, and in more than 13 scientific and academic publications.

Carolina Campos
Technical Staff, Macrosad Chair in Intergenerational Studies.

Carolina graduated in Occupational Therapy by the University of Granada, she is an

Specialist in Social Integration and got a Master Degree in Research and Innovation in Health, Care and Quality of Life through the University of Jaen. She has specific training in care for children and the elderly, as well as experience and a wide range of capabilities regarding the caring for people throughout their life cycle. She has as well training and experience as an expert in Animal Assisted Therapy, which has allowed her to further expand the range of her abilities to provide care and attention to people.

With regard to the intergenerational field, in March 2019 she joined the Macrosad Chair in Intergenerational Studies' team as Technical Staff. In this context, she has gained expertise in intergenerational projects through multiple formal training (e.g., the "Together Old and Young: An Intergenerational Approach" online course, the "International Certificate in Intergenerational Learning").

She provides technical support in research, training, dissemination, and other activities carried out by the Macrosad Chair.

Chapter 7

Intergenerational Practice in a Digital World

Ryan McKay

Denise Milne

Old's Cool

Old's Cool is an award-winning programme which brings older and younger people together in Leith, an area of economic deprivation in Scotland. The programme has run through 2 cycles, first funded by The Paul Hamlyn Foundation [1] and the second funded by The National Lottery [2]. During the current round of Lottery funding, 57 young people and 10 older people have taken part. Ryan McKay, a development worker at the Citadel Youth Centre has facilitated partnerships with schools and local agencies to support the intergenerational practice advocated by the *Old's Cool* programme. Young people, aged 12-16 who are considered to be at-risk, defined by McWhirter et al. (1998) as those who are likely to require intervention to avoid one of the following at risk behaviours: school drop-out, substance abuse, teen pregnancy, delinquency and violence and teenage suicide. Young people from this category are matched with older people and embark upon an 10-12 week programme of activities together which aligns with the Curriculum for Excellence (CfE) which is the national curriculum in Scotland for ages 4-18. During the project the young people are awarded time out of school to participate in the programme. At the end of the project the young people go back into school and may be offered the opportunity to attend 'New Spin' an intergenerational community cafe delivered in partnership with the Pilmeny Development Project [3], which takes place on a Friday afternoon. This allows

1 The Paul Hamlyn Foundation is an independent funder and the largest grant maker in the UK. Their focus is on creating a just society with a priority on helping young people realise their full potential (Phf, accessed 2021)

2 The National Lottery is a state-franchised lottery in the United Kingdom. The public can buy tickets to win cash prizes with money raised being distributed to grants which can be applied for by charities and community groups (The National Lottery, accessed 2021)

3 The Pilmeny Development project is a community based voluntary organisation which has been working with older and younger people in Leith and Edinburgh since 1979 (Pilmeny Development Project, accessed 2021).

the younger and older people to stay in touch and further benefit from intergenerational activity within their wider community.

Data collection

The data collected for this case study is in the form of observations, reports from the groups, self-evaluation forms and school attendance data. The group sessions, though organised and facilitated with a structured plan can evolve and develop spontaneously meaning that each session and interaction can have unexpected outcomes. Therefore it is essential to adopt a flexible approach to data collection when engaging in intergenerational practice within community spaces.

Benefactors of intergenerational practice

It is widely accepted that intergenerational practice should be mutually beneficial to both older and younger participants (Larkin & Rosebrook, 2002; Chung, 2008; Carr & Gunderson, 2016). However, through the *Old's Cool* programme it has been observed that the benefits associated with intergenerational practice extend beyond the immediate participants and include the staff and volunteers as well as the wider community. Additionally, it has been noted by the researchers that funders typically request that the positive impact on young people be recorded with no required measurement for older people. This suggests that, at least within a British context, funders look at intergenerational activity as something that is principally for the benefit of younger people. This is an inconsistency and perhaps a misconception of the power potential of this type of practice on wider social capital. Newman (2008: 33) describes intergenerational practice in communities as a form of social capital where people with non-familial connections connect and work towards a common goal with collective responsibility. This is pertinent within communities such as Leith where *Old's Cool* is based as nuclear families are less common in areas of economic deprivation (Brown et al., 2015) and therefore the inter-familial intergenerational knowledge sharing is notably absent in these areas due to more complex family structures reducing the likelihood of cross-generational contact. Through formalised intergenerational practice people from all generations can come together for a transformative knowledge exchange and resulting increase in social capital.

Older people experience

In one of the *Old's Cool* groups that ran in 2018 a group of 5 young people and 5 older people did some design workshops aimed at designing objects that were inspired by the stories shared between the younger and older people. Towards the end of this group's time together they were invited to visit a maker-space for a day of making and crafting their own designed objects. While there everyone was able to make use of tools such as 3D printers, laser cutters and vinyl cutters. One of the older people, Wilma was telling one of the younger people about her friend who is blind. Wilma explained that despite advances in technology aimed to improve communication for the visually impaired, her friend struggled more due to buttons and the way things work changing rapidly. Wilma posed the question- could they design and make something which used technology to design a more inclusive form of communication? The younger partner asked if there was a way to print Braille. As they were having this conversation in a maker-space, they were able to play around with the 3D printers and 3D printing pens. Over the course of a few hours the younger person supported Wilma in making a modular Braille postcard which Wilma could customise and send to her friend through the post. Wilma was delighted with the outcome of the project and the young person said she was proud that she had helped Wilma find a way to stay connected to her friend. Gauntlett (2011) discusses the feeling of connection and capacity experienced when engaging in the process of making. This is something that Wilma and the young person expressed in this example (2011: 69).

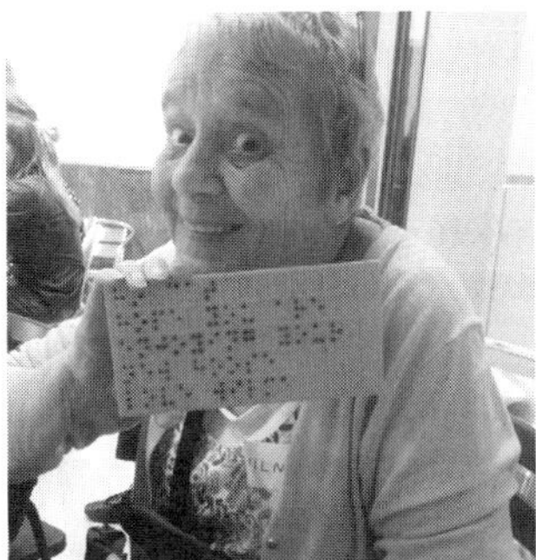

Figure 1: Wilma with the 3D printed Braille postcard that she designed with one of the younger people (Author: Milne nee Allan, 2018).

Wilma has taken part in many of the Old's Cool groups and during an evaluation session she said,

"One thing that I've found that makes me quite emotional actually is that I've been accepted with my disability...I've absolutely loved being with the children".

The sessions provide space and time for the younger and older people to become comfortable with each other and despite the challenges associated with working with at-risk groups the older people are tolerant of rowdy behaviour and the younger people are interested and non-judgemental in the way they interact with the older people and some of the issues that they face. Tolsma et al., (2009) discuss the acculturation that intergenerational social mobility facilitates. Their research suggests that those who come into contact with a variety of people from different backgrounds and generations are more tolerant and less likely to hold antagonistic attitudes. This confirms the observation that participation in intergenerational practice increases cross-generational tolerance.

Another older person, Robin said that before he participated in *Old's Cool*, he had spent 18 months in his home recovering from an operation. He explained that he was in a bad way emotionally and physically. He said that after Ryan invited him to take part in *Old's Cool*, he started getting out more and thoroughly enjoyed his time with the *Old's Cool* group. He also said that he was able to reduce the medication he was taking for depression which he thinks is because of his participation in *Old's Cool*. This highlights the powerful potential of intergenerational work on older people and tangible and transformative benefits it can have. This relates to The Transformative Learning Theory framework which posits that people interpret their circumstances and the world around them using their background and prior experience. Aguilera-Hermida (2020) says that intergenerational activities have the potential to provide transformative learning experiences for those who participate by empathising, connecting and being exposed to the hardships and difficulties faced by their counterparts (2020: 8).

Younger people experience

The benefits that intergenerational activity has on younger people is tangible to see through what they say, how they behave and an improved attendance and engagement record at school. The project was awarded an Intergenerational Excellence award for promoting achievement and attainment in school.

The risk of antisocial behaviour and dropping out of school correlates with truancy and poor engagement (Gubbels et al., 2019). Therefore, it is pertinent that to improve the future outcomes for these young people that they be supported in finding a way that makes school feel like a place for them. Learning from the stories of the older people and experiencing personal responsibility as they work with and support the older people offers the opportunity to change attitudes and to help the younger people to see themselves differently leading to increased confidence and improved self-esteem.

In one of the sessions in 2017, a group of younger and older people were working together to use a 3D printer and CAD modelling software for the first time. Allan (2018) describes the scenario where the younger people took on the role of 'teacher' when using the laptops to design CAD files to 3D print. One of the older men spoke about a computer literacy class that he was attending, and the young people listened with interest and shared words of encouragement without being impatient or condescending. The next week one of the older people brought in photographs from when he was younger. There was a photo of him on a motorbike and one of the younger people was particularly impressed. They worked together to design a model of a motorbike to be printed on the 3D printer. The photo provided the two with a common interest from which they could work and build a connection.

As Allan (ibid) highlights, this group experienced improved confidence and communication skills. Using attendance data, it was shown that 75% of the young people across 8 different *Old's Cool* groups had sustained improved attendance in the 3 months after the completion of the project.

Figure 2: A younger person taking on the role of 'teacher' to help Support the older person. (Author: Milne nee Allan, 2018)

Once the younger people are settled into the intergenerational group, they exhibit an improved attitude towards the older people and staff as well as demonstrating greater tolerance and thoughtfulness in general. One of the younger people said that they enjoyed participating in *Old's Cool* because,

"It's given us a chance to meet the old people...it's really good for the children for generations to pass down what used to happen"

This comment highlights the value that young people place on the interaction between them and the older people and an appreciation for understanding how things have changed over time.

Gordon et al. (2016) discuss Teaching Personal and Social Responsibility (TPSR) in the context of a boy's club. They had similar findings to those of *Old's Cool* in that when young people are trusted and given responsibility within a structured setting, they develop their Social-emotional learning (SEL) and demonstrate great self-awareness and desire to avoid antisocial situations.

Impact on Staff and volunteers

During the Covid-19 pandemic facilitating intergenerational work became more difficult due to isolation and lack of access to digital platforms as well as poor digital literacy. Digital exclusion has been an issue facing older people in areas of deprivation for many years (Gallistl et al., 2020) however, the pandemic proved to be a catalyst in trying to address some of these issues. During the first lockdown in Scotland from March-July 2020, one of the volunteers at the Citadel Youth Centre, Victoria was inspired to help one of the older people, Mary who was provided with a laptop by the Citadel. Victoria helped Mary learn how to use the laptop to access resources online and stay in contact with family, friends, and her community. Victoria and Mary began using Google Maps every week to visit somewhere new. They would phone each other and 'visit' different places across the world such as the Niagara Falls through Google Maps.

Figure 3: Digital intergenerational work: exploring the world together through Google Maps. (Author: McKay, 2020)

Impact on community

As *Old's Cool* was launched in 2015, the young people who took part in the first groups are now adults and it has been noted that many have gone on to positive destinations with *Old's Cool* playing a role in supporting their engagement and attendance at school. Therefore, it is hoped that with wider access to intergenerational activity young people can be supported to have more positive constants in their teenage years leading to less instances of anti-social behaviour and a community that feels safer.

Additionally, there is an intergenerational café, called New Spin that takes place in the Citadel Youth Centre. *Old's Cool* supports this by introducing more people from the local area and schools to intergenerational activity and strengthening the existing café by ensuring that a constant stream of new young people see this as a place they want to spend their Friday afternoons, in the company of older people.

Kaplan (1997) considered how intergenerational work would continue into the future. He was concerned that it would simply be seen as a fad by social researchers of the future unless the impact was well documented. Now that the future he discussed is the present, it is interesting to reflect back on the past 25 years. Kaplan (Ibid) noted that intergenerational programmes within communities had a 'significant impact on the lives of the participants but also generate community improvements and help establish a sense of cultural identity and continuity.'

Studies by others in the last 25 years (Lawrence-Jacobson, 2006; Hye-Kyung Kang, 2015; McKay, 2015; McKay 2022) indicate that the fear that intergenerational practice would not be recognised for its significant impact were unfounded and that the number of people documenting the success of intergenerational programmes is growing. It is the responsibility of the practitioners and funders of today to ensure that they continue to share best practice and provide a platform for intergenerational programmes to continue throughout communities across the world so that people of all background benefit from the transformative impact of intergenerational practice.

Conclusion

This case study has shown how intergenerational practice with a focus on technology can lead to mutual benefits between the younger and older people but also for the staff and volunteers as well as the community as a whole. The pandemic has led to people living in isolation, and those who are already digitally excluded are worst affected by this. *Old's Cool* showed how intergenerational practice can be flexible and adaptive providing new and interesting ways for younger and older people to connect and go on journeys together across the world while physically distanced. The data collected for this case study has been grounded within existing literature to convey the relevance of this study to other research and contribute to the growing evidence of the positive impact that intergenerational practice has on people and communities.

Message to Japanese practitioners:

For practitioners the most important thing is to provide a safe space, physically or digitally to allow intergenerational relationships to flourish.

References

Aguilera-Hermida, A.P. (2020). Fighting Ageism through Intergenerational Activities, a Transformative Experience. *Journal of Transformative Learning. 7*(2), 7-18.

Allan, D. (2018). Making as a means to re-engage disengaged young people back into education: a case study. https://makersdiyparticipatorydesign.files.wordpress.com/2018/04/allan_cameraready_denise.pdf

Barrie, G., Wright, P., & Jacobs, J., (2016). Social and Emotional Learning Through a Teaching Personal and Social Responsibility Based After-School Program for Disengaged Middle-School Boys. *Journal of Teaching in Physical Education*. DOI: 10.1123/jtpe.2016-0106

Brown, S.L., Manning, W.D. & Stykes, J.B. (2015). Family Structure and Child Well-Being: Integrating Family Complexity. *Journal of Marriage and*

Family. 77(1), 177-190.

Carr, D.C. & Gunderson, J.A. (2016). The Third Age of Life: Leveraging the Mutual Benefits of Intergenerational Engagement. *Public Policy & Aging Report, 26*(3), 83-87.

Chung, J.C. (2008). An intergenerational reminiscence programme for older adults with early dementia and youth volunteers: values and challenges, *Scandinavian Journal of Caring Sciences, 23*, 259-264.

Gauntlett, D. (2011) .*Making is Connecting*. Polity Press.

Gallistl, V., Rohner, R., Seifert, A. & Wanka, A. (2020).Configuring the Older Non-User: Between Research, Policy and Practice of Digital Exclusion. *Social Inclusion. 8*(2), p233-243.

Gubbels, J., van der Put, Claudia E. & Assink, M. (2019). Risk Factors for School Absenteeism and Dropout: A Meta-Analytic Review. *Journal of Youth and Adolescence. 48*, 1637-1667.

Kang, H. (2015). "We're Who We've Been Waiting For": Intergenerational Community Organizing for a Healthy Community. *Journal of Community Practice, 23*(1), 126-140, DOI: 10.1080/10705422.2014.983214

Kaplan, M. (1997). The Benefits of Intergenerational Community Service Projects. *Journal of Gerontological Social Work, 28*(3) 211-228, DOI: 10.1300/J083v28n03_06

Larkin, E. & Rosebrook, V. (2002). Standards for intergenerational practice: A proposal, *Journal of Early Childhood Teacher Education, 23*(2), 137-142, DOI: 10.1080/1090102020230205

Lawrence-Jacobson, A.R. (2006). Intergenerational Community Action and Youth Empowerment. *Journal of Intergenerational Relationships, 4*(1), 137-147, DOI: 10.1300/ J194v04n01_15

McKay, R. (on behalf of the Citadel Youth Centre) (2015). Olds Cool Intergenerational Practice Toolkit.https://generationsworkingtogether.org/downloads/5b1e757652795-OLDSCOOL_TOOLKIT_.pdf

The National Lottery (n.d.) Everytime you play, the UK wins. Retrieved from: https://www.national-lottery.co.uk/life-changing[Accessed 10th Aug 21].

Newman, S. (2008). Intergenerational Learning and the Contributions of Older People. *Ageing Horizons, 8*, 31-39.

Paul Hamlyn Foundation (n.d.) About PHF. Retrieved from: https://www.phf.org.uk/about-phf/ [Accessed 10th Aug 21].

Pilmeny Development Project (n.d.) About the Pilment Development Project. Retrieved from: http://www.pilmenydevelopmentproject.co.uk/start [Accessed 10th Aug 21].

Tolsma, J., de Graaf, N.D., & Quillian, L. (2009). Does intergenerational social mobility affect antagonistic attitudes towards ethnic minorities? *The British Journal of Sociology 60*(2), 257-277.

Summary

This case study article is about an award-winning intergenerational project called Old's Cool based in Leith, an area of economic deprivation in Scotland. The article first considers the benefactors of intergenerational practice and looks at how it can improve and enhance the lives of both, the young people and the older people by facilitating a transformative knowledge exchange.

Next the article discusses the impact that Old's Cool and the embedded technology focussed activities have had on older people. By working with the young people, the older people were supported in their learning to use a variety of technologies include drawing software and 3D printers. In this example one of the older people, Wilma is supported in designing and manufacturing a customisable braille postcard. The older people describe the positive impact that Old's Cool has had on their well-being.

Next the article discusses some benefits that Old's Cool has had on the younger people. In the example shared the young people play the role of 'teacher' in supporting the older people in their use of technology. This experience led to improved confidence and self-esteem, which resulted in less anti-social behaviour and an improved attendance at school.

This article then highlights the positive role that Old's Cool has had on staff and volunteers who work on the project. The example discussed explains how, during the Covid-19 pandemic, one of the volunteers, Victoria supported one of the older people, Mary to become more comfortable with her laptop. This helped her to stay in contact with her friends, family and community. Victoria and Mary would share phone calls and while talking would each go onto Google Maps and virtually visit different places around the world together, while they were apart. This example demonstrates how Old's Cool's embedded technology focussed activities helped the participants to adapt to the changing circumstances brought about by the pandemic enabling them to feel more comfortable using their devices to communicate.

Finally, the article discusses the impact that Old's Cool has had on the community in Leith, Scotland since it began in 2015. It highlights that many of the young people involved who are now adults have gone on to have positive futures supported by their improved engagement and attendance at school. Additionally, New Spin another intergenerational project based in

Leith, supports ongoing intergenerational practice and the legacy of Old's Cool.

要約

このケーススタディは、スコットランドの経済的窮乏地域であるリースを拠点とし、受賞歴も有する「Old's Cool」というプロジェクトを取り上げたものです。本稿では、世代間交流の恩恵を受けている人々について検討し、知識変換を世代間交流が促すことによっていかに若者と高齢者双方の生活を改善・向上できるかを考察します。

次に、Old's Cool と組み込まれたテクノロジーに焦点を当てた活動が高齢者にもたらした影響について論じています。若者と一緒に活動することで、高齢者は描画ソフトや3D プリンター等の様々なテクノロジーの使用方法を学ぶことができました。この例では、高齢者の 1 人であるウィルマが、カスタマイズ可能な点字ポストカードをデザイン・製作するための支援を受けています。プロジェクトに参加した高齢者の方々は、Old's Cool が自分達の幸福感にポジティブな影響を与えたと述べています。

続いて、Old's Cool により若者にどのような好ましい影響があったかについて触れています。紹介された例において、若者は、高齢者のテクノロジー利用をサポートする「先生」の役割を担っています。この経験により自信や自尊心が向上し、結果として反社会的な行動の減少や学校での出席率の改善につながりました。

さらに、本稿では、Old's Cool がプロジェクトに携わったスタッフやボランティアに与えたポジティブな役割についても明らかにしています。例として、新型コロナウイルス流行下において、ボランティアのヴィクトリアが、高齢者であるメアリーを、ノートパソコンを使いこなせるようサポートしたことが紹介されています。これよりメアリーは友達や家族、コミュニティーと連絡を取り続けることができました。ヴィクトリアとメアリーは電話で話しながら各々で Google マップにアクセスし、離れた場所にいながらもコンピューター上で世界中の様々な場所を共に訪れました。この例は、いかに Old's Cool に組み込まれたテクノロジーに焦点を当てた活動が、コミュニケーション用デバイスを使いこなせるよう支援することで、パンデミックにより変化した環境に参加者が順応する手助けになったかを示すものです。

最後に、2015 年の発足以降、Old's Cool がスコットランドのリースにおいてコミュニティーにもたらしてきた影響について論じています。Old's Cool に参加し、現在では成人となった若者の多くが、学校において積極的に学習する態度を身につけ、出席率が改善したことで、前向きな将来を歩んでいることが強調されています。さらに、リースを拠点とした別の世代間プロジェクトである「New Spin」が、現在進行中の世代間交流の実践と Old's Cool のレガシーを支えています。

Author

Denise Milne

Dr Denise Milne lectures in Digital Interaction Design at DJCAD, University of Dundee. Her research focuses on the role that digital technology can play in social relationships, particularly in healthcare and well-being settings. She was awarded her PhD in 2020 for a thesis which explored the potential of 3D printing within educational settings, particularly the applications of this technology for building confidence and developing skills relevant for contemporary society.

In 2018 she was part of a research team that received the Elsevier Grand 3D Printing Challenge Innovation Award for their development of 3D printing filament made from recycled ocean plastic. This project involved community work with local school children, and so provided hands-on experience in the remanufacturing process for young people and contributed to a better understanding of issues surrounding waste. Denise is a member of Studio Ordinary which offers a shared research and creative space to both disabled and non-disabled researchers across DJCAD and so unites colleagues with expertise including design, disability studies, illustration and social policy. Denise also leads the Critical Making module at DJCAD, which hosts a collaborative brief in partnership with Scotland's largest paediatric hospital, allowing students to develop practical experience with design in a healthcare setting.

Ryan McKay

Ryan McKay is a youth and community worker with a background in Community Education, based at the Citadel Youth Centre in Edinburgh, Scotland. Since 2015 he has been the lead worker for their award-winning *Old's Cool Intergenerational Project*, as well as their *New Spin Intergenerational Café* which they deliver in partnership with the Pilmeny Development Project. Ryan is a passionate advocate for the use of intergenerational practice as a way of enabling communities to become better connected. He is also interested in digital intergenerational practice and new ways of hybrid delivery.

Chapter 8

Intergenerational Learning for Senior Learners with Young "Teachers" in Singapore

How Sammy
Lim Wei Loong

"They [young people] know us more, we also know them more. The gap becomes narrower. It becomes easier to get along. The one most important thing is human relationship......Understanding each other is the most important thing." (A senior who participated in the Intergenerational Learning Programme)

The Singapore population is aging rapidly, and multi-generational households where seniors live with their children and grandchildren are becoming less common. This trend is set to intensify according to the Singapore Census of Population 2020, which reveals increasing numbers of singles and childless couples amidst a rapidly aging population. This implies that many among future generations of seniors will not have grandchildren. Their opportunities to interact with the younger generation will diminish and they risk losing touch with the younger generation and the society at large. Therefore, programmes that promote regular intergenerational bonding are important for seniors to remain connected with the society and form new social network through common interests, so that they can remain active and healthy. In this chapter, we provide an overview of Singapore's Intergenerational Learning Programme which is an important initiative to promote intergenerational understanding and bonding to attain active aging for seniors.

In 2011, the Council for Third Age (C3A), a government linked agency tasked to promote active aging, piloted the Intergenerational Learning Programme (ILP) to promote intergenerational bonding and enhance social cohesion between generations by matching senior learners with young "teachers" in a classroom-based group learning environment. The learning was to take place in schools and conducted by students. This model took reference from Hong Kong's Elder Academy scheme, which was launched in 2007 by the Elderly Commission. Elder academies are set up in schools and non-governmental organisations where senior learners are taught by student volunteers. So unlike existing peer-learning programmes, the uniqueness of the ILP lies in having students teaching seniors. Apart from providing learning opportunities for seniors, the ILP also present youths with an experiential learning platform whereby seniors share life experiences, knowledge and skills with them informally.

In June 2013, Family Central, a service by Fei Yue Community Services (FYCS), was officially appointed by C3A as the implementor to scale up ILP to benefit more seniors. At Family Central, we have been actively promoting the ILP among schools from primary to tertiary levels, and other community-based organisations, so as to engage them on board as partners. The schools provide the student teachers (school students), venues, facilities, and conduct the lessons, while Family Central recruits seniors (aged 50 and above) from the public and community-based organisations, and provides the framework and methodology, capacity building through training, consultancy and sharing of best practices. Participating schools can choose to develop their own programmes or adopt our pre-developed course curricula. Most of the schools have initiated new programmes, such as cooking, music, gardening, social media, and digital learning based on our recommendations. Participating schools can count the ILP as part of their schools' service-learning initiatives. In order to enrich the ILP content, we have also formed partnerships with government agencies such as Health Promotion Board (HPB), National Library Board (NLB), National Heritage Board (NHB) and Infocomm Media Development Authority (IMDA).

Currently, the ILP is conducted in English and Mandarin. The teaching takes place one-to-one where a student teacher is matched with a senior learner as buddies. The recommended duration for an ILP is 1-4 sessions and 2.5 - 3 hours per session. The sessions can be held during or after school hours. On the actual day of the sessions, senior learners travel to the school where they will be received and greeted by participating students who will be their student teachers. Seniors will then be guided to their respective classes for their ILP sessions. Every session begins with an icebreaker activity, followed by the lesson proper, and a refreshment break. A survey is administered to both seniors and students at the end of each ILP to probe attitudinal and perception changes.

As can be seen, through interactive, hands-on sessions that include digital learning, cooking, gardening, photography, managing heath, arts and craft, seniors acquire new knowledge while youths get an opportunity to share their knowledge and have their character moulded. Intergenerational understanding is promoted and intergenerational friendships formed. The benefits are expected to enrich students' relationships with their own grandparents and seniors' relationship with their own grandchildren, as well as intergenerational interactions among young people and seniors residing in the same community.

In 2016, we conducted a study to review the ILP. The review sought to find out how seniors benefited from the ILP, their views on the areas that have been done well, and what could be done differently. The study adopted a qualitative approach where seven focus group discussion sessions were conducted with 61 seniors who were ILP participants. There were 14 males and 47 females, and their ages ranged from 53 to 79 years old. In addition, an online feedback form was also administered to four ILP site coordinators and 17 schoolteachers.

First of all, study participants shared that the primary motivation for them joining the ILP was to learn new knowledge and skills, particularly IT-related skills such as using a mobile phone and social media. With this end in mind, seniors found it important that the students were sufficiently equipped to teach them and there are opportunities for them to practice the skills after the programme. The other motivations for participating in the ILP was wanting to interact with young people and wanting to get to know other seniors.

When it comes to how they had benefitted from the ILP, participants described that they had experienced personal growth through the ILP in two main ways. Firstly, they had gained new knowledge and skills; Secondly, their social network expanded as they got to know other seniors in the programme and continued to keep in touch with one another via social media after the programme.

Many study participants also described positive changes in their perceptions of young people as a result of the ILP. For instance, one participant remarked that before the ILP, he thought youths were very occupied with their schoolwork. But through the ILP, he discovered that the students were very keen to interact with him and were very patient in helping him to learn. Another senior who did not have children mentioned that the ILP helped her learnt about children and their school life.

In addition, intergenerational friendships were also formed. Participants enjoyed interacting with the students. After getting to know one another, the conversations between seniors and students went beyond merely discussing the content of the activity to sharing about their family and school lives. School teachers and onsite coordinators who completed the online feedback form also observed that the seniors and students had enjoyed both the learning and the interactions, and that intergenerational rapport were formed during the activity. Both teachers and coordinators found the programme meaningful in connecting the two generations.

The study also uncovered mutual understanding and effective communication between seniors and youths as the main ingredients that contributed to the ILP's positive outcomes. Participants in the focus groups mentioned that they appreciated students who were thoughtful in assisting them, and showed patience while teaching them as those students understood seniors' slower pace of learning. They could recall incidents such as students patiently repeating the same learning point to them until they grasped it, and a student who printed the handouts in larger fonts once she discovered that her senior learner had difficulties reading smaller fonts. On the seniors' part, they were also aware that they had to take the initiative to understand young people, be open and flexible to accommodate young peoples' interaction styles, and avoid imposing their own views or demands on the youths. Many seniors saw that the students regarded them as role models, hence the need to be more nurturing towards the students.

Generally, the findings showed that the programme has met its objectives as both seniors and students had benefited from it in ways that were consistent with the intended outcomes. Mutual understanding between seniors and students was an essential ingredient that contributed to the attainment of the outcomes. The finding thus implies that in order for the ILP to be effective, both students and seniors must be well-prepared to interact. As a result, all students now attend a soft skills training workshop prior to the start of the learning sessions. The training aims to help them gain better understanding of the ageing process, dispel myths and stereotypes about ageing, address unspoken fears and questions about seniors and improve communication skills for intergenerational interactions. For seniors, information packages were sent to them before the ILP sessions to help them understand what the programme is about and what to expect from the programme. The study also reveals that lower-primary school students (age

7 to 9 years old) might not be ready to teach seniors, so the current student-led teaching model might not suit these students. Thus a trainer/teacher-led teaching model was introduced to facilitate learning and bonding between the senior-student dyad for lower-primary students.

The ILP is currently in its 10th year (2011 to 2021). It continues to be offered free-of-charge for Singaporeans and Permanent Residents aged 50 and above. More than 20,250 seniors and 28,000 students from over 158 schools have benefited from the programme. The programme is also now offered as a course under the National Silver Academy (NSA), which is a lifelong learning initiative under the Government's Action Plan for Successful Ageing administered by C3A.

When the COVID-19 pandemic struck, we made ILP available on a virtual platform with the aim of enabling seniors to continue to form meaningful connections while remaining at home. At Family Central, we diligently worked out and tested a new set of operational procedures to ensure the feasibility of conducting ILP virtually. A series of trials with the main virtual meeting room used for the lesson, the breakout rooms for the senior-youth pairs, and the use of broadcast messages across all rooms to provide important instructions were carried out successfully. This virtual option was finally rolled out and offered to schools from July 2020. In addition, the soft skills training that has usually been conducted onsite was also converted to a pre-recorded video, thereby allowing students the flexibility to watch it at their own time. Despite these efforts, critical gaps remain with regards to serving seniors who prefer physical interactions and seniors who do not know how to access online learning.

To encourage more youths (aged 16 to 25) in Singapore to step forward to contribute to seniors' active ageing and lifelong learning journey, we have recently expanded the ILP by introducing the "Youths for Seniors" initiative. This is a volunteering initiative for youths to impart skills and knowledge to seniors, and bond with seniors through virtual workshops. It affords an opportunity for youths who are passionate about serving seniors to reach out to seniors and form friendships with them. Till date, 17 youths have conducted 15 virtual ILP sessions and reached out to more than 800 seniors.

To conclude, for the past ten years, the ILP has played an instrumental role in promoting intergenerational understanding and bonding, as well as lifelong learning. Looking forward, C3A is looking beyond schools and other formats of IG learning and working with implementors like Family Central to evolve the ILP and meet the needs of a new generation of seniors who are better educated, more digital savvy, yet has diminishing opportunities to interact with younger generations within their own families.

Acknowledgement

We thank Mr Mervyn Chua and his team at C3A for their helpful comments on the draft.

Summary

This chapter introduces the Intergenerational Learning Programme (ILP) launched and commissioned by Singapore's Council for Third Age (C3A), a government linked agency, and implemented by Fei Yue Community Services (FYCS), a social service agency.

The ILP aims to promote intergenerational bonding and enhance social cohesion between generations. In the programme, senior learners were matched with junior "teachers" in a classroom-based group learning environment. The learning takes place in schools and is conducted by students. Besides seniors, the ILP also present youths with an experiential learning platform whereby seniors share life experiences, knowledge and skills with them. Therefore, through interactive, hands-on sessions that include digital learning, cooking, gardening, photography, managing heath, arts and craft, etc, seniors acquire new knowledge while youths get to share their knowledge and have their character moulded. Through the ILP, intergenerational understanding is promoted and intergenerational friendships formed.

A 2016 review by FYCS showed that both seniors and students had benefited from the ILP in ways that were consistent with its intended outcomes. Based on the findings, some changes were introduced to improve ILP. These included pre-programme soft skills training for students to help them understand and interact with seniors better, ILP information packages for seniors to help them understand what the programme is about and what to expect from the programme, and adopting a trainer/teacher-led teaching model to facilitate learning and bonding between the senior-student dyad for lower-primary students. When COVID-19 struck, ILP was made available through a virtual platform and hence was able to continue enabling seniors and students to form meaningful connections while remaining at home. In addition, to encourage more youths (aged 16 to 25) in Singapore to step forward to contribute to seniors' active ageing and lifelong learning journey, ILP has recently introduced the "Youths for Seniors" initiative. This is a volunteering initiative for youths to impart skills and knowledge to seniors, and bond with seniors through virtual workshops. Till date, 17 youths have conducted 15 virtual ILP sessions and reached out to more than 800 seniors. In summary, ILP has played an instrumental role in promoting intergenerational understanding and bonding, as well as lifelong learning.

要約

本章では、シンガポールの政府関連機関であるCouncil for Third Age (C3A) が立ち上げ、委託を受け、社会福祉法人Fei Yue Community Services (FYCS) によって実施された世代間学習プログラム (ILP) を紹介します。

ILPは、世代間の結びつきを促進し、世代間の社会的結束を強化することを目的としています。このプログラムでは、シニアの学習者がジュニアの「先生」とマッチングされ、教室でのグループ学習が行われました。学習は学校で行われ、学生によって実施されます。また、ILPは、シニアが人生の経験や知識、技術を若者と共有する体験学習の場でもあります。そのため、デジタル学習、料理、園芸、写真、健康管理、美術工芸など、双方向の体験型セッションを通じて、シニアは新しい知識を身に付け、若者は知識を共有し、人格を形成することができます。ILPを通じて、世代間の理解が促進され、世代を超えた友情が形成されていくのです。

2016年に行われたFYCSのレビューでは、シニアと生徒の両方がILPの意図する成果と一致する形で恩恵を受けていることが示されました。この調査結果に基づき、ILPを改善するためにいくつかの変更が導入されました。

その内容には、生徒がシニアを理解し、よりよく交流できるようにするためのプログラム前のソフトスキル研修や、シニアがプログラムの内容やプログラムから何を期待するかを理解するためのILP情報パッケージ、小学校低学年児童の学習とシニアと児童の絆を深めるためのトレーナー / 教師主導の指導モデルの採用などが含まれています。

COVID-19が発生した際も、ILPはバーチャルプラットフォームを通じて提供されるようになったため、シニアと児童は、在宅のまま、有意義なつながりを形成することを可能にし、継続させることができました。

さらに、最近、ILPは、高齢者のアクティブ・エイジングと生涯学習の旅に貢献するため、シンガポールのより多くの若者 (16～25歳) に参加を呼びかけるため、「ユース・フォー・シニア」という取り組みを導入しています。これは、若者がシニアに技術や知識を伝授し、バーチャル・ワークショップを通じてシニアとの絆を深めるためのボランティア活動です。現在までに17人の若者が15回のバーチャルILPセッションを実施し、800人以上のシニアにコンタクトを取ってきています。

このように、ILPは世代間の理解や絆、生涯学習を促進する上で重要な役割を担っています。

Author

How Sammy

Sammy How is a Senior Manager of Fei Yue Community Services in Singapore, and currently heads the Elder Education department to promote lifelong learning, active ageing and intergenerational learning. In 2005, he inspired his department to three consecutive years' awards for initiating innovative Inter-Generational Bonding (IGB) programmes. Sammy has more than 17 years of experiences involving in talks, workshops and programmes relating to ageing, mental health, intergenerational bonding, parenting and self defence for seniors. His noteworthy projects include "Innovate!Sculpey" – a polymer clay programme for seniors, setting up of Active Ageing Academy, Singapore Silver Cosplay Club and The Arts Market (TAM) for seniors. He has won praises from the community and the media for implementing creative seniors programme. Sammy holds a Master degree in Polymer Technology from Loughborough University, UK.

Lim Wei Loong

Wei Loong is a Principal Research Executive at Fei Yue Community Services in Singapore, where he is actively involved in conducting social service research and evaluations, and supporting the agency in utilising research to inform practice. He has been involved in several research that examine the experiences of older adults in different life situations, such as living alone, divorce and widowhood, caregiving, intergenerational interaction, and access to social care services. Wei Loong completed an MPhil in Social and Developmental Psychology from the University of Cambridge, an MSc in Evidence Based health Care from the University of Oxford, and a Graduate Diploma of Social Science in Professional Counselling from Swinburne University of Technology.

Chapter 9

Intergenerational Housing Plaza de America Building

Gaspar Mayor Pascual

The Plaza de America Building Project is the first one on an ambitious programme of the Alicante Town Hall which pretends, using public plots, to build buildings that contains flats or apartments to rent for elderly people, with an intergenerational nature, and proximity services to attend the local elderly neighbourhood where the building is located, and with a special attention to the Community Centres destined to assist and take care of elderly people.

The Alicante Town Hall, through the Housing Department in close collaboration with the Social Department, present a programme with a 50.000.000 € of total investment, and using public plots to built 3 buildings "Plaza América", "Benalúa" y "Lonja – Mercado", but with the best intention to extend this project to other neighbourhoods.

Elderly people financial problems due to their low incomes, their poor living and accessibility conditions of their current houses, the afraid and the loneliness are some of the factors that lead most of our worth elderly to end living with their sons or to admit in a premature way in a geriatric centre. In view of this situation we have set as a programme objective to have a well-balance rent of the flats we offer and besides this flat must have safety, comfort and protection conditions to allow old people to live in a pleasant and independent way.

The supportive participation of young people, who live in one of every four flats, is based on its involvement in the whole living organization and mainly on the culture and leisure activities that with an intergenerational nature will take place in the common spaces or lounges. Besides there is a commitment, which we have called “the good neighbour”, in which every young take care of four elderly of his floor, they help them in some punctual domestic duties, they give them company and other important activities like alert us to every situation that can be consider as a risk.

The Plaza de America building, the first project consolidated, contains 72 intergenerational apartments or flats, a community centre for day time care, a complete equipment health centre and a parking for 250 cars. The building residential area contains spacious lounges dedicated to common services (library, computing rooms, handicrafts, garden and laundry).

These houses are state subsidized housing to rent.

The rent set for this first project in Plaza America Building, is 169 € monthly for a 40 squared meters apartment, that means a 35 % discount over the maximum rent allowed for these kind of apartments by the Housing State Planning .

The Valencia Region supports this project with a specific subsidy for the apartments and another one for the Community Centre, that means that both area are fundamental for each other.

The architecture project follows these premises which allow us a better understanding of this project:

- To make relationships easier between different age people by helping each other in a home environment.
- To disposal different services which extend an independence situation and gives safety.
- To encourage relationships between building neighbours and with the neighbourhood local people.
- To introduce new technologies which improve them welfare state and comfort in a simple and natural way.
- To give a warm environment by using friendly building materials, not sophisticated.

- To introduce a softly control and vigilance through the young cooperation, this will improve at the same time the intergenerational relationship between them.
- To create workshops for occupational, training and leisure programmes.

Municipal Intergenerational Houses and Proximity services

The Plaza de America Building contains 72 intergenerational apartments to rent for elderly and young people; there are 56 flats for elderly and 16 for young people.

This project was built in a public plot and with an intergenerational nature, also contains proximity services to attend the local elderly neighbourhood where the building is located; these services are a community centre (1st and 2 nd floor)and a medical centre (ground floor and 1st floor) and a parking to rent for a 256 cars in the basement.

Houses Typology

The intergenerational houses are 40 squared meters apartments with a multifunction space conception, with one bedroom, a living room, a kitchen and an adapted bathroom. These apartments take up four floors in the building, and are communicated with two elevators. Also they have three halls for residents: an audio and movie hall, a computer and reading hall and a workshop hall where young people develops occupational, training and leisure programmes for elderly people. This conception has one meaning, to improve the elderly people quality life based in the relationship between the actors and the experience and knowledge exchanges.

Financing

- Municipal contribution for the Medical Centre: 3.457.168, 52 euros.
- Qualified mortgage loan by *Patronato Municipal de la Vivienda de Alicante*: 2.532.494,72 euros.
- Housing state planning subsidy: 1.266.247,46 euros.
- Valencia region subsidy for the community centre: 995.000,00 euros.
- Parking dealership: 3.336.076, 80 euros.
- Municipal contribution: 766.803,71 euros.

Intervention Projects

Our social programme in this building must establish the rules for young people who are in charged to organize the intergenerational activities in their own building and the possible collaboration with other public or private organizations out of the building. This programme wish to be accessible to others and to be enjoined by everybody in the building, even with the community services for the neighbourhood which is located in the same building. These programmes are developed by the Patronato Municipal de la Vivienda Social Department with the residents' collaboration.

1. **"Vuelta a la tierra"**: "A return to the land", this is a real return to the land because they can work in it again through the gardening and a vegetable garden which are in the building. In this programme you will find three residents in charge of it:
   One elderly resident in the vegetable garden
   One elderly resident in the gardening
   One young resident supporting the gardening and the vegetable garden,

who is in charge of this area in the community blog, so must inform everybody about the growing through this blog.

They have promoted a seed nursery to obtain different cultivations.

2. **"De lo cultural a la información"**: "From the culture to the information" this programme is
   based in 4 different workshop with different actors.
   - Video library
   - Library
   - Music
   - Press

3. **"La Fiesta"**: Every year they celebrate 6 different parties in the building: Carnival, the European Intergenerational Day, the garden harvest day, Hogueras de San Juan (Local Festival), the building anniversary and Christmas. And of course, they have the possibility to organize community and private parties; there are two areas in the building that can be used for parties: a terrace in the top (during the summer) and the workshop hall (during the winter). If it is a community party there must be two residents in charge, for personal or private parties the resident who organize it will be in charge. Also they have a weekly dance for elderly and young's.

4. **"La tecnología en tu mano"**: "a technology on your hands", they try to bring old people to new technologies, not only computers, all the daily equipments or machines that are common or ordinary for young people but not very friendly for elderly people like air condition, mobile phone, computers, internet... they couldn't access to them and don't know how it works and it benefits.

   They also updated all the information in the building blog, and have contact with the

   Intergenerational Programme IMSERSO, they inform them about experiences and activities organized in the building, and also they made a monthly report about their activities.

   Plaza América blog: http://plazaamerica.wordpress.com

5. **"El buen vecino"**: "the good neighbour" is a programme were young people help elderly in some punctual domestic duties, they give them company, and if they need it , they can go to the doctor with them, to the pharmacy, and other important activities like alert us to every situation that can be consider as a risk. That doesn't mean to supply their families but means to return to the old neighbourhoods where they help each other in normal duties.

   Besides there is a commitment, in which every young take care of four elderly of his floor, and there is a coordinator in every floor.

Specific Workshops: every year specific workshops are planning by young and elderly people.

Running by elderly people:

- Home cooking
- Specific cleaning for clothes and other materials
- Ironing
- Domestic Economy

Running by young people:

- First Aid
- Home repairs
- Electrical household appliances manage

Organazation and Functioning:

The Social Department designs the intergenerational programme and put it into operation:

- They have monthly meetings with young people for the programme coordination and monitoring.
- Young people have a weekly meeting to be coordinated.
- Besides they organize different committees.
- All of them are part of this neighbourhood.

The resident's participation is a priority.

Committee functions:

- Coordination Committee: weekly meetings between young and elderly people.
- Participation Committee: to follow, evaluate and improve the participation in activity programmes.
- Communication Committee: coordination and organization of media visits: press, television ...
- To prepare the Articles of Community presented by Patronato Municipal de la Vivienda in the Municipal Registry Office.
- To participate in developing the Articles of the Intergenerational Association.

Summary

The Plaza de America Building Project is the first one on an ambitious programme of the Alicante Town Hall which pretends, using public plots, to build buildings that contains flats or apartments to rent for elderly people, with an intergenerational nature, and proximity services to attend the local elderly neighbourhood where the building is located, and with a special attention to the Community Centres destined to assist and take care of elderly people.

The Alicante Town Hall, through the Housing Department in close collaboration with the Social Department, present a programme with a 50.000.000 € of total investment, and using public plots to built 3 buildings "Plaza América", "Benalúa" y "Lonja – Mercado", but with the best intention to extend this project to other neighbourhoods.

Elderly people financial problems due to their low incomes, their poor living and accessibility conditions of their current houses, the afraid and the loneliness are some of the factors that lead most of our worth elderly to end living with their sons or to admit in a premature way in a geriatric centre. In view of this situation we have set as a programme objective to have a well-balance rent of the flats we offer and besides this flat must have safety, comfort and protection conditions to allow old people to live in a pleasant and independent way.

The supportive participation of young people, who live in one of every four flats, is based on its involvement in the whole living organization and mainly on the culture and leisure activities that with an intergenerational nature will take place in the common spaces or lounges. Besides there is a commitment, which we have called "the good neighbour", in which every young take care of four elderly of his floor, they help them in some punctual domestic duties, they give them company and other important activities like alert us to every situation that can be consider as a risk.

The Plaza de America building, the first project consolidated, contains 72 intergenerational apartments or flats, a community centre for day time care, a complete equipment health centre and a parking for 250 cars. The building residential area contains spacious lounges dedicated to common services (library, computing rooms, handicrafts, garden and laundry).

These houses are state subsidized housing to rent.

The rent set for this first project in Plaza America Building, is 169 € monthly for a 40 squared meters apartment, that means a 35 % discount over the maximum rent allowed for these kind of apartments by the Housing State Planning .

The Valencia Region supports this project with a specific subsidy for the apartments and another one for the Community Centre, that means that both area are fundamental for each other.

The architecture project follows these premises which allow us a better understanding of this project:

- To make relationships easier between different age people by helping each other in a home environment.
- To disposal different services which extend an independence situation and gives safety.
- To encourage relationships between building neighbours and with the neighbourhood local people.
- To introduce new technologies which improve them welfare state and comfort in a simple and natural way.
- To give a warm environment by using friendly building materials, not sophisticated.
- To introduce a softly control and vigilance through the young cooperation, this will improve at the same time the intergenerational relationship between them.
- To create workshops for occupational, training and leisure programmes.

要約

Plaza de America は、アリカンテ市役所による最初の意欲的なプロジェクトです。

これは、公共用地を利用して高齢者向けの賃貸アパートやマンションを建設し、世代間交流の環境や、特に高齢者の支援・ケアを目的とするコミュニティセンターを含む近隣の高齢者向けのサービスを作り出すものです。

アリカンテ市役所は、住宅局と社会局の緊密な協力のもと、総投資額 50,000,000 ユーロのプログラムを発表し、公共区画を利用して「Plaza America」「Benalua」「Lonja - Mercado」の３棟を建設しましたが、他の地区にもこのプロジェクトを拡大することを念頭に置いています。

高齢者における低所得に伴う経済的な問題、現在の住居の劣悪かつ不便な生活環境、不安や孤独感などが、多くの高齢者が息子との同居を解消したり、老人医療センターへの早期入所を余儀なくされている要因となっています。このような状況を踏まえ、私たちは提供する住居の家賃をバランスよく設定し、さらに高齢者が快適かつ自立して生活できるような安全性、快適性、保護条件を備えた住居にすることをプログラムの目標にしました。

4戸に1戸の割合で入居している若者の参加は、生活組織全体への参加と共有スペースやラウンジで行われる世代を超えた文化・余暇活動への参加が基本となっています。さらに、「良き隣人」と呼ばれる取り組みがあり、若い人は自分のフロアに住む4人の高齢者の世話をし、一定の時間に家事を手伝い、彼らの仲間を作り、その他、危険と思われるあらゆる状況に注意を払うなどの重要な活動をしています。

最初のプロジェクトとして建設されたPlaza de Americaには、72戸の世代間交流アパートまたはマンション、デイケア用のコミュニティセンター、設備完備のヘルスセンター、250台収容の駐車場があります。建物の居住エリアには、共用サービス(図書館、計算室、手工芸、庭、洗濯機)専用の広々としたラウンジがあります。

これらの住宅は、国からの補助による賃貸住宅です。最初のプロジェクトであるPlaza America Buildingの家賃は、40平方メートルのアパートで月169ユーロであり、国の住宅計画で認められているこの種のアパートの最大家賃より35%割引となっています。

バレンシアでは、このプロジェクトにおいて、アパートとコミュニティ・センターに対して補助金を出しており、この2つのエリアは互いに重要な役割を担っています。

この建築プロジェクトは、以下のような前提に基づいており、これによってこのプロジェクトをより良く理解することができます。

- 異なる年齢の人々が、家庭的な環境の中で助け合うことによって、人間関係をより円滑なものにします。
- 自立を促し、安全を確保するための様々なサービスを提供します。
- 建物内の隣人や近隣の地域住民との関係を促進します。
- シンプルかつ自然な方法で、福祉と快適さを向上させる新しい技術を導入します。
- 洗練されたものではなく、親しみやすい建材を使用し、温かみのある環境を提供します。
- 若者の協力によるソフトな管理と警備を導入し、同時に世代間の関係も改善します。
- 職業訓練や余暇プログラムのためのワークショップを企画します。

Author

Gaspar Mayor Pascual

Qualifications: Degree in Economics (University of Valencia. 1969-1974).

Main areas of past experience:

a. Head of the economic section of a general information magazine (1975- 1977).
b. Economist in a major banking group in Madrid (1975-1977).
c. Manager of a food products manufacturing company (1977-1988).

Current professional situation:

1. Manager of the Housing Department (City of Alicante) since 1988.
2. Manager of the Comprehensive Projects Office for the Old Town Rehabilitation Plan since 1992, City of Alicante and Region of Valencia.
3. Member of the Municipal Culture Hall governing board (City of Alicante).

European and International Collaboration Programs:

1. Head of European programs related to housing and neighborhood rehabilitation for the City of Alicante.
2. Head of International collaboration programs related to housing andneighbourhood recovery for the City of Alicante.

Professional Associations:

1. Vice President of the Spanish Public Housing and Land Developers Association, from 2001 to 2003 and President from 2003 to 2006.
2. President of the Public European Coordinating Committee for Social Housing (CECODHAS) from 2004 to 2006.

Non-profit private activities:

Since February 2002, Vice President of a private foundation dedicated to caring for people with severe mental disabilities.

Academic activities:

1. Lecturer on a Master's Degree in Urban Planning and Housing (University of Alicante).
2. Lecturer on a Master's Degree in Housing (Catholic University of Murcia).
3. Lecturer on a Master's Degree in social housing management (University of Sevilla).

Publications and Seminars:

Publication of a book about the City of Tartous (Syria). Publications in professional journals and a speaker at numerous seminars and conferences related to the rehabilitation of historic centres, social housing, immigration, disadvantaged groups, etc

Chapter 10

Generations Connect: Strengthening Community Connectedness

Kristin Bodiford
Cory Elliott

We are grateful to learn with our colleagues in Japan and around the world about how intergenerational exchanges can contribute to the creation of a new society. We hope the experiences in this series can spark conversation about what might be useful to help shape our collective future. This chapter shares the experience of an intergenerational pilot project called Generations Connect that ran from January and June 2021. You will find lessons youth learned in this project, in their own words.

Generations Connect brings together people of different ages to strengthen community connectedness, learn about online safety, and prevent interpersonal violence. It is based on the belief that everyone at every age can help build communities where people can feel safe in their relationships, families, and communities. Generations Connect helps people to recognize our "shared fate" and creates a range of opportunities to learn together and deepen skills as leaders and network-builders.

I used to think the voices of the older generation were outdated and weren't really important to the improvement of our society. However, I've realized that one day I will be an older person and I would want my voice to be appreciated. I've learned that as long as we converse with each other, we will find common ground and deepen our understanding which in turn will benefit our society. Phoenix (age 16)

This work helps us to appreciate different perspectives and bridge intergenerational divides to make a meaningful impact.

Intergenerational connections are important because they let us view different ideas from different perspectives. It's important to empathize with other people and understand, not only across ages but also across race and gender, that people have different perspectives. Max (age 18)

When we intentionally invest in strong networks across generations, we strengthen our capacity to recognize our interconnectedness and apply cross-generational strategies and values to many issues (Henkin et al., 2012).

Generations Connect was developed as part of a countywide strategy in Contra Costa County in California (similar to a prefecture in Japan, with a population of 1.1 million) to prevent interpersonal violence called the *Call to Action*.[1] The *Call to Action* is a collective commitment to a safe and healthy community for all people, of all ages. Generations Connect ties directly to the *Call to Action* Goal 3: Encourage community trust and connectedness. It recognizes that interpersonal violence affects people across and between all ages, thus requiring life course and intergenerational solutions. Generations Connect focuses on neighborhood and cross-community efforts to bring multiple generations together, foster strong connections across ages, race/ethnicity, socioeconomic classes, and other factors.

During the height of the COVID pandemic, we knew that this was even more essential, as people faced increasing rates of isolation and risk for interpersonal violence. We also knew we would need to innovate to bring people together online to do this work. We are grateful to Generations United and a major tech company partner as they supported us to test a pilot program to bring youth and older adults together online to learn about online safety, increase social connectedness/decrease loneliness, and strengthen intergenerational relationships. We adapted the program to include a capstone project with the focus on intergenerational community building to prevent interpersonal violence.

Background

Regardless of age, across the world, especially in the midst of COVID-19, younger and older people are experiencing risks of online safety, loneliness, and social isolation (Barreto, 2020; Gloria, 2020). [2]

Research shows that both younger and older generations are often the most at risk for online safety issues such as scams (Guzman, 2018). This is especially important as the number of older adults ages 60-79 in Japan using the internet increased by 12% over the last decade, putting them at increased risk of online scams (Japan Cabinet Office, 2020). Young people are also at

1 http://www.contracostaalliance.org/

2 In this article, social isolation is defined as an objective lack of social contact with others and loneliness is defined as the subjective feeling of being isolated.

risk of online safety issues including cyberbullying and mental health issues related to internet, social media, and online gaming use.

In the global BBC's Loneliness Experiment, 40% of 16 to 24-year-olds reported they often or very often feel lonely with higher levels of loneliness in young people (Hammond, 2018). Older adults also face an increased risk of loneliness due to factors such as living alone or the loss of family or friends, with significant potential impacts on mental and physical health and mortality (Holt-Lunstad, 2018). Social isolation and negative social attitudes, including ageism, racism, and ableism reduce opportunities for people of all ages to be socially engaged in the community (Sellon, 2019).

Yet, people also experience increasing psychosocial health, happiness, and wisdom as they age, which presents an opportunity for older adults to connect to each other and youth to decrease social isolation and loneliness for themselves and for others.

Intergenerational programs value people at all ages and stages of life and increase connectedness.

- Intergenerational programs are those that intentionally connect young people and older adults in meaningful, purposeful activities together.
- Relationships are at the core of intergenerational programs.
- Bringing generations together to support each other and address critical issues helps improve lives, build caring relationships, and strengthen the fabric of our society.

These kinds of opportunities for connection and contribution are foundational to promoting resilience in the face of challenges. This focus on resilience helps us shift from a deficit-orientation to approaches that focus on strengths and well-being (Masten & O'Dougherty Wright, 2010). Across the life course, resilience is enhanced when people are able to:

- come together in safe and nurturing environments,
- feel a sense of belonging and connection to caring relationships,
- develop skills and capacities, and
- engage in opportunities to participate and contribute (Benard, 2004).

Our families and communities are richer and stronger as a result (Butts & Bodiford, 2019).

Bridging the gaps that separate us

The primary prevention of interpersonal violence requires us to focus on the multiple priorities of the United Nations Sustainable Development Goals to realize the vision of "peace and prosperity for people and the planet, now and into the future". Addressing the SDGs helps to reduce the risk factors that promote violence such as economic and gender inequality, and increase access to healthcare, food security, and quality education. We must do this together, by bridging gaps through sharing knowledge and practices across the globe as this series, *Intergenerational Exchange Activities as a Social Network toward the Creation of a New Society* has invited us to do.

I wasn't expecting to learn that making connections with people who are much older than you are can be kind of hard. I was thinking 'Oh, I'm good at talking with people and connecting, so this will be really easy'. But through talking to my grandparents or other older people, I realized that people have different spectrums of how open they are and how willing they are to have deep and meaningful conversations. But that also taught me that's what makes it so much more valuable and meaningful. These relationships and conversations are so important because I feel like in society, we have this big divide when it comes to certain things and if we just talk to each other and try to understand that we can really bridge those gaps and have a better future for all of us. Sarah (age 17)

Generations Connect Activities

Generations Connect weaves learning with action—understanding topics of online safety and safe and healthy relationships and taking action through intergenerational leadership and community building.

A youth leadership team advised on implementation, developed a recruitment plan, and actively reached out to other youth to participate. There was also a team of adult allies who also supported the process of advising and supporting the youth team and connecting to organizational partners.

Although not everyone's the same or comes from around the same place, I really found a connection that I didn't expect. I was truly grateful for her elderly sister advice. Giselle (age 17)

The curriculum we used integrates social gaming and discussion-based activities to increase knowledge and skills covering topics such as basic online safety, emotional resilience, media literacy, and recognizing and avoiding scams. The goal is to create a connecting and nourishing use of technology.

We also focused on building intergenerational leadership through sessions on topics such as connecting and communicating, healthy relationships, understanding ourselves and our community, creating change, and storytelling.

Intergenerational connections are important because older people teach us younger people something that they've learned during their life. So, we can use it in our personal experiences, so history doesn't repeat itself. Like, if someone older than you made a mistake in their life and learned from it, they can pass it on to you. And you can use it in your own experiences, so you know what to do. Jorge (age 16)

The youth and adult allies then engaged in a design thinking process - a human-centered approach to solve problems. Design thinking starts with developing empathy and understanding what is important for other people. It uses creative thinking to develop many ideas for solutions that can be tested and improved upon.

My favorite part of the design thinking approach is that it allows us to focus on what we are most passionate about and build ideas to take action! Sarah (age 17)

Youth started by interviewing people of other generations in their families about what could be done so that we can all have safe, connected, healthy relationships. From what they learned in these interviews, the youth developed several main themes that they then developed into How Might We questions that turn challenges into opportunities for design.

- How might we create spaces for generations to **listen deeply to each other and develop more understanding and connection?**
- How might we **provide support** for other generations and be there for them during difficult times?
- How might we **build trust and respect** between generations?
- How might we develop strategies that **connect people and promote healthy relationships**?

I've learned to communicate better with people and support each other. Anamaria (age 18)

The youth invited their adult allies to form intergenerational teams to brainstorm ideas for projects around these How Might We questions. They developed three project areas including: 1) holding conversations together,

2) doing activities together, and 3) creating media together. Then the youth started implementing the following prototypes in each of these project areas.

They hosted intergenerational conversations with older adults in Spanish and English focusing on the questions: "What has allowed you to remain strong in your life? What can we do to strengthen intergenerational relationships in our families and communities?"

What I've learned from this project is that the older generation were once younger, like me. They had their own lives, their own friends, their own experiences. I'm like - that's so cool. I always saw them as just like, oh, these are older people. I never saw them as like they are just like me, but they have more experience. Phoenix (age 16)

They hosted a food giveaway in which they gave 165 boxes of food away to families and older adults.

I feel like I learned not to judge people. When we did a food drive, I didn't think I would learn anything from anybody. But they really taught me so many things. I feel like when we are so reluctant to talk to people, we miss out on a lot of opportunities and information. Kristina (age 13)

They also engaged in an intergenerational storytelling project based upon the belief that the shortest distance between two people is a story. From these conversations they developed digital stories in partnership with Story Center. [3, 4]

I learned everyone has a story. Donovan (age 16)

With a successful launch of Generations Connect, a youth leadership team is developing a toolkit for youth-led intergenerational community building and a roadmap for the future of this work.

I think that there's a lot of issues between different generations and we should learn how to bridge the gap between them. Now, I am more aware of the issues, and I am striving to change

3 https://www.storycenter.org/

4 Generations Connect digital stories can be found here-
https://youtube.com/playlist?list=PLjIM3nc48YLShmhuAfpnu3Onp3qewUsmL

those. Dylan (age 16)

Citations

Barreto, Manuela, et al. "Loneliness around the World: Age, Gender, and Cultural Differences in Loneliness." Personality and Individual Differences, 26 Apr. 2020, p. 110066., Retrieved from doi:10.1016/j.paid.2020.110066.

Benard, Bonnie. Resiliency: What we have learned. San Francisco, CA: WestEd, 2004.

Butts, Donna M., and Kristin J. Bodiford. "Family and Intergenerational Relationships." Social Isolation of Older Adults: Strategies to Bolster Health and Well-Being, by Lenard W. Kaye and Clifford M. Singer, Springer Publishing Company, 2019, pp. 197–217.

"Catalyzing Change." Connect2Affect, AARP Foundation, 24 Mar. 2020, Retrieved from connect2affect.org/for-researchers/.

Gloria, Kristine. "Lessons in Loneliness: A Report from Roundtables on the Future of Social Connection, Loneliness, and Technology." Aspen Digital, The Aspen Institute and Facebook, Oct. 2020.

Guzman, Zack. "Millennials Fall for Financial Scams More than Any Other Age Group." CNBC, CNBC, 7 Mar. 2018. Retrieved from www.cnbc.com/2018/03/07/millennials-fall-for-financial-scams-more-than-other-age-groups.html.

Hammond, Claudia. "The Anatomy of Loneliness - Who Feels Lonely? The Results of the World's Largest Loneliness Study." BBC Radio 4, BBC, Oct. 2018. Retrieved from www.bbc.co.uk/programmes/articles/2yzhfv4DvqVp5nZyxBD8G23/who-feels-lonely-the-results-of-the-world-s-largest-loneliness-study.

Henkin, Nancy, et al. Intergenerational Community Building: Lessons Learned. June 2012. Retrieved from www.gu.org/resources/intergenerational-community-building-lessons-learned/.

Holt-Lunstad, Julianne. "The Potential Public Health Relevance of Social Isolation and Loneliness: Prevalence, Epidemiology, and Risk Factors." Public Policy & Aging Report, vol. 27, no. 4, 2 Jan. 2018, pp. 127–130. Retrieved from doi:10.1093/ppar/prx030.

Japan Cabinet Office, Annual Report on the Ageing Society (2020). Retrieved from https://www8.cao.go.jp/kourei/english/annualreport/2020/pdf/2020.pdf

Masten, Ann & O'Dougherty Wright, Margaret. "Resilience over the Lifespan: Developmental perspectives on resistance, recovery, and transformation." Handbook of Adult Resilience, by John W. Reich, Alex J. Zautra, and John Stuart Hall, The Guilford Press, 2010, p 215

Sellon, Alicia M. "Grand Challenge: Eradicate Social Isolation." Gerontological Social Work and the Grand Challenges, edited by S Sanders et al., Springer Nature Switzerland AG, 2019, pp. 61–74.

Summary

Regardless of age, across the world, especially in the midst of COVID-19, younger and older people are experiencing risks of online safety, loneliness, and social isolation (Barreto, 2020). In addition, different generations may have a harder time understanding each other. They might have different experiences and perspectives which can lead to different mindsets and expectations. By understanding each other better, we can develop better connections, bridge gaps, create stronger relationships, learn from each other, and work together to create change in our communities.

Generations Connect, in California, USA, brings together people of different ages to strengthen community connectedness, learn about online safety, and prevent interpersonal violence. It is based on the belief that everyone at every age can help build communities where people can feel safe in their relationships, families, and communities.

Generations Connect weaves learning with action—understanding topics of online safety and safe and healthy relationships and taking action through intergenerational leadership and community building. The curriculum we use integrates social gaming and discussion-based activities to increase knowledge and skills covering topics such as basic online safety, emotional resilience, media literacy, and recognizing and avoiding scams. The goal is to create a connecting and nourishing use of technology.

We also focused on building intergenerational leadership through sessions on topics such as connecting and communicating, healthy relationships, understanding ourselves and our community, creating change, and storytelling.

Generations Connect helps people to recognize our "shared fate" and creates a range of opportunities to learn together and deepen skills as leaders and network-builders. This work helps us to appreciate different perspectives and bridge intergenerational divides to make a meaningful impact. These kinds of opportunities for connection and contribution are foundational to promoting resilience in the face of challenges.

Intergenerational programs help reduce social isolation that younger and older generations experience by increasing connectedness and valuing people at all ages and stages of life. Intergenerational opportunities also tap into the wisdom and strengths of younger and older people.

While this chapter is focused on how intergenerational strategies can contribute to efforts focusing on preventing interpersonal violence, we hope it will be a resource for any issue that multiple generations face.

要約

年齢に関係なく、世界中で、特にCOVID-19の感染拡大が続く中、若い人も年配の人もネット上の安全、孤独、社会的孤立のリスクを経験しています(Barreto, 2020)。さらに、世代が異なるとお互いを理解するのが難しくなることもあります。彼らは異なる経験や視点を持っており、それが異なる考え方や期待につながる可能性があります。お互いをよりよく理解することで、よりよいつながりを築き、溝を埋め、より強い関係を作り、互いに学び協力してコミュニティに変化をもたらすことができます。

米国カリフォルニア州にあるジェネレーションズ・コネクトは、さまざまな年齢の人々が集まり、地域社会のつながりを強め、オンラインの安全性について学び、対人暴力を防止することを目的としています。この活動は、どの年代の人においても人間関係や家族、地域社会で安心して暮らせる地域社会の構築に貢献できるという信念に基づいています。

ジェネレーションズ・コネクトは、オンラインの安全性や安全で健康的な人間関係を理解し、世代を超えたリーダーシップやコミュニティ構築を通じて行動を起こすといった学習と行動を織り交ぜたプログラムです。私たちが使用しているカリキュラムは、ソーシャルゲームとディスカッションベースの活動を統合し、基本的なオンラインの安全性、感情のレジリエンス(回復力)、メディア・リテラシー、詐欺の認識と回避といったトピックに関する知識とスキルを向上させます。このカリキュラムの目標は、テクノロジーとつながり、それを活用することにあります。また、つながりやコミュニケーション、健康的な人間関係、自分自身とコミュニティの理解、変化の創出、ストーリーテリングといったテーマでセッションを行い、世代を超えたリーダーシップの育成に力を入れました。

ジェネレーションズ・コネクトは、私たちが「運命を共有している」ことを認識し、共に学び、リーダーやネットワーク構築者としてのスキルを深めるためのさまざまな機会を提供します。この活動により、私たちは異なる視点を理解し、世代間の溝を埋め、有意義な影響を与えることができるようになります。このようなつながりと貢献の機会は、困難に直面したときに回復力を促進するための基礎となります。

世代間交流プログラムは、あらゆる年齢やライフステージの人々とのつながりを強め、人々を大切にすることで、若い世代や高齢者が経験する社会的孤立を減らすのに役立ちます。また、世代間交流の機会は、若い世代と高齢者の知恵や強みを活用することにもつながります。この章では、世代間交流戦略が対人暴力の防止に焦点を当てた取り組みにどのように貢献できるかに焦点を当てていますが、複数の世代が直面するあらゆる問題のリソースとなることを期待しています。

Author

Kristin Bodiford

Kristin Bodiford, Ph.D. brings experience and knowledge working with systems, communities, organizations, groups, teams, and individuals addressing opportunities for learning, innovation, and transformation. Kristin is passionate about strengthening relational resources in an "intergenerative" way to create positive change. Intergenerative approaches aim to construct a meaningful fusion of conversations and experiences among often disconnected sources of human creativity (e.g., generations, disciplines, or nations) that inspire new possibilities and innovative actions. Kristin is a Taos Associate, Research Faculty at Portland State University Institute on Aging, Senior Fellow and United Nations Representative for Generations United, and Adjunct Faculty at Dominican University School of Social Work.

Cory Elliott

Cory Elliott is an independent consultant from Richmond, California. He works with cities & agencies to provide community, leadership, & violence prevention programs to the youth. Before consulting, Cory was a special education teacher in Brooklyn, New York; he received a Master's Degree from Relay Graduate School in Manhattan, NY. Working with young people, elderly, and the overall community are extremely important. Cory is the President and Co-founder of a non-profit organization called The Black Neighborhood. The organization focus on community building, youth development and mental health.

Find out more about Cory Elliott & The Black Neighborhood at:
cory.e.elliott@gmail.com
theblackneighborhood.org
IG: theblackneighborhood

第３部

Part 3

メッセージ

Message

Intergenerational Exchange Activities as a Social Network Towards Creation of a New

Donna M. Butts

executive director, Generations United

The world is unsettled shaken by a global pandemic, grappling with climate change and much more. Challenges, however, offer opportunities. Looking to the future, the solutions that will help us navigate these extreme challenges require innovative intergenerational approaches that value and engage all ages working together to better rebuild our countries and communities.

Investments and exchanges between younger and older people result in vibrant, respectful societies. This social fabric is woven with the threads that bind generations together passing on culture, sharing stories, growing deep roots, building resiliency and creating a hopeful future for everyone. It will take practitioners, researchers and people of all backgrounds to usher in a new era that recognizes we are all stronger together.

The time to begin is now. I am grateful to Atsuko Kusano, Kazushige Mizobe, Hayato Uchida, Yo Murayama, and Harumi Sakuda for creating this important guide to light the path forward.

新たな創造に向けたソーシャルネットワークとしての世代間交流活動

ドナ・M・バッツ

世界的なパンデミックや気候変動など、世界は不安定な状況にあります。しかし、困難に挑戦することはチャンスを与えてくれます。未来に目を向けると、このような極度な困難を乗り越えるための解決策は、国やコミュニティをより良く再構築するために、すべての年齢層の価値を認め、協働するような革新的な世代間アプローチを必要としています。

若者と高齢者間で時間や精力を傾け交流することは、活力と敬意に満ちた社会をもたらします。このような社会構造は、世代間を結びつける糸で織られています。そしてそれは文化を継承し、物語を共有し、深く根を張り、弾力性を作り、すべての人にとって希望に満ちた未来を創造するのです。実務家、研究者、そしてあらゆるバックグラウンドを持つ人々は、私たちすべてが共により強い存在であることを認識する新しい時代を先導する必要があります。

今こそ、その時です。草野篤子さん、溝邊和成さん、内田勇人さん、村山陽さん、作田はるみさんには、前途を照らす重要な指針を作成していただき、感謝いたします。

Growing an Intergenerational Community from Child-care Center as the Core

Leng Leng Thang
National University of Singapore

In Eastern part of Singapore, a little garden space outside a childcare centre has seen itself transforming into an intergenerational contact zone, becoming a gathering place for grandparents after dropping off their grandchildren or before fetching them.

Although the informal group has developed out of chance encounters, it will be great if there can be more intentional efforts to integrate the garden space outside by connecting the growing informal group with the children, such as having gardening activities where the group can work with the children, getting together for tea time with the children, recruiting grandparents skillful in certain activities to share with the children and teachers.

The blossoming of an intergenerational community from intentional integration of spaces and groups grown out of childcare centre as the core have the potential to promote neighborliness, build security and warmth for all generations living in the vicinity.

チャイルドケアセンターを核とした世代間交流コミュニティの構築

リン・リン・タン

シンガポールの東部では、チャイルドケアセンターの外にある小さな庭が、孫を送った後や迎えに行く前の祖父母たちの集いの場となり、世代を超えた交流の場に変わってきました。

このインフォーマルなグループは、偶然に人々が出会ったことから発展したものですが、もっと意図的に外にある庭のスペースを統合して、増大するインフォーマルなグループと子どもたちを結びつける努力があれば素晴らしいと思います。

例えば、グループが子どもたちと一緒に活動できるようなガーデニングをしたり、子どもたちと一緒にティータイムを過ごしたり、特定のアクティビティに長けた祖父母を募って子どもたちや先生と共有したりするようなことです。

チャイルドケアセンターを核として、そこから生まれた空間やグループを意図的に統合することで、世代を超えたコミュニティが花開くことは、近隣の人々の交流を促進し、周辺に住むすべての世代に安心と温もりを与える可能性があります。

Intergenerational Studies: A Multi-Pronged, Yet Unified Field of Inquiry and Practice

Matt Kaplan, Ph.D.,

Professor, Intergenerational Programs and Aging, Pennsylvania State University

In 1989, when I attended Generations United's second annual conference, I noticed that most of the participants had "arrived" at the intergenerational studies field from disciplinary backgrounds rooted in psychology, social work, human services, and education.

Over the following 30 years of involvement in GU conferences and other initiatives, I noticed a steady increase in the diversity of participants' academic and professional backgrounds. I met new colleagues and lifelong friends from fields such as anthropology, architecture, urban/community studies, parks and recreation, workforce development, environmental sciences, and medicine.

Certainly, growing a field that cuts across so many disciplines, sectors, and perspectives has its challenges. Nevertheless, I advocate for framing and maintaining "intergenerational studies" as a unified field of practice and inquiry spanning intergenerational engagement focal points related to learning, caregiving, recreation, and community/societal development. Herein lies the field's significance for addressing broader questions related to human thriving and ecological sustainability.

世代間交流研究：多方面にまたがる研究と実践が統合された研究分野

マット・カプラン

1989年、私がジェネレーションズ・ユナイテッドの第2回年次大会に参加したとき、参加者のほとんどが、心理学、ソーシャルワーク、ヒューマンサービス、教育などの分野から世代間研究の分野に「たどり着いた」ことに気づきました。

それからの30年間、GUの会議や他の活動に参加しているうちに、参加者の学問的・専門的背景の多様性が着実に増していることに気づきました。人類学、建築、都市・コミュニティ研究、公園・レクリエーション、労働力開発、環境科学、医学などの分野の新しい同僚や生涯の友人に出会いました。

確かに、非常に多くの分野、セクター、そして視点を横断する学問分野を構築するのは困難なことです。しかし、私は、「世代間交流学」を学習、介護、レクリエーション、コミュニティや社会の発展に関連する世代間交流の関わりの中心を網羅する、統合された実践と探究の分野として構築し、維持することを提唱します。人間の繁栄と生態系の持続可能性に関連するより広い問題に取り組むためにこの分野の意義があるのです。

The intergenerational learning circle in cooperation between the school and the community

Shih-Tsen Liu,

Associate Professor, Master's Program of Environmental Education and Resources, University of Taipei

Imagine the elders in our society are no longer just the burden of the aging society, but our educational resources. Such ideals are already happening. The principal and teachers look for groups near the school to cooperate, such as religious temples or mother's kitchen, and invite the elders among them to come to the school, or take the students to these elders' activity sites.

The form of activity can be a single local studies; a community tour throughout the weekend, a large-scale Spring Festival event; or a traditional music club for the entire semester. Apply the talents of the elders to educate our next generation.

Over the years, residents of the community, not only the school students, but also the families of the elderly, regardless of age, have been integrated in the intergenerational learning circle.

学校と地域が連携した世代間交流学習サークル

シン・セン・リー

想像してみてください。社会の中のお年寄りが、もはや高齢化社会の重荷ではなく、教育の資源になることを。そんな理想がすでに実現しつつあります。校長と教師達は、学校の近くにあるお寺や料理ボランティアなど、協力してくれるグループを探し、その中のお年寄りを学校に招待したり、生徒をそのお年寄りの活動場所に連れて行ったりしています。

活動の形態は、一つの地域研究になり得ます。例えば、週末を利用した地域ツアー、大規模な春のイベント、学期を通した伝統音楽クラブなどが考えられます。お年寄りの才能を次の世代の教育に生かしましょう。

数年にわたって、学校の生徒だけでなく、年齢に関係なく、高齢者の家族も含めたコミュニティの住民が、世代間学習の輪の中で一体化されてきています。

Intergenerativity for the future

Peter Whitehouse, MD-Ph.D.,

Transdisciplinary Professor Case Western Reserve University and University of Toronto

Intergenerational exchange programs around the world are the seeds of the cultural change we need to survive and thrive in the future.

In Japan, these activities are leading to Society 5.0. Some people, including myself, refer to the emerging civilization as "cosmodernity". This is a rekindled world, underpinned by indigenous sources of knowledge and illuminated by a collective wisdom based on humility and solidarity in nature.

The concept of intergenerativity can deepen and broaden intergenerational work and play by encouraging us to "go beyond (the) sources of creativity" (our current limited techno-scientific neoliberalism). The climate crisis is the perfect storm (floods, droughts, hurricanes, typhoons, fires) and demands that we think more deeply about and value what kind of future we want to share with all living things, including those yet to be born.

Intergenerational conversations about shared responsibility, so-called seven-generation thinking, are essential to creating a "new story".

未来のためのインタージェネラティヴィティ

ピーター・ホワイトハウス

世界各地で行われている世代間交流プログラムは、これからの時代を生き抜き、繁栄するために必要な文化変容の種となっています。

日本では、これらの活動がSociety 5.0につながっています。私を含めて、到来しつつある新しい文明を「コスモダニティ」と呼ぶ人がいます。これは、再燃した世界のことです。つまりそれは、その地域固有の知識源に支えられ、自然の中での謙虚さと結束に基づき、みんなで作り上げてきた知恵に照らされたものなのです。

インタージェネラティヴィティという概念は、「創造性の源泉」(現在の限られた科学技術によるネオリベラリズム)を超えることを促すものであり、世代間の仕事や遊びを深め、広げることができます。

パーフェクトストーム（洪水、干ばつ、ハリケーン、台風、火災）である気候危機は、まだ生まれていないものも含めたすべての生物とどのような未来を共有したいのかをより深く考え、大切にすることを求めています。

「新しい物語」の創作には、いわゆる第７世代の思考と言われる責任共有に関する世代を超えた会話が不可欠です。

Three Future-oriented Personal Reflections

Mariano Sánchez

Head, Macrosad Chair in Intergenerational Studies, University of Granada

After a couple of decades as researcher and practitioner in the international intergenerational field, I'd like to share with colleagues in Japan three future-oriented personal reflections.

Firstly, both our research methods and programmes are not still able to capture well enough the relational nature at the center of any intergenerational endeavor. Many of our logic models are just lineal, not relational, and in terms of research identifying individual changes is not enough to unveil and understand the relational processes at stake.

Secondly, we would need to pay much more attention to the spatial component in any international intergenerational interaction. To this regard, the study of intergenerational contact zones would be a helpful way forward.

Finally, we do need more quality and sustained international collaboration. How? The setting of an international network and community of practice connecting intergenerational practitioners and researchers is an urgent task that I invite you to consider and get involved in.

未来を志向する３つの個人的な考え

マリアーノ・サンチェス

国際的な世代間交流の分野で研究者として、また実践者として 20 年を過ごして、私は、未来志向の個人的な考えを３つ、日本の同僚たちと共有したいと思います。

第一に、私たちが取り組んできた研究手法やプログラムは、あらゆる世代間交流の試みの中心にある関係性の本質をまだ十分に捉えているとは言えません。私たちの論理モデルの多くは、関係性についてのものではなく、単に直線的なものであり、個人の変化を特定するという研究の観点からだけでは、問題となっている関係性のプロセスを明らかにし、理解するには不十分です。

第二に、あらゆる意図的に実施される世代間交流の相互作用における空間的要素にもっと注意を払う必要があります。この点については、世代間の接触領域（コンタクト・ゾーン）研究が前進するために有益なものとなるでしょう。

最後に、より高い質と、持続的な国際共同が必要であるということです。どのようにしていくのか？それは、世代間交流の実践者と研究者をつなぐ国際的なネットワークとコミュニティの設立です。これは、緊急の課題であり、皆さんにもぜひ検討していただき、参加していただきたいと思っています。

おわりに

本書は、『世代間交流の理論と実践』シリーズ3として編集している。その構成は、日本編：16編、外国編：10編であり、52名（のべ人数）によって手がけられている。そして、最後は6名によるメッセージで締め括られている。編著者の数も含めると実に60名を超える方々の叡智によって仕上がってきている。シリーズ2の倍近くの人数であった。当然、その内容も実に多様で参考になる具体的実践やその背景となる理論にふれることができる。振り返ってみると、シリーズ1では、「あとがき」にも記したように、「場」「対象」「コンテンツ」を柱として「世代間交流」のあり方を検討する契機を用意したと主張する。それによって「人を結び未来を拓く」世代間交流をとらえるとしている。集まった内容からしても、シリーズ1の役割は十分果たしたと思っている。ここに携わってくださった執筆者は、日本人のみであったが、一部に外国の実践が掲載されていた。それがおそらく伏線となって、シリーズ2が構想されたように記憶している。そしてシリーズ2では、国際的な感覚に目覚めた編集スタッフによる、ユニークな二か国語併記にチャレンジしている。アメリカのGU (Generations United) といった国際的なカンファレンスにも関心が寄せられ始めた時期とも近接しており、グローバル化に移行してきたと言える。シリーズ2の刊行からやや時間的経緯が見られるものの、それが熟成期間とすれば、シリーズ3では、さらに視野に広がりと深まりが増し、日本の実践的な展開や理論的な考究も世界標準として他国のそれらと肩を並べ､いよいよ対等に議論するところに達してきたのではないかと考える。「世界標準」化の完成とまで言えないかもしれないが、シリーズ1をはじめ、シリーズ2および3に至る執筆者の方々の弛まぬ研鑽と長きにわたるシリーズへの協力が実を結んだ結果と理解する。編著者の一人として、その熱き思いに感動するとともに心より深く感謝する次第である。

シリーズ3の第2部：外国編執筆者の顔ぶれは、シリーズ2と比べるとほとんどが変わっている。しかしながら、本書のメッセージの部に寄稿してくれているメンバーは、シリーズ２で執筆者となっていた５名に新しい１名を加えた構成になっている。また、こういう形で、著名な方々からのメッセージを集めることができたことは、誠に嬉しいことであり、私たちにとっても誇りとなっている。ここで、紙面の許す限り、個人的な思いも含めながら、各氏のメッセージの受け止めを述べることで、感謝の意を表しておきたい。

Donna Butts 氏は、前のシリーズ２で第１章を飾ってくれており、その際も世代間交流のあり方を熱く語ってくれた (pp.2-12)。GU の代表幹事でアメリカでも著名であり、多忙を極める中で、2020 年、JSIS (日本世代間交流学会：オンライン開催) の招待講演 (ビデオメッセージ) を受けていただけた。内容も大変わかりやすく、学会参加者へ広く動画配信することができた。個人的には、GU に参加した際も気さくに声をかけてくださり、常にポジティブで笑顔の絶えないところが印象的である。今回も世代間交流という糸を紡ぐことの社会的影響をしっかりと受け止め、実践に活かすことへの示唆が受け取られる。また、それは具体的展開を模索していこうとする私たちの原動力につながるメッセージと解することもできよう。忘れないように心しておきたい。

Leng Leng Thang 氏は、いつも流暢な日本語で話しかけてくれる、世代間交流に精通する National University of Singapore の研究者である。彼女もシリーズ２の執筆者であり、その際には、世代間交流における接触空間 (ICZ：Intergenerational Contact Zone) についてその重要性を語ってくれている (pp.126-135)。ICIP (International Consortium for Intergenerational Program) の重要なメンバーであり、2020 年でも JSIS の大会にも関わっていただいた。本書においては、世代間交流のコミュニティとしてのチャイルドケアセンターの重要性がメッセージとして込められている。日本においても、私個人にとっても示唆的で、大切にしていきたいと感じるところである。日本とシンガポール間でとても素敵なコラボレーションができるかもしれない。大いに楽しみである。

Matt Kaplan 氏は、ペンシルベニア州立大学 (Pennsylvania State University, USA) の教授であり、長年にわたって世代間交流学を実践的に、かつ学究的に取り組む研究者である。幅広い見識を有する研究者だからこそ、他分野に広がり、深まりをめざす世代間交流という広大な分野の意義を述べようとする本書でのメッセージには、含蓄がある。JSISの研究大会では基調講演（2013年）を受けていただくとともに、企画セミナーでは、2020年、2021年と2年連続して、研究交流の一翼を担っていただいた。もちろん、彼のオープンマインドなところも魅力だが、日本びいきであることは疑いの余地もなく、JSIS設立当初からの顧問としてサポートしてくれている、日本にとってとても大切な人材と言える。今後も彼のメッセージを受け止め続けたいと思うところである。

Shin-Tsen Liu氏は、台北大学の准教授として精力的に研究を展開してきている。本書で述べる「学習サークル（learning circle）」は、地域の高齢者を教育資源としてとらえ、さまざまな活動シーンで活かされることの重要性とこれからの学校と社会とのつながり方を示唆してくれている。私自身にも刺激になるこの「世代間で展開される学びの多層性」は、魅力的であり、かつ実行可能性が高く、近未来の学校の意味が見える社会モデルになるのではないかと考える。教育という観点から考えれば、学校制度の編み直しの機会提供と言えそうである。またアジア諸国の特徴ではなく、世界に通じるものと期待するところでもあり、今後の彼女の活躍に期待するとともに目を離さないでおきたい。

Peter Whitehouse氏は、大学教授（Case Western Reserve University, University of Toronto）であり、妻のCatherine夫人とともに設立した世代間交流学校（Intergenerational Schools International）の校長でもある。数年前、オハイオ州のクリーブランドにある、その学校を個人的に視察訪問させていただいたことは、今でも記憶として鮮明に残っている。その学校については、彼自身がシリーズ2でしっかりと記している（pp.144-157）。それらの取り組みの中からも、"Intergenerativity" のキーワードが見られ、未来創造に向かう世代間交流という本書のメッセージにもつながっていることがわかる。JSISの研究大会での講演（2017年）をはじめセミナー（2020年）などどのような形式であっても世代間交流に対する彼の情熱は変わらず、そしてしっかりと伝わってくるところは、尊敬の一言に尽きる。

Mariano Sánchez 氏は、スペイン、グラナダ大学 (University of Granada, Spain) に所属し、世代間交流の実践者・研究者としてグローバルに活動を続けてきている。シリーズ２では、同僚と共著し、世代間交流における今日的課題を整理してきている (pp.108-125) 。Matt Kaplan 氏と同様、JSIS の顧問である彼は、2021 年 JSIS のオンライン全国大会においても登壇し、世代間交流の議論を盛り上げてくれた。「関係性」というキーワードの探究と「コンタクトゾーン」のあり方をメッセージの中に組み入れている点は、本質を明らかにしたいという私たちの欲求を方向付けてくれたと感じる。さらに国際的ネットワークをつくり出すコミュニティの設立・参加の呼びかけは、誰もが認める喫緊の課題と受け止められる。コミュニティ設立の早期実現に助力したい思いが湧き起こる。常々、スペインの世代間交流の第一人者だと思っていたが、昨年秋の韓国であった大会でシンポジストとして同席した際､その語りから確信へと変わった。エールを送り続けたい。

以上、十分に意が尽くせませんが、本シリーズに関係された全ての方々のご支援･ご協力に対するお礼とさせていただきます。本当にありがとうございました。

最後になりましたが、本書出版に際し、草野博志・ヨシエ記念財団の援助を受けましたことに厚くお礼申し上げます。また、三学出版株式会社・中桐和弥様には、シリーズ完結まで長期にわたり多大な尽力を賜りましたことに心より感謝申し上げます。

2022 年春

編著者を代表して　溝邊和成

＜シリーズの紹介＞

草野篤子・溝邊和成・内田勇人・安永正史・山之口俊子編著『世代間交流の理論と実践 1　人を結び、未来を拓く世代間交流 The Theory and Practice of Intergenerational Learning; Series 1 Intergenerational Exchange Connects People and Opens the Future』三学出版、2015 年

草野篤子・溝邊和成・内田勇人・安永正史編著『世代間交流の理論と実践２ 世界標準としての世代間交流のこれから　The Theory and Practice of Intergenerational Learning; Series 2 Future of the Intergenerational Exchange as the World Standard』三学出版、2017 年

Afterword

This book is edited as Series 3 of Theory and Practice of Intergenerational Exchange. It consists of 15 Japanese and 10 foreign editions, written by 52 people (total number of contributors). The book concludes with a message from six authors. Including the editors, more than 60 people have contributed their wisdom to this work. This is nearly double the number of people who contributed to the second series. Naturally, the contents of the book are very diverse, and you will be able to learn about specific practices and the theories behind them.

We would like to express our deepest and most sincere gratitude to all those involved in this series. Thank you very much.

Finally, as a way of expressing our gratitude to those who have sent us messages of support, I will share my personal thoughts.

Ms. Donna Butts wrote the first chapter in the previous Series 2, in which she also spoke passionately about the state of intergenerational exchange (pp. 2-12).

She is the executive director of Generations United (GU) and a well-known figure in the U.S. She was extremely busy and gave an invited lecture (video message) at the JSIS (Japan Society for Intergenerational Studies) conference in 2020. The content was very easy to understand and the video message was widely distributed to the conference participants. Personally, I was impressed by her friendly approach to me when I attended the GU conference and her constant positive attitude and smiling face. From the messages in this book, I receive suggestions for taking a firm hold of the social impact of spinning the thread of intergenerational exchange and applying it to practice. This message can also be interpreted as a motivation for those of us who are seeking concrete developments. We should keep this in mind.

Dr. Leng Leng Thang is a researcher at the National University of Singapore who is well versed in intergenerational exchange and always speaks fluent Japanese. She is also the author of Series 2, in which she talks about the importance of Intergenerational Contact Zones (ICZ) in intergenerational exchange (pp.126-135). She is an important member of ICIP (International Consortium for Intergenerational Program) and was also involved in the JSIS conference in 2020. In this book, her message is to keep in mind the importance of child care centers when creating communities the create and nurture intergenerational exchanges. For Japan and for me personally, it is very thought-provoking and something I feel we should cherish. It could be a very nice collaboration between Japan and Singapore. I am very much looking forward to it.

Dr. Matt Kaplan is a professor at Pennsylvania State University, USA, and a longtime practicing and scholarly researcher in intergenerational studies. As a researcher with a wide range of insights, his message in this book has implications as he attempts to describe the significance of the vast field of intergenerational exchange as it seeks to expand and deepen into other fields.

He was a keynote speaker at the JSIS conference (2013) and was part of the research exchange in the planned seminars (2020 and 2021). Of course, his open-mindedness is appealing, but there is no doubt that he is a Japanophile, and he is a very important person for Japan, having supported us as an advisor since the establishment of JSIS. We hope to continue to receive his message in the future.

Dr. Shih-Tsen Liu is an associate professor at Taipei University, where she has been actively developing her research. The "learning circle" described in this book suggests the importance of considering the elderly in the community as an educational resource to be utilized in various activity scenes and how schools and society can be connected in the future. I believe that this "multi-layered nature of learning that develops between generations," which is inspiring to me personally, is both attractive and feasible, and may become a social model that will allow us to see the meaning of schools in the near future. From an educational perspective, it seems to offer an opportunity to re-knit the school system. We hope that this will not be a characteristic of only Asian countries, but rather a global phenomenon, and we will keep a close eye on her current and future endeavors.

Dr. Peter Whitehouse is a university professor (Case Western Reserve University, University of Toronto) and the founder, with his wife Catherine, of Intergenerational Schools International). Several years ago, I had the privilege of personally visiting the school in Cleveland, Ohio, which remains a vivid memory for me to this day. He himself wrote about that school well in Series 2 (pp. 144-157).

The key word "Intergenerativity" can be found there, and it is clear that it is connected to the message of this book, "Intergenerational exchange toward the creation of the future.

One word of respect is that his passion for intergenerational exchange remains unchanged and comes across well in any format, including his speech at the JSIS convention (2017) and in seminars (2020).

Dr. Mariano Sánchez is affiliated with the University of Granada, Spain, and has worked globally as a practitioner and researcher in intergenerational exchange. In Series 2, he has co-authored a book with a colleague (pp. 108-125) that lays out today's challenges in intergenerational exchange; like Matt Kaplan, he is an advisor to JSIS and was a speaker at the 2021 JSIS online national conference. He enlivened the discussion. We feel that the exploration of the keyword "relationship" and the incorporation of the "intergenerational contact zone" concept into the message oriented our desire to clarify the essence of intergenerational work. Furthermore, the call for the establishment and participation of a community that creates an international network is accepted as an urgent issue that everyone recognizes. The desire to help in the early realization of the establishment of the community is aroused. I have always thought of him as a leading figure in intergenerational exchange in Spain, but when I sat with him as a symposium presenter at a conference in Korea last fall, his words convinced me of this. I would like to continue to send him my respect and encouragement.

Kazushige Mizobe
Editor
2022 Spring

編著者紹介（Editors）

草野篤子（Atsuko Kusano）

担当箇所(Chapter)：はじめに Preface, 第６章 Chapter6, 第10章 Chapter10

白梅学園大学子ども学部(〒187-8570 東京都小平市小川町1-830)。白梅学園大学名誉教授、博士(医学)東北大学。日本世代間交流学会(JSIS)会長、特定非営利活動法人日本世代間交流協会(JUIA)理事、International Consortium for Intergenerational Programs(ICIP)運営委員、Journal of Intergenerational Relationships 編集委員。米国テンプル大学世代間学習センター上席研究員、信州大学教育学部教授を経て、白梅学園大学教授。著書には、『インタージェネレーション：コミュにテーを育てる世代間交流』(現代エスプリ No.444)至文堂、“Intergenerational Programs: Support for Children, Youth and Elders in Japan” State University of New York Press, “Linking Lifetimes: A Global View of Intergenerational Exchange”, University Press of America,『グローバル化時代を生きる世代間交流』明石書店、『世代間交流効果：人間発達と共生社会づくりの視点から』三学出版、『世代間交流学の創造－無縁社会から世代間交流型社会実現のために』あけび書房、『世代間交流の理論と実践シリーズ１－人を結び未来を開く世代間交流』三学出版、『世代間交流の理論と実践シリーズ２－世界標準としての世代間交流のこれから』三学出版　ほか多数。

Faculty of Child Studies, Shiraumegakuen University, 1-830 Ogawacho, Kodairashi,Tokyo,187-8570 JAPAN, Tel +81-42-346-5639, FAX +81-42-346-5644, E-mail: kusano@shiraume.ac.jp

Dr. Atsuko Kusano, Ph.D, is a Professor Emeritus of Shiraumegakuen University and a chair of Japan Society for Intergenerational Studies (JSIS). Ex-chair of Japan Intergenerational Unity Association (JIUA), Member of Managing Committee of International Consortium for Intergenerational Programs(ICIP), Editorial Member of Journal of Intergenerational Relationships etc.

溝邊和成（Kazushige Mizobe）

担当箇所 (Chapter)：第 16 章 Chapter16, おわりに Afterword

兵庫教育大学 (〒 673-1494 兵庫県加東市下久米 942-1)。兵庫教育大学大学院学校教育研究科教授、博士 (学術) (神戸大学)。小学校教論、広島大学大学院教育学研究科講師、甲南女子大学教授を経て現職。専門は、小学校生活科・理科・総合学習実践論・カリキュラム論。最近では、世代間交流の視点からの教育実践に注目。日本世代間交流学会副会長 (2010-)・同学会誌編集委員長・同学会事務局長 (2010-2020)。『多様化社会をつむぐ世代間交流　次世代への「いのち」の連鎖をつなぐ』(編著) 三学出版 (2012)、『世代間交流の理論と実践シリーズ 1 －人を結び未来を開く世代間交流』(編著) 三学出版 (2015)、『世代間交流の理論と実践シリーズ 2 －世界標準としての世代間交流のこれから』(編著) 三学出版 (2017) など。

Graduate School of Education, Hyogo University of Teacher Education,942-1, Shimokume, Kato, Hyogo, 673-1494, JAPAN Tel&Fax +81-795-44-2197 E-mail: mizobek@hyogo-u.ac.jp

Dr. Kazushige Mizobe is a Professor of Hyogo University of Teacher Education, Japan. His major is the curriculum and practice for Living Environment Studies, primary science, and the integrated study of elementary school. Recently, he is interested in the educational research at the view of intergenerational exchange. He is a co-chair of Japan Society for Intergenerational Studies (JSIS).

内田勇人 (Hayato Uchida)

担当箇所 (Chapter)：第 11 章 Chapter11, 第 13 章 Chapter13

兵庫県立大学 (〒 670-0092 兵庫県姫路市新在家本町 1-1-12)。兵庫県立大学・大学院教授、博士 (医学) (岡山大学)。環境人間学部長兼同研究科長。専門は健康教育学、公衆衛生学、老年学。日本世代間交流学会理事 (2010-)・同学会事務局長 (2021-)。現在、児童養護施設入所児童と高齢者との交流効果等に関する研究等に従事。「世代間交流の理論と実践 (2) 世界標準としての世代間交流のこれから」(編著)、三学出版 (2017 年) など。

School of Human Science and Environment, University of Hyogo, 1-1-12, Shinzaike-honcho, Himeji, Hyogo, 670-0092, JAPAN Tel&Fax +81-79-292-9367 E-mail: uchida@shse.u-hyogo.ac.jp

Dr. Hayato Uchida is Dean and Professor of the School of Human Science and Environment, University of Hyogo Japan. His major is Health Education, Public Health and Gerontology. His latest research is about the educational support program for the children in a child welfare institution offered by the senior volunteers. He is a board member of Japan Society for Intergenerational Studies (JSIS).

作田はるみ（Harumi Sakuda）

担当箇所（Chapter）：第 13 章 Chapter13

神戸松蔭女子学院大学人間科学部食物栄養学科（〒 657-0015 神戸市灘区篠原伯母野山町 1 丁目 2-1）准教授、管理栄養士、病院の給食マネジメントに携わったのち、行政や福祉施設での管理栄養士業務、管理栄養士養成課程で助手としての勤務を経て現職。行事食や郷土料理についての調査研究を行っている。「次世代に伝え継ぐ日本の家庭料理」（農山漁村文化協会, 2017-2021）などの著作がある。

Faculty of Human Sciences, Kobe Shoin Women's University
1-2-1 Shinoharaobanoyama-cho,Nada Ward, Kobe City,657-0015,Japan
TEL+81-78-882-6419　E-mail:sakuda@shoin.ac.jp

Dr.Harumi Sakuda is an Associate Professor of Kobe Shoin Women's University. Her major is food service management and Registered Dietitian, Japan. She is promoting research on event foods and local cuisine.She has written books such as "Japanese Home Cooking Passed on to the Next Generation" (Rural Culture Association Japan, 2017-2021).

村山　陽（Yoh Murayama）

担当箇所（Chapter）：第 14 章 Chapter14

東京都健康長寿医療センター研究所（〒 173-0015 東京都板橋区栄町 35-2）。東京都健康長寿医療センター研究所 社会参加と地域保健研究チーム 研究員（主任）、博士（社会学）（慶応義塾大学）。専門は、社会心理学。世代間交流の視点から、単身高齢者の社会参加に着目。日本世代間交流学会理事（2019-）・同学会編集委

員 (2018-) 。発表論文には、

Murayama Y et al (2015) The effect of intergenerational programs on the mental health of elderly adults, Aging Ment Health,19. Murayama Y et al (2018).The impact of intergenerational programs on social capital in Japan, BMC public health, 19. Murayama Y et al (2022). The effects of reciprocal support on mental health among intergenerational non-relatives, Arch Gerontol Geriatr 99. など。

Research Team for Social Participation and Community Health, Tokyo Metropolitan Institute of Gerontology, 35-2, Sakae-cho, Itabashi-ku, Tokyo, 173-0015, JAPAN Tel+81(3)3964-3241, E-mail: yhoyho05@tmig.or.jp

Dr. Yoh Murayama, Ph.D, is a Chief Researcher at Tokyo Metropolitan Institute of Gerontology. His major is social psychology. He focuses on social participation of single elderly from the perspective of intergenerational exchange. He is a director and editorial board member of Japan Society for Intergenerational Studies (JSIS).

メッセージをお寄せいただいた方々 (People who sent us messages.)

Donna Butts
Executive Director, Generations United

For over 35 years, Generations United has championed programs and public policies that support connecting generations. Intergenerational shared sites, where young and old receive services and engage together under one roof, and grandparents and other relatives raising children are two significant areas of work. Generations United's biennial global conference provides the only international forum for practitioners to come together, learn from each other and connect with others in the intergenerational field.

Dr. Leng Leng THANG
Department of Japanese Studies and Next Age Institute (Co-Director), National University of Singapore

A pioneer in the study of intergenerational approaches in Singapore, she started her interest in intergenerational work from her PhD ethnography of

Kotoen in Tokyo (see her book “Generations in Touch: Linking the old and young in a Tokyo neighborhood. Cornell University Press, 2001” She believes that besides programming, we need to expand Intergenerational contact zone in multiple dimensions in making place for the promotion of intergenerational encounters and bonding.

Dr. Matt Kaplan
Professor, Intergenerational Programs and Aging, The Pennsylvania State University (U.S.A.)

Dr. Kaplan has published several books, including: Intergenerational Contact Zones: Place-based Strategies for Promoting Social Inclusion and Belonging (with Thang, Sanchez and Hoffman, 2020), Intergenerational Pathways to a Sustainable Society (with Sanchez and Hoffman, 2017), Linking Lifetimes: A Global View of Intergenerational Exchange (with Henkin and Kusano, 2002), and The Role of Intergenerational Programs for Supporting Children, Youth and Elders in Japan (with Kusano, Tsuji, and Hisamichi, 1998).

Shih-Tsen Liu
Associate professor, Master program of environmental education and resources
University of Taipei, Taipei, Taiwan

Shih-Tsen Liu is the first scholar who combines intergenerational exchange with environmental education. In addition to looking at the influence of intergenerational activities on participants in schools or nature centers, her research interests have been tracked over years to discover the long-term impact on communities. Shih-Tsen has also responsible for the international Study Tour project in Taiwan.

Peter Whitehouse MD-PhD
Transdisciplinary Professor at Case Western Reserve University and University of Toronto and founder Intergenerational Schools Cleveland and Internationally (InterHub).

He is an Intergenerative designer and activist whose fields include cognitive/brain health, integrated health care, intergenerational learning, interprofessional practice, deep bioethics, organizational aesthetics, narrative epistemology, transmedia arts, and play. His recent accomplishments focus on political action (with Third Act and Right Care Alliance) concerning improving health in a time of crisis. His most recent book with Danny George is American Dementia: Brain Health in an Unhealthy Society (Hopkins Press, 2021)

Mariano Sánchez (See p.215)

＜関連図書の紹介＞

草野篤子・溝邊和成・内田勇人・安永正史編著
世代間交流の理論と実践２　世界標準としての世代間交流のこれから
The Theory and Practices of Intergenerational Learning; Series 2
Future of the Intergenerational Exchange as the World Standard
三学出版社、2017 年

本書は、世代間交流の理論と実践２として、編集されている。前シリーズ１の編集方法とは異なり、諸外国の最前線で取り組まれている方々からのメッセージを第一部で紹介し、第二部では、日本から世界へのメッセージとして、日本人９名による報告がなされている。もちろん、英語と日本語の二か国語併記の編集によって、その意図が互いに伝わるよう工夫を凝らしている。また、タイトルとして掲げる「世界標準」は、日本で新しい学問的潮流が誕生したことを世界に発信する点に加え、世界各国からのメッセージを受けることにより、世界に通用する「世代間交流」を磨き上げ、世界の標準的なモデルプランをめざす意思表示ととらえている。したがって、国際的な「世代間交流」に関心を寄せる読者にとって、本書との出会いが、日本のみならず、諸外国での実践報告や研究交流につながり、国際レベルでの活躍を積極的に進める原動力になることを期待している。

目次

草野篤子・溝邊和成・内田勇人・安永正史・山之口俊子編著
世代間交流の理論と実践１　人を結び、未来を拓く世代間交流
三学出版社、2015 年

科学技術のめざましい進歩・発展によって、人を取り巻く環境が日々変化し、身近なコミュニティから国際社会まで、近未来に向かってさまざまな制度の編み直しや概念の再構築が起こっている。そんな中で2010年より世代間交流学会がスタートした。小さな一歩ではあるものの、その成果は着実に得られてきている。もちろん、他の学問がその体系づくりに多くの時間と地道な努力を注いできているように、この分野においても絶え間ない理論と実践の往還的検討の継続が求められる。そこで、「理論と実践」をシリーズ化し、近未来の「世代間交流学」確立をめざした本書を刊行するに至った。

本書に収録されている内容は、そうした意味においても多岐にわたっている。執筆者の主張もさまざまに受け止めることができる。だからこそ、初学の読者にも自分の意見と比較しやすく、受け入れやすい。また、本格的にこの分野の開発に寄与しようとする読者にも、研究・実践の状況がとらえやすく、味わい深いものになっている。いずれの読者においても、未来の国際社会における「世代間交流」をイメージする端緒が、ここにあるといえよう。

目次

草野篤子・内田勇人・溝邊和成・吉津晶子編著
多様化社会をつむぐ世代間交流　次世代への『いのち』の連鎖をつなぐ
三学出版社、2012 年

本書名の一部でもある「多様化社会」は、いうまでもなく、価値観が「多様」になった社会を示している。国際化（internationalization）とは異なる地球規模化（globalization）とともに「多様性」や「多様化」は現代社会を語るキーワードとして受け止められる。そして「多様化社会」をつむぐ「世代間交流」といったとき、「多様化社会」を成立させる枠組みとして、「世代間交流」をどのようにセットしていくのがよいかを議論しようとする意図が見られる。ここでは、ソーシャルキャピタルの紹介をはじめ、エンパワーメント、ジェネラティビティ、世代間交流アジェンダ、アクティブエイジングといったことが話題となっていることからも、諸外国とともに日本の「世代間交流」が容易にイメージされる。未来社会を考えたい方には、立ち止まって一読をすすめたい書である。

目次

世代間交流の理論と実践３
新たな社会創造に向かうソーシャルネットワークとしての
世代間交流活動

The Theory and Practices of Intergenerational Learning; Series 3
Intergenerational Exchange Activities as a Social Network
toward the Creation of a New Society

2022年 11月 10日初版印刷
2022年 11月 20日初版発行

編著者　草野篤子　溝邉和成　内田勇人　村山陽　作田はるみ
発行者　岡田金太郎
発行所　三学出版有限会社
〒520-0835 滋賀県大津市別保３丁目 3-57 別保ビル３階
TEL 077-536-5403　FAX 077-536-5404
https://sangakusyuppan.com

亜細亜印刷（株）印刷・製本